Praise for *Make Sure It's Deductible*

Evelyn Jacks is well-deserving of her reputation as Canada's most trusted tax advisor. This book could save thousands of tax dollars for anyone who is self-employed, runs a small business, or is thinking of starting one.

GORDON PAPE

The day you opened your small business is the day you stepped up to the plate to play ball with the Canada Revenue Agency. In characteristic friendly style, Canada's foremost tax author lays out the rules of the game so that you and your family can minimize stress and maximize deductions. Prepare to be surprised and rewarded.

MICHAEL KANE, *The Vancouver Sun*

Ms Jacks draws on her expertise in a way that makes the argument for self-employment in this tax-oppressed country almost compelling.

JONATHAN CHEVREAU, *The National Post*

For guidelines on the home office and all self-employment issues, I would recommend you read Evelyn Jacks' book Make Sure It's Deductible as a really good general and specific guide.

DAVID CHRISTIANSON, *Winnipeg Free Press*

Evelyn Jacks knows tax and writes about it in a way the average person can understand. That's a very unusual combination. Reading her advice will make you richer, especially if you deduct business expenses the way she tells you to in this book.

ELLEN ROSEMAN, *The Toronto Star*

Jacks' style is direct and concise. For the answer to "What does this line on the tax return mean?" it is where I would turn first.

GEORGE HARTMAN, *Investment Executive*

MAKE SURE IT'S DEDUCTIBLE

Third Edition

Little-Known
TAX TIPS
for Your Canadian
Small Business

Evelyn Jacks

**McGraw-Hill
Ryerson**

Toronto   Montréal   Boston   Burr Ridge IL   Dubuque IA   Madison WI   New York
San Francisco   St. Louis   Bangkok   Bogotá   Caracas   Kuala Lumpur   Lisbon
London   Madrid   Mexico City   Milan   New Delhi   Santiago   Seoul
Singapore   Sydney   Taipei

McGraw-Hill
Ryerson Limited

A Subsidiary of The **McGraw·Hill** Companies

Copyright © 2007 by Evelyn Jacks Productions

This edition has been carefully researched and verified for accuracy; however, due to the complexity of the subject matter and the continual changes occurring in law and its administration, neither the author nor the publisher can be held responsible for errors or omissions, or consequences of any actions resulting from information in this book. Examples discussed are intended as general guidelines only, contain fictional names and characters, and any resemblance to real persons or events is purely coincidental. Tax law and policies referred to in this book include proposals of recent federal and provincial budgets. The reader is urged to seek the services of a competent and experienced professional should further guidance in income tax preparation, tax planning, or financial planning be required.

ISBN-13: 978-0-07-148446-6
ISBN-10: 0-07-148446-9
1 2 3 4 5 6 7 8 9 0 DOC/DOC 0 9 8 7 6

National Library of Canada Cataloguing in Publication Data

Jacks, Evelyn.
    Make sure it's deductible: little-known tax tips for your Canadian small business

3rd ed.
Includes index.
ISBN: 0-07-148446-9

1. Income tax – Law and legislation – Canada – Popular works.
2. Small business – Taxation – Law and legislation – Canada – Popular works. I. Title.

HJ4662.A45J32 2001   343.7105'268   C2001-903894-1

Printed and bound in the United States of America.

For Cordell and Don

You and the brilliance of your future inspire me daily.

xoxo

Contents

Introduction

An effective tax system is one which promotes the ideals of fairness and equity, simplicity and compliance. Unfortunately for taxpayers, some of these ideals are at odds with one another, as illustrated below:

- Our tax system is based on *self-assessment:* taxpayers are expected to voluntarily comply with the requirement to file a tax return, correctly assess taxes owing, and pay them on time. However, tax law is often legislated retroactively.
- Taxpayers expect equity: that others in like circumstances pay similar taxation levels.
- To be completely fair, however, one must put into place special provisions for special groups of people—the sick and the disabled, the elderly, families, business people, employees, and investors.
- The fairer the tax system, the more complex it will be.
- Complexity, often caused by the quest for fairness, can make compliance difficult.
- Without compliance there is no equity.

You can see what we mean.

As a result, it is not necessarily true that two neighbours, each earning gross revenues of, let's say, $50,000, will pay the same level of tax. In fact, it's not always income level that determines the after-tax result. . . it's income *source* that will have the biggest bearing on your family's real wealth over the long run, a fact that few Canadians consider seriously.

What's more, the type of income earned, when it's earned, and by whom, together with the application of generous rules for the expenses of earning certain income sources, will determine your family's after-tax status.

Take Jean-Paul, for example, a 35-year-old self-employed electrical contractor, who suffered through a devastating divorce over a year ago. You could see the pain on his face as he spoke of missing his eight-year-old son, who moved with his mom to a small town over four hours away. His commitment to the boy was unfaltering. Every weekend he drove the four-hour trek to visit with his son, and then back home again.

"It's worth it to see my boy," Jean-Paul sighed, "but I am exhausted and the travelling is costing me a fortune. Is there any way I could write some of this off?"

At first glance, the answer would be no. Driving to and from the small town to visit one's own child is considered to be a personal expense; not deductible.

But wait. Jean-Paul was self-employed. Did he ever bid on work in the area in which his child lived? No. Could he? Yes. In fact, a new school was expected to be built in the vicinity very soon. Was it too late to bid on the work? No.

Jean-Paul could now legitimately write off the cost of driving to and from the town in which the work would be completed. Trips to place the bid, negotiate with the parties, supervise his work crew, etc., would all qualify for expense deductibility. So would the hotel bills he incurred to perform the work. His travel now had a dual purpose. Deductibility of at least a portion of the trip could be justified to the CRA (Canada Revenue Agency*), as there was a reasonable expectation of profit in the future.

Only a few miles away, driving for visits with his son would be considered a personal expense. But Jean-Paul took this into account when filing his tax return, and accomplished his goals: the majority of his expenses were now tax deductible, leaving more in his pocket to spend on his beloved son. He now makes a point of looking for work in the area over the weekends, so that he can better balance business and personal resources, *and arrange his affairs within the framework of the law to pay the least taxes legally possible.*

Often, taxpayers can increase their tax write-offs, without dramatically changing their lifestyles. It's all in the way you think about the time and money you have. If you can make a business case for the expenditure — even if you have to prorate the cost for a personal component — the after-tax benefits will accumulate in double-digit yields.

That's the primary purpose behind this little book — to urge you to re-evaluate your existing income sources and annual expenditures. Is there a business purpose to any of them? Could there be? If so, what do you have to do to conform to CRA's audit requirements to ensure their acceptance? How can you plan to make decisions throughout the year to enhance your lifestyle with increased after-tax dollars? How can you be more astute and vigilant about claiming every tax deduction and credit you are entitled to?

---

* Formerly known as Revenue Canada and Canada Customs and Revenue Agency.

Be sure to check out the history of significant personal and small business tax changes we have prepared for you in Chapter 12, to help you discuss key tax savings with your professional advisors, and record savings from your voluntary compliance or adjustments for errors or omissions.

With marginal tax costs in the range of 22% to 50% or more of every dollar you earn (depending upon your province of residence and your exposure to social benefit Clawbacks), it makes absolute "cents" to aggressively pursue your legal rights to pay only the correct amount of tax and not one cent more.

You *can* take control of the taxes you pay! Make the decision today to take a fresh look at your next financial commitment and. . .

. . . *Make Sure It's Deductible*!

CHAPTER 1

Key Reasons Why Canadians Pay Too Much Tax

"The greatest discovery of my generation is that human beings can alter their lives by altering their attitudes of mind."
WILLIAM JAMES

KEY CONCEPTS

- There are 10 key reasons why taxpayers overpay their taxes
- Tax can be reduced in multiple ways by operating a small business
- Documentation is necessary
- Small business owners face a higher audit risk than other taxpayers
- A reasonable expectation of profit is necessary to legitimize tax write-offs
- The key to tax savings over time is tax efficient decision-making all year long.

REAL LIFE: David groaned as he completed this year's tax return. He thought he was doing well, supporting his family on his $45,000 of employment income. David scrutinized his simple tax return: one T4 slip and not much else. He had paid close to $7000 in taxes this year, and his take-home pay of about $2,900 a month (after source deductions for Canada Pension Plan (CPP) and Employment Insurance (EI)) barely seemed to cover all the expenses of running a household with a stay-at-home mom and two small kids. How could this be? David, a typical Canadian dad, wondered whether he needed a second job, or perhaps, a self-employment opportunity.

THE PROBLEM

Canadians who pay too much tax face the following challenges. They:

- Earn the majority of their income from one source (e.g., employment or pensions)

- Have one person in the family who earns significantly more than the others
- Pay too much to the government through tax withholding or tax instalments all year long
- Fail to build equity
- Have no long-term savings goals
- Have no estate planning goals
- Have trouble keeping records
- Don't know themselves, their investments or their business well enough
- Don't effectively communicate their current and future tax and financial affairs to their professional advisors; failing to ask effective questions about current and future tax-savings planning, and/or demanding the answers to help themselves make tax-wise decisions.
- Look at tax filing/tax planning on an annual basis only

THE SOLUTION: START A BUSINESS

There are millions of small businesses thriving in Canada today, owned and operated by entrepreneurs, professionals, commission salespersons, farmers, fishers, and revenue property owners.

They are people who invest their time and money first, to reap the rewards of profit and equity in their enterprises later, and in fact, they are tax advantaged! Owners of a small business can have both: tax efficient income today, and the potential to substantially enhance their net worth by building equity for tomorrow.

Tax efficiency comes from numerous opportunities to do the following:

- Diversify income sources from their efforts
- Control the tax timing of income and expenses
- Split income with family members, thereby reducing the household's marginal rate of tax
- Increase their working capital by reducing or eliminating the withholding taxes
- Think tax first with every expenditure, and then decrease personal living costs by writing off the business portion of such expenses
- Average their tax costs over a period of years
- Build equity with the goodwill and other assets of their business
- Leverage their productivity by taking pro-active control of their retirement income and the size of their estate.

You too could reap the benefits of these opportunities; however, as a small business owner you must know the rules of the tax-filing game. That includes an understanding of the new relationship you will have with the tax department, something that will be discussed throughout this book. To begin, consider these preliminary concepts to help you prepare to save tax dollars through your new business venture.

THE PARAMETERS

In order to take advantage of the benefits provided to the self-employed under the law, a new approach must be taken to the tax-filing ritual. Three basic parameters must be observed.

1. Family First—Reassess Your Tax and Financial Affairs   To maximize tax advantages, and smooth out income fluctuations, the small business owner must look not only at his/her own individual return, but to the returns of each family member as an extension of the economic activities produced within the family unit, *in the current year and over a period of years.*

2. Have a Source of Income From the Business   To make sure your claims for expenditures made to start and grow your business are deductible, a specific requirement must be met. That is, it's not enough to simply start an economic activity, no matter how simple or small. One must start earning *income* from it, now *or in the future.* That's the key. Those who can show the potential for earnings from a new source of income resulting from from their commercial activities, legitimize the deductions they are allowed under the Income Tax Act. That revenue source will help to prove that your business has *a reasonable expectation of profit.*

3. Leverage Risk, and Make a Tax-efficient Profit   Earning business revenues is a process that evolves—generally you spend first, earn later. Therefore, the tax-filing profile of the self-employed requires an assessment of profitability over time. This is a distinct difference from the earning of employment income, which occurs regularly, and generally without risk to the employee.

The Income Tax Act recognizes this evolutionary income-producing process for enterprises that can show a reasonable expectation of profit: business losses from a proprietorship may be deductible against other income of the year, and in carry over years. However, sometimes such losses can be disallowed retroactively; this despite the fact that claims are fully supported by documentation. This will be discussed in detail in subsequent chapters.

The self-employed, who must self-assess income and deductions, and collect withholding taxes and sales taxes for CRA, are subject to a great risk of scrutiny by tax auditors. They therefore have even more compelling reasons to learn more about tax compliance. Here are some "starter tips:"

Who Files a Return?

Canadian residents must report their taxable income to the government annually. Your obligation to file a Canadian tax return usually ends when you leave the country permanently, unless you continue to earn certain Canadian-source income after you leave, including Canadian business income.

What's Taxable Income?

For Canadian residents, that's world-wide income, in Canadian funds, after allowable deductions and credits. You should also know that income sources are classified and subject to varying tax treatment. In other words, not all income is taxed in the same manner, and that can have advantages for the taxpayer who diversifies income sources.

How Is Employment Income Taxed?

Income and deductions from employment, including salary, wages, gratuities, bonuses and vacation pay, are specifically defined and outlined in the Income Tax Act, leaving little room for flexibility or interpretation. Income must be reported on the return in the year received, and includes taxable benefits and employee stock options.

Can Employees Claim Tax Deductions?

Sometimes, yes. Employees, however, may not take tax deductions for any expenditures except those listed by the Act; even if the taxpayer legitimately makes the expenditure in pursuit of his/her duties from an office or employment. A good example of these restrictions concerns the acquisition of certain equipment, computers or cell phones. An employee may not claim a deduction for the cost of depreciating assets — known as Capital Cost Allowance (CCA) — on any assets other than motor vehicles, aircraft or musical instruments used in pursuit of income from their office or employment. Certain special provisions exist for tradespeople's tools, however.

Another example concerns the deductibility of meals consumed by the employee while away on company business: that employee must be absent from the employer's place of business for a period of not less than 12 hours in order to claim his/her meal expenses. Further, to claim any deductible expenses, a certificate signed by the employer (Form T2200, *Declaration of Conditions of Employment*) must be available for CRA to verify that the employee was required, under the employment contract, to pay the tax-deductible expenses being claimed, and was not reimbursed for the costs.

How Is the Income of the Self-Employed Taxed?

The Income Tax Act states that a taxpayer's income for the year from a business or property is the taxpayer's "profit." This word is not specifically defined in the Act, but does infer that the activity conducted has a business purpose. It encompasses the concept that those expenditures that cause the taxpayer's gross income to be reduced to the taxable net income are legitimate, provided that they have an income-earning purpose and are not personal in nature. Professionals will look to Generally Accepted Accounting Principles (GAAP), as defined in the Canadian Institute of Chartered Accountants' *CICA Handbook,* in computing profits.

However, sometimes the Act itself sets out exceptions to those rules. For example, the deduction for meals and entertainment expenses is usually limited to 50% of their cost. Most importantly, the income or loss a taxpayer reports on the tax return can be challenged by CRA if there is no "reasonable expectation of profit" over time from the business venture. This is a "grey area" of interpretation that has led to hundreds of challenges in the courts (for a discussion, see Chapter 11). It is particularly problematic because the pursuit of profit can result in the creation of a source of income in the future. *In other words, often the pursuit comes before the income.* Despite this, the onus is always on the self-employed taxpayer to show that a legitimate source of taxable income exists from the activities of the business within the audit period and in the future, in order to ensure the deductibility of the costs of pursuing that income.

It is also important to understand that the Income Tax Act separates the sources of income from a business — which is actively pursued — from sources of income from "property," which occurs with only a passive effort by the taxpayer. Income from property generally includes dividends, employee profit-sharing plans, retirement compensation arrangements, income from royalties, interest from investment contracts. Capital gains are classified separately, as discussed later.

What Deductions Can Be Claimed by the Self-Employed?

Here is the general rule for claiming deductions of a small business: if you can show that your expenditures were made or incurred to produce income, now or in the foreseeable future, and the amount of the expenditure was reasonable, and did not include any personal and living expenses, CRA must allow the claim. However, this is also where the "onus of proof" arises: it is your responsibility to show both potential for profit now or in the future and reasonableness in all documentation. You must also make allowances for any personal components of the cost. *Do this by prorating your total costs according to their relevant business/personal use components.*

This includes the deduction for interest expenses. In the case of those who borrow funds to invest in their enterprises or property, it is important to note that there must be potential for income from the property — profits, rents, dividends or interest — for the interest amounts to be deductible at all.

You should also know that "capital appreciation" is not considered to be business income. That's important.

How Is Capital Appreciation Taxed?

Currently, the Income Tax Act requires only 1/2 of capital gains received in the year to be included as income, and that these gains can be offset by capital losses of the current year, or any prior year since 1972, adjusted for changes in income inclusion rates.

There are certain tax-free exceptions to this rule, which include gains on the sale of the principal residence, the reporting of gains when replacement properties are acquired, and tax-free rollovers to children and/or spouses in certain cases.

Striving to earn profits from the disposition of capital assets is wise. The reason? (1) Asset appreciations is never taxed until disposition, which can include "actual disposition" sale, gift, or "deemed disposition." An asset is deemed to be disposed by way of transfer, conversion to personal use, emigration, expropriation or death. (2) gains usually qualify for a tax exemption of 50% and, (3) in certain cases, a further capital gains deduction. Also, except in the case of death, you do have some control over when you sell or otherwise dispose of an asset.

For example, you could reduce your tax burden by disposing of the asset over two tax years (half in December, half in January) or by offsetting capital gains in the year with capital losses, and so on.

TAX ADVISOR

Before any taxpayer begins a new small business, it is important to go through a personal income assessment procedure. Start this procedure as follows:

Complete a Current Year Tax Review

Prepare a Tax Summary to confirm how your current year income sources are earned and how they are taxed. A sample plan for Linda Baker, who started an unincorporated small business during the tax year follows.* Note the following:

- She has a tax refund originating from the tax deducted from her employment income. This refund represents the tax savings produced by the loss reported from her business.
- Her total amount payable for the year represents approximately 12% of her total income.
- Her RRSP contribution limit for next year is calculated as 18% of her earned income of the current year. This represents some potential for real tax savings in her future.

Know Your Current Average and Marginal Tax Rates on Income Types

In Linda's case, her employment income, as well as her net business income (in this case a loss) will be taxed at her **marginal tax rate**—the rate of tax she pays on the next dollar of income earned in her tax bracket. Her **average tax rate** on total income, however, will be less. This is the total amount of tax she actually pays on her total income. The difference takes into account her eligibility for non-refundable tax credits, such as the Basic Personal Amount, or "tax free zone", her contributions to the Canada Pension Plan and premiums for employment insurance contributed through her employer.

Remember that income from different sources attracts different rates of tax. It is interesting to note that in her current tax bracket, dividends Linda might earn from a private small business corporation would be taxed at a much lower rate (in fact starting in 2006 even more advantageous tax treatment is extended to shares held in large corporations subject to

* Figures for tax year 2006 are used in the example

tax at general rates). Her capital gains on any asset dispositions would be taxed at one half her marginal tax rate on ordinary income. This illustrates the difference in taxation of a diversified income portfolio, which can lead to lower average taxes payable over a lifetime.

Marginal and average tax rates change continuously both on the federal and provincial level. For an updated look at the current rates, visit www.knowledgebureau.com and click on the Make Sure It's Deductible mini-site.

Analyze Current RRSP Contribution Room

Small business owners often have "all their eggs in one basket" in terms of their investment in their enterprises. For this reason—and all the other good ones that strike a chord with average taxpayers—the RRSP is a "must-have" investment. It provides a way for you to invest your profits in a tax-deferred savings vehicle that can enable a legitimate way to split income with your spouse* (through a spousal RRSP), while reducing the taxes you pay today and deferring your investment earnings to the future. The table below shows Linda's approximate tax savings at different levels of RRSP contributions. Remember: to contribute, you must have filed a return in prior years, and reported the qualifying "earned income" from active sources like employment or business income. Had Linda planned to save through an RRSP, she would have reaped double-digit returns on her investment this year—just through her tax savings.

RRSP Contribution	Tax Savings
$ 500	$135
$1,000	$254
$1,500	$360
$2,000	$467
$2,500	$576
$3,000	$680
$3,500	$786

Prepare a Tax Review for Each Family Member

One of the objectives you should have whenever you file a tax return is to attempt to reduce taxes not just for each individual, but for the family unit as a whole. You should look into the legitimate ways to split income with family members, take advantage of transferable deductions and credits, and tax deferral opportunities.

* or common-law partner

| Sample 1.1 | **Tax Summary** |

2006 Tax Summary
for
Linda Baker

Calculation of Taxable income	
Income	
Employment Income	$ 25,000.00
Business Income	–$ 4,320.60
	Total Income $ 20,679.40
Deductions from Total Income	
None	
	Net Income $ 20,679.40
Deductions from Net Income	
None	
	Taxable Income $ 20,679.40

Calculation of Federal Tax			
Federal Tax on Taxable Income		$ 3,153.70	
Federal Non-Refundable Credits			
Basic Personal Amount	$ 8,839.00		
CPP through employment	$ 1,064.35		
EI premiums	$ 467.50		
Total non-refundable credits	$ 10,370.75		
Total non-refundable credits × 15.25%		$ 1,581.54	
Federal Tax		$ 1,572.16	$ 1,572.16

Calculation of Ontario Tax			
Ontario Tax on Taxable Income		$ 1,251.14	
Ontario Non-Refundable Credits			
Basic Personal Amount	$ 8,377.00		
CPP through employment	$ 1,064.25		
EI premiums	$ 467.50		
Total non-refundable credits	$ 9,908.75		
Total non-refundable credits × 6.05%		$ 599.48	
Ontario Health Tax		$ 40.80	
Ontario Tax		$ 692.46	$ 692.46
Total payable			$ 2,264.62

Calculation of Refund or Balance Due			
Refundable Credits			
Income tax deducted		$ 3,575.00	
Total Credits		$ 3,575.00	$ 3,575.00
Refund			$ 1,310.38
2007 RRSP contribution Limit		$ 3,722	

Assess Previous Errors and Omissions

Because a small business owner is subject to greater scrutiny by tax auditors, it is important for you to clean up any past filing problems with CRA before you start your business. For example, if you have failed to file tax returns in the past, you may wish to consider filing them now. CRA may owe you money with regard to overpaid taxes at source, or refundable tax credits you may be eligible for. If you had eligible earned income in those years, you will also create increased RRSP contribution room, which CRA will not yet have calculated.

Also, if you voluntarily comply with the law, you will avoid gross negligence and tax evasion penalties. It is always important to clear up your tax-filing status, and it could pay off for you in the future. For example, you may have to rely on CRA's Fairness Committee to grant you a waiver of interest and penalties should a severe hardship occur in your circumstances in the future. More on that later.

And, if you find you have missed an important provision in your prior filed returns — like GST rebates on employment expenses, medical expenses, charitable donations, disability tax credits, safety deposit box charges, or moving expenses — file Form T1 ADJ to request an adjustment. You can do so over a prior 10 year period for most federal provisions.

Find Out More: Incorporated or Proprietorship?

If you are serious about running a for-profit business, be aware that a business can be formed in a variety of organizational structures. For most people who begin an owner-operated business, an unincorporated structure is best at the start. Also known as a *proprietorship*, the income, expenses and capital transactions are reported on the T1 General personal tax return and added to other income of the year, in the case of net profits. Losses from the business offset other income of the current year, or if excess losses exist after this, these non-capital losses can offset other income of the previous three years or income in the next 20 years. They can, therefore, be lucrative.

The incorporated company, on the other hand, is a separate legal entity. Under this scenario, legal liability is limited, and earnings may be retained in the company, or distributed on an after-tax basis to shareholders; losses, however, stay within the corporate structure. The shareholder, who is generally also the owner-manager, can earn salary, dividends or other income from the business.

A third form of business organization is the partnership, which may be incorporated or not. We'll discuss the tax implications in more depth later; however, unless otherwise stated, we will assume our reader is operating an unincorporated small business.

Plan to Tax Cost Average

Once you have all the steps above in place, you can integrate tax efficiency into your normal business planning activities. In fact, you can plan to average your tax costs for the current year, the prior years, and future years, by applying the provisions available to you within the Income Tax Act. We'll show you how in Chapter 2, How to Tax Cost Average.

RECAP. YOU NEED TO KNOW:

1. How diversifying your income can decrease taxes payable
2. What Onus of Proof is
3. How to prorate costs incurred for both business/personal use
4. The difference between business income and capital appreciation
5. How gains on a principal residence are taxed
6. The difference between marginal and effective tax rates
7. How to account for previous errors and omissions on tax returns
8. The difference between incorporated and unincorporated enterprises
9. The importance of RRSP contributions for small business owners

YOU NEED TO ASK: Your tax advisor to help you

1. **Assess your current tax-filing profile:** What you want to know is how your current income sources are being taxed. Make sure you know what your marginal tax rates are on all new dollars earned in the future. And finally, find out what deductions and credits apply to you.

2. **Find new money:** Many people overpay their taxes every year, and then fail to go back and ask for a refund due to errors and omissions on their returns. This is possible by requesting a formal adjustment to returns — filed over a prior 10 year period. Ask your tax advisor to prepare a thorough prior-filing review for each family member. This is particularly important if you have been changing advisors from year to year, or have missed filing tax returns in any prior years. Make sure you ask for your overpaid dollars back, if applicable.

3. **Launch future RRSP tax savings:** Make sure you isolate the ways to reduce future taxes now. One way to do this is to have your tax advisor prepare an RRSP contribution room analysis for each family member. You'll want to receive a tax refund for every dollar contributed, as this new money can be used to finance your business or personal expenses or split retirement income with your spouse. It also diversifies your investments and maximizes your personal productivity. Carry forward undeducted contributions in cases where income is too low to derive a benefit from the RRSP contribution. Where income levels are high, make sure RRSP deductions are taken.

4. **Prepare to tax cost average:** Some carry-over provisions are available to taxpayers to average tax costs over time. Those are the ones to isolate and record now. Examples are prior capital and non-capital loss balances, unclaimed moving expenses or unused medical expenses and charitable donations.

5. **Do some "tax planning R & D:"** Find out how your self-employment can help you diversify income first from the operations of the enterprise; second, by building a potentially saleable concern. Talk to your tax advisor about your proposed business plans, your business structure at start up and in the future. Receive information about obligations to CRA, for income taxes, source deductions and GST/HST remittances, as well as business name licensing, trademark applications and the like. It is important to protect all of your equity in your income-producing assets.

6. **Plan to split business income with family members:** By starting a home-based business, you have the potential to reap double-digit returns in tax savings, simply by giving family members an opportunity to work for you. Try not to earn all the profits yourself. Find tasks within your business that can be delegated to others; then consider employing family members who are willing to take on the job a stranger would normally be hired for, and pay them at fair market value to do so. More detail later.

7. **Be vigilant about keeping track of all expenditures:** Start a document filing system and open a separate bank account. Small business owners can reap double-digit tax savings on each dollar they *spend* in their small business ventures, depending on their income levels and marginal tax rates in their province of residence. But to deduct costs you must keep track of all money spent in the establishment of your business enterprise, even if you are not yet earning revenues. Store your receipts.

8. **Get ready to give birth to your business:** Remember that the birth of a small business requires careful nurturing to grow into a profitable entity. Both money and time must be expended in advance for revenues to begin to flow. This involves the formalization of the financial path your business will take to its maturity as well as an injection of capital. CRA will want to know the details of that birth and its growth patterns when assessing your tax return. Keep track of all initiatives that precede the revenue flow in your business.

CHAPTER 2

···

How to Tax Cost Average

"We make our habits, and then our habits make us."
JOHN DYDEN

KEY CONCEPTS

- Control the tax you pay with a detailed tax and business plan which anticipates your income, deductions, and credits
- Review your tax filing results over a 10- to 20-year period
- Consider saving permissive deductions — like Capital Cost Allowance — for the future
- Claim every deduction you are entitled to, by accounting for full business and mixed business/personal components
- Split income with family members but watch the CPP costs, which affects each lower income earner
- Defer taxable income to the future, if possible

REAL LIFE: How would you like to save tens of thousands of dollars in taxes over the next several years? What would you do with the extra money? How would it change your life? The good news is that it's possible, you can do it and it's easy. In fact, this recently happened to Mary, a single entrepreneur living in Ontario.

Unable to afford a dream camping trip to beautiful BC with her boyfriend, Mary decided to have her tax advisor prepare a current year tax review. Perhaps there was something she was missing out on by filing her own return. Mary makes $40,000 a year from her efforts as a manufacturer's agent, which is shown on the T4A slip sent to her at the end of the year. She reports the amounts as self-employment income on her tax return, and that's it, she's done. "A simple return," she'd say every year; "no hassles."

Turns out, Mary's erroneous self-assessment has extracted a costly fee. She is dramatically overpaying her taxes. In preparing her return as she described it — which is perfectly legal and correct, by the way — she owes close to $10,000 at year end. Let's project that liability forward for a moment. Should her income stay constant over the next ten years, she'll have paid over $100,000 in taxes — more than what's left to pay on her home mortgage.

In addition, because the annual amount she owes the government at year end is over $2,000, she is required to make quarterly tax instalment payments throughout the year. This will take approximately $2400 out of her pocket *every calendar quarter*. What does this mean to Mary's lifestyle? No holidays this summer. . .fall, winter, or spring.

THE PROBLEM

Most people overpay their taxes year in and year out because they think about their tax liabilities only once a year. . .at tax-filing time. Unfortunately, at this point you are usually only reconciling history. Aside from maximizing every tax deduction and credit you and your family are entitled to, there are few proactive measures available to reduce the tax burden of the tax year in question.

In fact, the difference between a "taxpayer" and a "tax saver" lies in the desire to gain control of his/her future tax bill by planning all year long. A Tax Saver also controls the amount of taxes being paid to the government over a period of years — looking back and forward — to get a new result: *a tax cost that on average is significantly lower than the current liability.*

It is the self-employed who are in the best position to minimize tax in this way. As discussed in Chapter 1, business income, which is generally taxed within the calendar year in the case of proprietors, can be reduced by all reasonable expenses incurred to earn income from a venture that has a reasonable expectation of profit. Employees, on the other hand, are limited to writing off only a very specific group of itemized expenses, and then only with the certification of their employers. Proprietors can also utilize the loss application rules to their advantage.

So the Tax Saver's goal is to reduce the taxes paid over a period of years to avoid one of the taxpayer's greatest risks: the real dollar cost of under-utilizing available and legitimate tax provisions during one's lifetime.

THE SOLUTION

The key to reducing the taxes you pay is to put yourself and your family in the position of controlling the type of income earned, when it's earned, who reports it and how much of it is subject to tax. Your goal is to create an effective plan to increase after-tax wealth, implemented over a period of years, within the framework of the law. One way to do this is to *tax cost average*.

Your *tax cost* is the real dollars you send to CRA every year. If you net $40,000 a year from your small business, for example, your tax cost for the year will be about $10,000 (the exact amount depends on your province of residence).

Tax cost averaging is the calculated use of existing tax provisions to reduce the taxes you pay *over a period of years*. This involves the diversification of income sources, the application of all existing tax provisions to reduce your current tax bill, and the maximization of carry-over provisions to average out the good years and the bad.

Tax cost averaging begins with a "Tax Savings Blueprint". This is a projection of taxes payable through a multi-year overview, generally encompassing the tax results from:

1. the current year
2. the prior three years
3. the next 20 years

This can be a worthwhile endeavor that takes into account the maximum loss carry over periods.

The Tax Savings Blueprint is like a business plan—but focused on tax efficiency. It defines and brings structure to your after-tax results so that you can achieve them through your decision-making all year long. Anticipating and understanding the effects of those decisions on your after-tax dollars, within your 24-year window, can help you maximize all provisions that apply to your changing personal and business stages. Over time, this focus on tax position can return five and six figure tax savings—sometimes more—depending on the size of your business enterprise.

But, you likely can't maximize those opportunities alone. You'll need the help of an astute tax advisor with whom you are in sync with both tax law and the evolution of your business. The opportunity for tax savings often arises out of change—changes in tax law as well as changes in your personal/business life.

This, however, can also be difficult to manage, as tax law changes continuously—that's what you need your advisor to do for you, and then explain the implications to you.

You, on the other hand, are the expert at your business and therefore in control. When you combine a clear understanding of tax options with the vision you have for your business, you get tax efficient results. This is especially important when it comes to a tax audit. More about that later.

THE TAX ADVISOR

Mary was delighted to find out about the tax cost averaging process when she visited her tax advisor. He showed her how to reclaim some control over her tax costs. She hadn't known, for example, about the allowable claims for:

- automobile expenses (#2500)
- workplace in the home expenses (#1200, after personal use allocation)
- operating expenses, like promotions and travelling expenses (#3500)
- RRSP deductions, to maximize her RRSP room.

By drawing up a Tax Savings Blueprint—some "what if" scenarios—Mary's advisor illustrated the financial results available to a better informed taxpayer:

Current Year Investigation:

Mary's loosely kept books and records revealed the following:

- The additional deductions of $7200 above would save Mary close to $2500 in taxes
- Mary had never claimed any of these expenses before—a potential for recovery of overpaid taxes of the past
- Mary has accumulated $19,500 in unused RRSP accumulation room—a potential for future tax savings

Adjustments for the Past:

Mary's advisor can now take further action and request adjustments to prior filed returns where errors or omissions occurred. In looking over last year's return, he finds $2500 more in tax savings. Now it looks like Mary and her boyfriend can afford that holiday after all!

Adjustments for the Current and Future Years:

There is more good news. Thanks to her lower tax obligations on her current year return, Mary can reduce her quarterly tax instalment payment obligations throughout the next tax year—thereby increasing her cash flow by just over $600 each quarter or $200 a month. This gives Mary more cash to invest or grow her business with. Her tax savings opportunities now spanned three taxation years.

Mary's advisor wisely counsels her to consider all tax savings as a windfall to be used to accumulate her wealth. Her next logical step should be to invest part of this tax windfall into her RRSP. Given her plentiful RRSP room, Mary decides to contribute $3,000 to her RRSP this year and vows to do so every year. At her current income level, her taxes are now decreased by another $640, which further decreases her quarterly instalments by another $160. Again Mary has increased her cash flow.

In the second year, Mary uses the $640 refund resulting from the RRSP contribution along with some of the prior year tax savings to make a down payment on the new car she's wanted for years. That acquisition will give her further tax write-offs against her business income, based on both her fixed costs (like Capital Cost Allowance (CCA) and interest charges) and her operating costs (like repairs, car washes and parking).

By year three of her "tax enlightenment," Mary decides to use the tax savings from the increased Capital Cost Allowance write-offs to buy another asset—a new laptop computer. The CCA write off from this asset finances the cost of her office supplies. It just keeps getting better. . .tax savings from one business expenditure finances another! This is fun!

By the time Mary and her tax advisor were through analyzing "what if" scenarios on her Tax Savings Blueprint and putting them into action, Mary was paying approximately $4000 per year less in taxes than before they started. Mary could hardly believe that she could have been over-paying her taxes by $40,000 in ten years; $80,000 in 20 and so on. There is a trick to tax planning all right—you can't afford not to do it!

See the Big Picture—then Reinvest

It is important to see the big picture when it comes to your potential tax savings. Five-figure tax savings returns over a ten-year period are possible for some, and can translate into numerous new investments both inside and outside registered accounts, to send the taxpayer along the road to maximum wealth creation.

THE TAX PARAMETERS

If we've whet your appetite for tax savings, please take a moment now to learn more about the tax theory surrounding the *Tax Cost Averaging* process. Following are a series of parameters to help you understand the benefits of tax cost averaging.

Diversify the Types of Income You Earn Today and in the Future

Here's a quick look at different tax results stemming from your decision to earn a variety of different income types. (Ask your tax professional to prepare an exact computation for you as part of year annual Tax Savings Blueprint or use your favourite tax software program to do so):

Figure 2.1	Average Personal Tax Rates

Federal tax brackets in Canada are indexed according to increases in the consumer price index. The following table shows recent brackets and tax rates:

2006 Brackets	2006 Rate	Average Federal/Provincial
Up to $8,839	0%	
Up to $36,378	15.25%*	26.12%
$36,378 to $72,756	22%	35.84%
$72,757 to $118,285	26%	41.61%
Over $118,285	29%	45.14%

*Rises to 15.5% in 2007.

As you can see, those with income levels over $118,000 generally pay the highest federal marginal tax rates on taxable income levels... however, these results will differ from province to province, and over time with federal law change. The tax brackets are also indexed annually.

What we see in Figure 2.2 is the tax results obtained by a single taxpayer living in Ontario with income at the $40,000 mark; no tax credits other than the Basic Personal Amount and CPP/EI premiums. The example also assumes 100% of the income is earned from the source named. You might be surprised at the completely different tax results obtained from earning the same income but through different sources.

Figure 2.2	Diversification: Approximate taxes payable on $40,000

Income Type	Taxes Payable	% of income	Cost of $100	Marginal Tax Rate
$40,000 Employment	$9,518.10	23.79	$35.05	35.05%
$40,000 Net Business	$10,169.68	25.42	$44.16	44.16%
$40,000 actual dividends (small business)	$1,555.56	3.89	$15.87	15.87%
$40,000 Capital Gains	$2,405.24	6.01	$13.66	13.66%

*2006 figures, rounded. Taxes payable include CPP/EI premiums. Marginal tax rates vary by province.

It is interesting to see that income from dividends and capital gains earned produce the most advantageous tax result at this income level; in the case of dividends that's due to the effects of the dividend tax credit. This credit offsets the gross-up of dividends required under the personal tax system.

Capital gains on the disposition of assets produce the *next* most advantageous tax result. This is because of the 50% income inclusion rules. In addition, and just as important, you'll never be taxed on your appreciating value until disposition of the asset. That allows you the bonus of accumulating value on a tax-deferred basis. Finally, should you sell the shares of a qualifying small business corporation, fisher's farm property, you could, in fact, qualify for the $500,000 Capital Gains Exemption. . .and a largely tax free capital gain. More on this later.

Watch the CPP "Tax"

Figure 2.2 shows us that earning $40,000 of net business income costs you the most in real dollars. Why is this? The reason is not so clear: the numbers quoted include the cost of contributing to the Canada Pension Plan, and it's expensive: an annual total of over $3800 in 2006. That's because the proprietor must contribute both "employer" and "employee" portions to the plan. (This obligation can cause hardship for new proprietors, who may not expect to pay the CPP contribution all at once at tax time.)

So, while every tax dollar that you can split with family members may put the unit in a lower average tax position, this must be adjusted for the cost of CPP premiums, which affects every member with earnings between $3500 and around $40,000.

In 2006, for example, earnings subject to contribution were capped at an upper limit of $42,100 with a basic exemption of $3500, under which no premiums are paid. That means that there is a diminishing marginal cost for those whose incomes exceed the maximum contributory amount and an additional marginal cost to those whose incomes exceed $3500. See chart below:

Year	Maximum Pensionable Earnings	Basic Exemption	Contribution Rate	Maximum Employee Contribution	Max Self Employee Contribution
2006	$42,100	$3,500	4.95%	$1,910.70	$3,821.40
2005	$41,100	$3,500	4.95%	$1,861.20	$3,722.40
2004	$40,500	$3,500	4.95%	$1,831.50	$3,663.00

The employer must contribute a matching amount on behalf of the employee. In the case of a proprietor, 50% of his or her premium is deductible as a non-refundable tax credit; the other as a deduction which reduces net income. This tax treatment is on par with that afforded to other employees/employers.

Careful tax planning can help you reduce the tax burden of net business income and CPP obligations. You might consider planning to reduce net income subject to CPP contributions with your deductions for Capital Cost Allowances (CCA) for example. CCA is a deduction which accounts for the loss in value of your income-producing assets due to their ongoing use.

CCA is taken at the taxpayer's option and is used to reduce the net income of the business, upon which CPP premiums are based. This option provides you with some tax planning opportunities. For example, you may wish to elect to save your CCA deductions for future use if current income is low or you are operating your business at a loss. You can then reduce net business income later as CPP obligations rise. Then, to reduce this year's tax liability further, you'll want to maximize use of tax expenditures like RRSP contributions, medical expenses, charitable donations and so on, which can often be claimed in different tax years to maximize your tax benefits.

Split Income With Family Members

The chart in Figure 2.3 assumes the taxpayer has an unincorporated small business in the province of Ontario that grosses $125,000 and nets $75,000 after operating expenses. The illustration shows there are tax benefits of income splitting. In the first instance, the entire profits are earned by one spouse, while the other spouse has no income.

Figure 2.3   The Tax Effect of Income Splitting

Gross Profit	Net Profit	Tax Paid by Owner	Tax Paid by Spouse	Tax Paid by Child	Family Tax Liability	Tax Savings	CPP/ EI	Savings (Net)
$125,000.00	$75,000.00	$16,355.51	n/a	n/a	$16,355.51	n/a	$3,821.40	n/a
$125,000.00	$34,835.25*	$ 5,204.34	$6,175.63	n/a	$11,379.97	$4,975.54	$8,151.17	$ 645.77
$125,000.00	$21,562.50*	$ 2,397.27	$3,443.98	$3,443.98	$ 9,285.23	$7,070.28	$8,289.19	$2,602.49

* Scenario 1 takes into account a claim for the Spousal Amount; Scenario 2 and 3 take into account CPP/EI contributions by employer and employee. Figures are rounded and approximated based on tax rules at the time of writing.

In the second, the spouse is hired to work in the business full time. Salary paid out to that spouse is $37,500. Next, profit is split three ways, as the couple's 18-year-old child works full-time and draws a salary of $25,000; and the spouse works part-time drawing $25,000.

The family tax liability is reduced significantly, however, at these income levels, the high cost of CPP and EI eats up almost all the tax savings in Scenario 2 and a significant portion in Scenario 3. Results improve when employees are paid more than $42,100 or less than $3,500 — the CPP maximum contributory earnings and basic exemption in 2006.

The moral? When assessing your tax position, take into account the cost of the CPP and the results of your family's net income on refundable and non-refundable tax credits. To find out more about current tax credits, tax rates and clawback zones, visit www.knowledgebureau.com.

Defer Taxation of Income Into the Future

Try to invest the first dollar you earn, rather than the last one left over after taxation, by using your opportunities for tax deferral. Moving tax into the future increases your earning power today. There are several ways to accomplish this:

- Assess which of your potential income sources are taxed on a cash basis and which are taxed on an accrual basis. Capital transactions, for example, are taxed on the cash basis in the year the transaction actually occurs. Business transactions are generally subject to accrual accounting rules, which require reporting of income as it is earned, rather than when it is received, and expenses when they are incurred, rather than when they are actually paid.
- Time dispositions of assets advantageously, given the cash reporting rules. For example, you might choose to sell your revenue properties strategically if you expect a large taxable gain: one-half in the current year; one-half in the new year. The same logic could be applied to any capital or depreciable asset. The right price and willing buyer are, of course, prerequisites.
- In the case of depreciable business assets, try to push the disposition into the next taxation year, if the transaction will be happening late in the year, and the buyer is willing to wait. This could be especially wise if a recapture of previous CCA deductions will occur. More details appear in later chapters.
- When signing contracts for new work in your business, record start dates in the new fiscal year, if work on the project will not begin until then.

- Buy mutual funds in the new year, to push any potential distributions into the next taxation year.
- If incorporated, pay dividends in January rather than December.
- Time severance package receipts over two tax years or move into next year if that otherwise makes sense
- Take bonuses and raises in January rather than December.

Strive to Earn Profits and Build Equity That Will be Tax Free

Most business owners are so concerned about surviving the day-to-day challenges of making enough money to cover all expenses, that they often forget about the possible rewards, down the road, for the hours of unpaid labour they invest in their businesses in the start-up years. That is, if they build an entity someone else wants to buy in the future, they'll earn a capital gain that could be tax-free in some cases. Below is a true-to-life example.

REAL LIFE: Maggie, a 40-year-old mother, started a cleaning business last year. She started cleaning one house every Friday. After a while her integrity, work ethic, and reputation became well known, and within six months Maggie and her staff of three others were cleaning two houses a day, six days a week. After the first year, Maggie was grossing $60,000 a year and taking on even more staff to increase her revenues. Halfway through the second year, Maggie was offered $80,000 by a franchise company for her list of clients. She decided to sell her business. Not a bad return for a 24-month effort.

Had Maggie been operating a proprietorship,* she would have reported a taxable gain on goodwill.

However, had this business been incorporated, Maggie may have qualified for the Capital Gains Deduction and her gain on the sale of her shares would have been tax-free.

This scenario begs the question: *when should I incorporate?* This is an important question to discuss with your tax advisor. The factors to consider include the following:

- The importance of limited liability to the business owner
- The importance of income diversification: employment income, dividends from after-tax profits, bonuses paid out of the corporation
- Whether there are current year losses. Losses held in a proprietorship offset all other income in the year, the prior three years and for up to 20 years in the future
- The likelihood of a future sale of the business.

* other than a qualified farming or fishing operation.

These issues should be revisited with your tax advisor whenever you anticipate significant new opportunities, or at least annually. Also see Chapter 10.

Leverage the Cost of Time and Money Audit-Proof!

In our example above, taxpayer Maggie did an excellent job of leveraging time and opportunity for growth. After maximizing her own productivity, she hired one employee after another, and increasingly spent her time combing the neighbourhood for new houses to clean. The expenses of scouting out new business and earning revenues — salaries, car expenses, cleaning supplies, bookkeeping costs and so on — were all tax deductible. However, Maggie had no time to keep up with the books.

Realizing she possessed no skills for keeping track of receipts or numbers Maggie then did a wise thing. . .she hired a bookkeeper to do all of that for her. Now she need not fear a tax audit, an event that can reverse many of Maggie's carefully laid plans to tax cost average!

Make It Your Business To Know Tax Changes

Another great way to Tax Cost Average is to keep on top of all the most recent tax changes, announced with every federal and provincial budget. The documents often review prior provisions. You may find you've missed a few recoverable ones. If so, always go back and review prior-filed returns for any potential errors or omissions. But in addition, you may find some new tax write-offs and deferral opportunities. For the latest federal budget summary, visit www.knowledgebureau.com.

Retroactive Tax Adjustments May Have Limits

CRA may allow an adjustment for some of the unclaimed operating expenses of prior years, but special rules may apply. For example the Capital Cost Allowance deduction will not be allowed if the adjustment request comes more than 90 days after receiving a Notice of Assessment or Reassessment. However, taxpayers will be able to preserve the claiming of the Capital Cost Allowance deduction for next year in those cases. Home office and operating expenses will likely be allowed, retroactively, if receipts are provided. If the taxpayer is not claiming a loss, and/or shows that the majority of the income of the year is from the business, the question of "reasonable expectation of profit" will not be an issue. Otherwise, there is always the potential for a more thorough audit, if CRA suspects abuse. Therefore adjustment requests should never be made frivolously.

Always Have an Up-to-date Record of All Carry-Over Provisions

All taxpayers should make it their business to keep track of all carry-over provisions available over their tax-filing lifetime. Here are some common examples:

- Undepreciated Capital Cost (UCC) balances as well as costs of asset acquisition and disposition
- undeducted moving expenses
- undeducted home office expenses
- RRSP carry-forward room or undeducted contributions
- undeducted past-service contributions to Registered Pension Plans (RPPs)
- Capital Gains Deduction availability
- prior-years' capital and non-capital losses
- prior years' business investment losses
- undeducted medical expenses
- undeducted charitable donations
- undeducted tuition, education and text book amounts
- undeducted student loan interest
- minimum tax carry-overs
- undeducted Labour Sponsored Funds Tax Credits
- refunds of investment tax credits.

Maximize Opportunities to Build Tax-Exempt Income

Many people don't realize that there are certain income sources that are, in fact, completely exempt from tax. They include the following:

- Certain stock option benefits
- The Child Tax Benefit
- Gifts or inheritances (non-cash gifts from employers are generally tax free under $500)
- Goods and Services Tax credits (teenagers should be reminded to file a return for the year they reached age 18 in order to claim this credit for themselves the quarter after they turn 19)
- Income received as a personal injury award (income earned as a result of subsequent investment of such sums received by children under age 21 also will not be taxable)
- Life insurance policy proceeds on death of the insured
- Profit from the sale of a person's principal residence.

Further reinvestment of these sources generates taxable investment earnings in the hands of the recipient, unless invested in another tax exempt source.

TAX ADVISOR

To average out the money you will turn over to CRA over the long term, you'll need to be aware of the tax-planning choices available from the past, today, and, as time goes by, in the future. It is therefore important to have a good working relationship with a tax professional who clearly understands those tax parameters and how they affect your current and future financial planning goals and can discuss them in a way that makes sense to you. Look for a team of professional advisors: accountant, lawyer, financial planner, banker, life insurance advisor, who will inform you of all your options, so that you can make the most tax efficient decisions about your time and money.

Communication with your professionals begins with you, though. Be sure to provide the background information your advisors need to make the best recommendations for you. Here's a way you can facilitate the process:

Chart your tax cost over your carry-forward time frames, using historical data, current year data and projection for the future, using your own standard Tax Savings Blueprint. At the end of this process, you should have a basic understanding of the following:

- estimated tax calculations for the entire review period, using current tax law, and/or known proposals for change
- an analysis of the marginal tax rates paid or payable in the period
- a plan to average-out income, apply deductions and credits, as well as carry-backs and carry-forwards, so as to pay the least amount of tax, at the lowest average rate possible in the period, for the household as a unit.

RECAP. YOU NEED TO KNOW:

1. The difference between tax preparation and tax planning

2. How unused provisions can be carried forward or back to reduce taxes in carry-over years

3. Why loss carry overs and discretionary deductions like Capital Cost Allowances are particularly lucrative

4. How to use a Tax Savings Blueprint or "what if scenarios" to plan tax efficiency

5. How changing tax law— particularly tax brackets and marginal tax rates— affects your after-tax return on investment

6. How reinvestment of tax savings into tax deferral structures— like the RRSP— can produce even bigger tax rewards

7. What income sources are tax exempt

8. That quarterly tax instalments should never be overpaid

9. What to do when errors or omissions are made on your tax return

10. That tax efficiencies should be calculated forward over one's working lifetime to bring purpose to investigative tax queries between taxpayers and their advisors.

YOU NEED TO ASK: Get Tax Help to Ace Tax Cost Averaging and Cut Your Lifetime Tax Bill

1. **Work with a Tax Savings Blueprint** to make tax efficient decisions all year long. This blueprint—usually developed in conjunction with your advisor—is a standard format for "what if scenarios," which helps you understand marginal tax rates, and track carry over provisions, to help think about ways to reduce your taxes over a defined window of past, present and future tax years.

2. **Diversify the types of income you earn** today and in the future, and when you realize it for tax purposes. In this way you can average the taxes charged on your overall income portfolio.

3. **Minimize the CPP.** Take special note of the effect of Canada Pension Plan premium obligations over the next several years and plan your business deductions and income-splitting affairs with this liability in mind.

4. **Split income with family members** using all provisions available under the law.

5. **Defer taxation of income** into the future with registered retirement pension and/or education plans and by checking out tax-efficient investment strategies using capital asset acquisitions.

6. **Strive to do both—earn profits and build equity**—in all future business planning decisions.

7. **Leverage the cost of time and money with proper documentation**. . . miss no tax deductions due to poor bookkeeping skills.

8. **Understand how to make on-going retroactive tax adjustments** and then use them whenever the opportunity arises to reduce previously overpaid taxes, or to bring forward provisions that will reduce future tax liabilities.

9. **Have an up-to-date record of all carry-over provisions** available for reference at all times, and make sure that if you change accountants the new professional knows about these too.

10. **Build tax-exempt income sources.** Maximize opportunities to receive tax-exempt income now, in the future, and within your estate. This includes investments in tax-exempt principal residences and life insurance policies.

CHAPTER 3

How to Start a Tax-Efficient Small Business

"Ultimately we know deeply that the other side of every fear is a freedom."
MARILYN FERGUSON

KEY CONCEPTS

- Recognize a start up: is it a personal hobby or does it have a reasonable expectation of profit?
- Be ready to meet subjective and hard copy tests in an audit
- Formal business plans and cash flow projections help with the first
- Meet hard copy tests with documentation for amounts claimed
- Open a separate business bank account; use a separate credit card
- Classify expenses into operating and capital costs
- Strip out personal use components
- Claim your tax losses

REAL LIFE: Marlen Macleod loved to cook. Over the years she had invented a number of taste-bud tempting new creations, but a few stood out as memorable to her family and friends. There was the tomato aspic that was special at Thanksgiving, the miniature chocolate sculptures on her cream puffs at Christmas time and her crown roast of pork barbequed exquisitely for her mother's birthday bash, every August. In fact, after one particularly sumptuous girth-enhancing session, Marlen's friends remarked, "You know, you should really go into business!"

This common scene, played out daily in countless homes and workplaces throughout Canada often initiates entrepreneurship in those with both a product (or service) and vision. Yet, the flame of a small business owner's inspiration can quickly be doused if steps are not taken to shelter a fledgling enterprise from the gusts of CRA's audit department.

Marlen went on to become the town caterer and is today making plans to franchise her methods nationwide. However, she almost lost it all, when a tax auditor refused to see the potential in her and her start-up venture.

THE PROBLEM

Just when does a passion or a hobby become a viable business with a reasonable expectation of profit? The Income Tax Act provides limited guidance. It defines a business as follows:

> "A business includes a profession, calling, trade, manufacture or undertaking *of any kind whatever.* . . (including) an adventure or concern in the nature of trade, but does not include an office or employment."

This means that if you can make a profit from activities as diverse as gardening, walking your neighbours' dogs while they are on holidays, drawing ads or finding mates for the lovelorn, CRA will be obliged to agree that you are in fact in business. Unfortunately, the nature of business start-ups is usually such that you must spend both time and money before you reap the rewards. The risk hopefully will justify the rewards, which often are several years away.

In the meantime, CRA's auditors have a window of time in which to probe your affairs and make a judgement call on the deductibility of your expenditures. This is usually the current tax year and up to two years back. The bad news? CRA can choose to put the blinders on and take a narrow view of your business results to date. In fact, if you are writing off business losses resulting from legitimate deductions that are fully documented, an auditor can take a hard-nosed approach. . .that your intent is simply to take the expenses of a hobby, create a business loss and write it off to recover refunds of tax prepaid on other employment, pension or investment income. This is particulary true if you have a large component of personal use in your business costs.

However, the courts have consistently ruled in favor of the taxpayer when the Reasonable Expectation of Profit (REOP) tests have been invoked by the CRA, ruling that the REOP test must not be used to second-guess the business judgment of the taxpayer. Rather, it is the nature of the taxpayer's activity which must be evaluated. If the nature of those activities is clearly commercial, there should be no need to analyze the taxpayer's business decisions, as such activities *necessarily involve the pursuit of profit.*

THE SOLUTION

Start-up ventures can be a challenge for a CRA auditor and taxpayer alike. It's difficult, for example, not to get a little emotional when you've struggled to keep your enterprise afloat for a couple of years, only to find yourself nose to nose with an auditor who is inferring you are cunningly trying to avoid paying tax on the income from the day job that's keeping you all fed in the meantime. This can be particularly distressing if you've run into some unanticipated road blocks along the way. So to begin your new relationship with CRA, there are two things you need to understand up front:

Don't take it personally   Unfortunately there are those taxpayers who do try to bend the rules or cheat the tax system, and they are the very ones who validate the tax compliance activities at CRA. Tax auditing has its place in ensuring that small business in Canada competes on a level playing field; where honest taxpayers can rest assured that tax cheats aren't undercutting pricing. Your role in a tax audit is to provide the information required for the auditor to understand and agree that you have a viable business enterprise with a reasonable expectation of profit *in the future*. See it as an exercise in both communication and education, and approach this part of any audit with confidence. Remember, *it is usually the person with the most knowledge who is the most successful.* At this point, that's you, because no one knows your business and its future better than you do.

Know the rules and how to play the game   The day you decided to open your business is the day you stepped up to the plate to play ball with CRA. You're in the game, and it's more than just a pastime: you're in the big leagues now. Imagine for a moment a baseball player capable of hitting a home run. However, by not studying in advance the tendencies of the pitcher, he could easily strike out. Likewise, you could be heading for a lucrative dollar contract, but if you don't bother to know the tax rules, CRA could strike you out despite your skills, ability and work ethic. To that end, in the back of your mind in the pursuit of all of your business activities, you should be prepared to qualify that you are in fact, a pro, and know the batting range!

THE PARAMETERS

Professionals — those who get paid to do what they love to do best — conduct themselves in a *consistent*, professional manner. When business is your calling, your professional conduct is under scrutiny by your clients, your employees, your suppliers, your competitors, and yes, even CRA. For this reason, a specific code of conduct is required, particularly when it comes to your tax-filing obligations.

Open a Separate Business Bank Account

Never co-mingle personal and business funds. Also, obtain a separate charge card for the business. Never put business charges on your personal charge cards. In this way you can avoid "mixed use" and keep your personal (commercial activities) clearly separated.

Business Start Criteria

In order for any amount to be deductible on the tax return, the taxpayer must be found to be "carrying on business" in the fiscal period in which the expense was incurred. So when are you considered to be in business? Did the expenses you incurred precede the start of the business, or did they take place after the business had commenced? When did the business actually start? To assist taxpayers, CRA issues a number of "Interpretation Bulletins" on various grey areas. Here are some guidelines, based on CRA's IT 364; Commencement of Business Operations:

• A business starts whenever some significant activity that forms a regular part of the income-earning process takes place.
• There must be a specific concept of the type of business activity that will be carried on.
• An organizational structure must be in place to undertake the essential preliminaries, to show whether this is a one-time transaction, or an on-going enterprise.

The full utilization of start-up costs over the lifetime of your business is most important, as they can help you reduce profits in the future or reach back and gain access to past taxes paid. More on that later. Therefore, it is important not to lose this draw.

Some examples of activities that indicate whether or not business is considered by CRA to have started follow in Figure 3.1.

Hobby vs. Business

After determining a business start date, you'll have to convince CRA that you have a viable business that has a reasonable expectation of profit. This could be problematic in several areas, in which the taxman could take a hard line:

• The business is not making enough money to cover expenditures, and it looks doubtful it ever will
• The income from the business is not the chief source of income.

Figure 3.1 CRA's Considerations on Business Start-ups	
Type of Activity	**A Business Start?**
Purchase of materials for resale	Yes
Review of various business opportunities	No
Market surveys are undertaken to establish place or method of carrying on the business	Yes
Construction of a hotel has started, together with staff recruitment, training, advertising, purchase of supplies for bedrooms, restaurant, etc.	Yes
Overviewing preliminary plans and/or various sites to determine whether the hotel business was the right opportunity	No
Steps are taken to obtain a required regulatory licence in advance of business activities starting	Yes
Assurances were negotiated in advance of the commencement of business activities that suppliers would perform	Yes
Steps were taken to obtain a patent	No
Manufacture of the patented goods begins	Yes

To be fair, many successful businesses start out as a hobby. . .something you enjoy and at which you perfect your skills, only to find it produces a business case sometime in the future. There are many such examples:

- The professor of music who writes in her spare time, touring with a local band of musicians to summer folk festivals to build up her name and image
- The photographer who is employed by a newspaper during the day and takes breath-taking wedding photographs on the weekend
- The mechanic who has invested thousands of dollars in his video and computer equipment in order to document the history of his passion — vintage vehicles — in what he hopes will be a best-selling coffee table book next Christmas
- The farmer who works in the city as a teacher by day, and raises his prize exotic poultry — geese, ducks and ostrich — when he comes home
- The housewife and mother of four who has turned her recipe for after-school nutritional "candy" into a Christmas fair bestseller.

The best way to prove that a business emerged and has a reasonable expectation of profit in the future is to keep a detailed record of all the activities that you have performed in the past to cross the line from activities pursued "for pleasure" to those pursued "for profit." You can do this best by keeping a ***Daily Business Journal*** (see Figure 3.3). It also helps to show how close you are to landing the deals you need to make yours a profitable venture.

Establish Your Business Start and Your Fiscal Year End

Unincorporated small businesses must end their fiscal period for reporting business income and deductions at December 31. An election may be made to select an off-calendar year end in specific cases — when there is a bona fide business reason to postpone the business year end. This could happen in the case of a retail outlet, which experiences its largest sales of the year in the month of December. Corporations may choose any 12-month period in which to end their fiscal reporting period. This could be June 1 to May 31; February 1 to January 31, and so on.

Set up Your Tax-Filing Framework

For most businesses, there is a specific "framework" from which to work in approaching tax-filing obligations. This boils down to six easy parameters:

1. **Methods of Reporting Income.** There are two methods of reporting income:
   - **The cash method:** Income is reported for tax purposes when it is actually received, and expenses are deducted when they are actually paid. This method is usually only available to farmers and very small businesses.
   - **The accrual method:** Most businesses must use the accrual method of accounting. Income is reported when "earned" (rather than received) and expenses are deducted as they are "incurred" (rather than actually paid). Professionals, like doctors and dentists, may report on a modified accrual basis, to take into account "work-in-progress," while other businesses may take special reserves in certain instances.

2. **The Requirement to Collect and Pay the GST.** As a small business owner in Canada you may be required to collect the Goods and Services Tax (GST), if you make "taxable" goods and services in your business, also known as "supplies" for the purposes of this tax. Taxable supplies are taxed at a rate of 0% (if the supply is zero-rated), 6% or 14% (depending on whether the supply is made or in a participating province which charges the Harmonized Sales Tax (HST). The participating provinces are Nova Scotia,

New Brunswick, and Newfoundland and Labrador and include the Nova Scotia and Newfoundland offshore areas.

GST/HST is imposed on every taxable supply made in Canada. In addition, supplies which are made outside Canada but enjoyed in Canada will also be subject to tax when they are imported into Canada.

The recipient of the supply is the one who must pay the GST/HST. It is important to identify who the recipient of the supply is because it is generally only the recipient that can recover any GST/HST paid as an "input tax credit" (see below).

Although almost everyone pays GST/HST on taxable supplies, there are some exceptions. Certain organizations and groups including some governments and Indians may not have to pay this tax.

Small suppliers, those with gross revenues under $30,000 need not collect the tax (but may elect to). Specifically, a small supplier is defined as a person whose worldwide taxable supplies are equal to or less than $30,000 in either a calendar quarter or over the last four consecutive calendar quarters. This definition is used for sole proprietorships, partnerships, trusts, and corporations. In applying this definition, you are required to add together taxes collected on taxable supplies made by all persons with whom you are associated.

If the $30,000 threshold is exceeded in a calendar quarter, you are required to be registered to collect the GST/HST, starting with the supply that takes total revenue over $30,000. That is, there is no grace period allowed—you must register at that time, although 30 days are allowed for the registration form (RC1) to be submitted.

If the $30,000 threshold is exceeded over four calendar quarters, you cease to be a small supplier, and are required to be registered, on the first day of the second month following the end of the last calendar quarter. That is, a one-month grace period is allowed.

There are many rules around your GST/HST compliance obligations. Be sure to cover these with your tax advisor carefully.

3. **Deduction of Operating Expenses.** Operating expenses are also known as "business inputs" in GST jargon; or those expenditures that are necessary for you to produce the goods and services that bring in the revenues. These are items that are "used up," like supplies, advertising and promotions, rent, salary, communications costs, licences, etc., and are usually 100% deductible in the fiscal year in which they occurred, unless there are specific restrictions in place. When gross revenues earned are reduced by operating expenses the result may be either net operating loss or an operating profit.

4. **Computation of Capital Cost Allowances.** When you acquire an asset with a useful life of more than one year, you must classify that asset into prescribed classes set out in the Income Tax Act in order to get tax relief from their acquisition and cost of use. Prescribed rates of amortization are claimed for those assets and the result is a deduction for Capital Cost Allowance or CCA. This subject is discussed in more detail in Chapter 5. However, the key concept here is that you don't want to make the mistake of taking a 100% deduction for an expenditure that CRA is going to reclassify as a capital one. That can lead to expensive surprises later.

It is also necessary to keep track of asset values on acquisition and disposition, whether or not a GST/HST rebate or input tax credit was received, an Investment Tax Credit was claimed, or a special accelerated rate is available. Ask your advisor about these provisions.

The CCA claim also provides a series of tax-planning opportunities. For example, if operating expenses have already exceeded the gross revenues, it may be wise not to take the CCA deduction in the current year and "save" a higher undepreciated balance for use in the future. On the other hand, if the CCA deduction helps to increase or create a business loss that can be carried back to recover taxes paid in the prior three years, the taxpayer may wish to maximize the claim. Again, ask your tax advisor about this.

In addition, by reducing net business income with CCA, you may be able to save money on your CPP liability. This is significant for businesses in which net profit is in the $40,000 range.

5. **Computation of Auto Expenses.** One of the most common deductions of the home-based business owner, these expenses are usually computed on a separate worksheet. The reason for this is so that you can first total all operating expenses like gas and oil, and all fixed expenses like interest on your car loan, and then prorate them according to the business driving you did during the year. It's necessary to have an auto log that reports both business and personal driving in order for you to come up with the deductibility ratio. Details are discussed in Chapter 6. Note that certain expenses can be claimed on an unreceipted basis: coin parking, car washes, pay telephones or any other expenses incurred where it is not possible to receive a receipt. Keep a log of such expenditures.

6. **Computation of Home Workspace Costs.** Most home-based business owners will also be writing off home workspace costs, which is legitimate only if you have a separate area exclusively set aside for the business and if you regularly see clients or conduct your business

from there. This is also computed on a separate worksheet in order to properly accomplish the proration of all total expenses of the home, including utilities, interest, insurance, property taxes, etc. As well, there is a special restriction to be aware of: *home workspace expenses may not be used to create or increase an operating loss*. When this happens, the balance of the home workspace expenses must be carried forward for use in future years when there is an operating profit.

7. **Personal Use Allocation.** Most home-based business owners spend many long hours trying to get their businesses off the ground and use all the resources available to them to do so. This includes their own home, car, and other supplies, including the human resources inherent in available family members to get things off the ground. Many people make the mistake of underclaiming expenses that have a legitimate business component. We'll take a closer look at how to legitimize business-use components of specific expenses in Chapter 9.

To be sure, the Income Tax Act is very specific about personal or living expenses of the taxpayer. . .they may not be deducted, other than travel expenses incurred by the taxpayer while away from home in the course of carrying on a business.

Personal and living expenses are specifically defined in the Act in Section 248. They include the expenses of the personal property, costs of a life insurance policy or expenses of properties that are maintained by a trust.

However, what you need to know is that so long as you make proper allowances for any personal component of an expense, the business portion of the expenses should be tax deductible, provided that the expenses are connected to the earning of income from the business, which has a reasonable expectation of profit.

If you're in the business of selling cosmetics, for example, you might write off all the expenses of make-up and skin care products that are used for resale. But if you fail to add back into income a reasonable amount for personal consumption, you can expect trouble from tax auditors, unless you can prove you never use any of the products yourself.

In another example, a masonry contractor, who ships a portion of interlocking bricks to his new home, and a portion to his client's worksite, would need to allocate the personal use portion of the expenses, or write off only the portion of the expense that pertained to his client.

Similar adjustments must be made by those who run clothing stores, grocery stores, farms, fishing enterprises and the like. In addition, costs of using capital assets that have both a personal and business usage — example, a car or your home office — must reflect reductions for personal use. Expect to be asked for the personal use allocation during an audit.

Record Keeping: Meeting the Onus of Proof

For any expense to be deductible a couple of factors have to be in place:

- You have to meet an Onus of Proof, to show the amounts were actually incurred and are reasonable
- You have to incur the expense in order to produce income from your business.

Usually, you are considered innocent until proven guilty. However, compliance under the Income Tax Act has a slightly different twist: CRA doesn't have to accept your return as filed. Rather, you have the obligation to prove that every figure on that return was correct and legitimate. There are two sections of the Income Tax Act to look for guidance here:

- Section 67, which introduces the requirement for "reasonableness:"

  "In computing income, no deduction shall be made in respect of an outlay or expense. . .except to the extent that (it) was reasonable in the circumstances."

- Section 18, which zeros in on the concept of "intent:"

  "In computing the income of a taxpayer from a business or property, no deduction shall be made in respect of an outlay or expense except to the extent that it was made or incurred by the taxpayer for the purpose of gaining or producing income from the business or property."

To support your case for "reasonableness" you have to do two things:

- Keep meticulous records of all income and expenditures, including auto logs.
- Keep your personal and business affairs completely separate.

In addition, the auditor must consider the following: gross income, net income, cost of goods sold, capital investment, cash flow, personal involvement, experience and training, plans for future development, and all other relevant factors which will be used to determine whether business income is taxable, and consequently whether any losses will be deductible in full or in part.

When it comes to recordkeeping, it matters not how sophisticated your computer system and software is. The finest reports will not by-pass CRA's requirement for hard copy or microfilming. Guidelines for proper electronic imaging must be met, and can be obtained by calling the Canadian General Standards Board 1-800-665-2472.

You will be required to produce records, in an organized, retrievable and readable manner, including:

- Accounts
- Agreements
- Books
- Charts
- Tables
- Diagrams
- Forms
- Images

- Invoices
- Letters
- Maps
- Memoranda
- Optical Disks
- Plans
- Returns
- Source Documents*

- Statements
- Telegrams
- Vouchers
- Any other thing that contains information, whether in writing or any other form.

It is also necessary to keep an automobile distance log.

* Source documents include sales invoices, purchase invoices, cash register receipts, formal written contracts, credit card receipts, delivery slips, deposit slips, work orders, dockets, cheques, bank statements, tax returns, accountant's working papers and general correspondence, according to Information Circular 78-10R4.

Record Retention

Your records must be kept at your place of business or your residence, and must be available to tax auditors at reasonable times. CRA may reassess your tax returns at any time up to three years after the date on the original Notice of Assessment. If at any time fraud is suspected, however, the agency can go as far back in your records as it wants, subject only to the record retention period. That is, you are only required to keep books and records until six years from the end of the last taxation year in which the records and books relate. You can request permission to destroy your records earlier than that, using Form T137; however, this may be an invitation for a tax audit first. Note that electronic documents must be in a format readable by CRA auditors on CRA equipment. Contact CRA for more information.

Know the Value of Your Tax Losses

When your total business expenditures exceed your income for the year, the resulting non-capital loss can be used to offset all other income of the year. If there is an excess loss, the remaining balance can be carried back for up to three years, or carried forward for up to twenty years.

So let's say that last year your total taxable income was $115,000. This year after losing your job, you start a business and incur a $10,000 non-capital loss. What's the value of that loss if you carry it back and offset last year's income? Well, at a 45% tax bracket, that's $4,500. . .which can go a long way to financing continual growth in your business. So, you want to get this right!

But this is exactly the type of situation that can raise the flags in CRA's audit department, especially if you've been claiming these losses over a number of years. You'll need to be prepared to prove that the expenses were both reasonable and incurred to earn income from a business with a reasonable expectation of profit.

THE TAX ADVISOR

The following action items will be necessary to start your business venture. Do them on your own or together with your tax advisors.

Register Your Business

When you have determined your business start date, open a separate bank account for your business. Your next stop should be to your tax accountant and/or lawyer who will help you with the following compliance discussion points. Take Figure 3.2 along as a guide.

Tax Compliance Discussion Points

- Whether to obtain a Business Number, required if it is advantageous or necessary to collect and remit GST/HST and/or to make payroll remittances on behalf of employees
- When to make payroll, GST/HST and PST remittances to avoid late-filing penalties
- When tax instalment payments are necessary
- Whether to register business names, trademarks and copyrights
- Whether provincial sales tax collections and remittances will be necessary
- Whether family assets need further protection
- Whether life insurance, disability and medical insurance should be obtained
- How your estate planning will be affected by the start-up venture
- Parameters in writing contracts with others
- How to protect yourself and your family from lawsuits by others.
- Whether or not to incorporate

Write Your Business Start Plan

The checklist in Figure 3.2.1 should be consulted throughout the year to help you make major business start-up decisions.

By covering off the items in this Business Start Plan with your advisors, you will have most of the information a tax auditor will need to recognize you have taken steps not only to start a business formally,

Figure 3.2   Tax Compliance Discussion Points

Directions for Use: Discussion topics with taxpayers and their advisors.

A. Form of Business Organization: Incorporated or Unincorporated

Issues: Questions   Potential Solutions:

_____

_____

_____

_____

_____

B. CRA COMPLIANCE REQUIREMENTS

1. Business Number:

2. GST/HST Issues:

3. Provincial Sales Tax Issues:

4. Payroll Remittance Issues:

5. Taxable and Tax Free Benefits:

6. Requirements to Remit Instalment Payments

C. BUSINESS START PLAN

1. Fiscal Year End & Reporting Methods
2. Legal: Business Name, Trademarks, Copyrights, Asset Protection, Will Planning
3. Contracts Required, Formats
4. Business Plan, Budget, Cash Flow Plan
5. Capital Asset Acquisition Plan
6. Daily Business Journal & Aug Log
7. Sales and Marketing Plan
8. Separate Banking, Borrowing Schedules
9. Negotiate Terms of Payment
10. Home Workspace Sketch & Area
11. Owner-Manager Compensation Plan
12. Employee, Supplier, Client Contracts
13. Employee Role Descriptions
14. Training Programs
15. Risk Management: Personal Insurance, Disaster Recovery

Figure 3.2.1	Your Business Start Plan

Circumstance	Decision	Action Plan
Business Starts	Formalize Tax Position	- Prepare Business Plan: 1,3, 5 Years - Consult Professional Team - Prepare annual budget - Prepare cash flow journal - Start Daily Business Events Journal - Register business name/trademarks - Obtain Business Number - Start recordkeeping system, auto log
Obtain Assets Used in Business	Buy, Lease or Convert existing assets to business use.	- Obtain Fair Market Value of car, home computer, other assets to be used in business - Establish business location - Separate home workspace area - Obtain estimates on buying new or used - Obtain estimates on leasing options, tax advantages
Operating Expenses Commence	How Will Expenses Be Paid?	- Obtain Line of Credit or make equity contribution - Arrange terms from suppliers - Get business cards, design logos, letterhead printed - Establish separate business phone lines, fax/e-mail communications - Prepare marketing materials
Plan Owner-Manager Compensation	How Will I Be Paid?	- Proprietorship: remuneration, draw - Corporation: salary, bonus, dividends or shareholders loan?
Plan Income Splitting with Family Members	How Will I Pay Income to my Spouse or Children?	- Establish job descriptions, pay at FMV - Write employment contracts - Begin source remittances
Enhance Family Lifestyle	How Can I Utilize Company-Paid Benefits?	- Company Pension Plans - Company Group Health Plans - RRSP contributions, RPP, IPP Contributions* - Taxable/tax-free perks
Establish Operating Procedures	How Can I Expand?	- Document Policies and Procedures - Establish Organizational Structure - Prepare Marketing Plans - Prepare Development Plans - Prepare Product Distribution Plans - Prepare Quality Control Procedures - Prepare Follow-up Procedures - Prepare Client Relationship Procedures
Plan Equity Accumulation	How Will I be Paid Out?	- Establish family succession plans - Establish current valuation of business - Set a price. . .you never know when an offer may come along - Plan for tax-free capital gains
Plan for Your Demise	What Taxes Will Be Payable?	- Anticipate deemed disposition rules - Ensure life insurance will cover taxes - Family trust/testamentary trust planning

* Registered Retirement Savings Plan, Registered Pension Plan, Individual Pension Plan.

or to turn a hobby into a business, but also that there is a reasonable expectation of profit from your venture.

Start a Daily Business Journal

As you can tell by our previous discussions, even the commencement date of a business can be a debated matter when it comes to a tax audit. The best defense for the business owner to stay onside is to begin journalizing any and all activities that relate to the business as soon as possible. This can take any format you are comfortable with, but the key is to make notes of the following points:

- Every phone call made to do research, enquire about finding a supplier, get a business licence, lease a location, buy a computer, etc. Electronic calendars provide a great perpetual record
- Every networking appointment. Keep all business cards from potential customers, suppliers, or others who will be associated with you in your business, or keep an electronic contact record
- Every lead, meeting, conference, etc., which brings you to the next step in your business development
- Every hour worked on the project
- All distances driven in pursuit of your business activities.

A sample format follows in Figure 3.3.

This Daily Business Journal can be your key to tax audit survival. It shows intent and reasonableness at the same time. It helps you meet your subjective audit test.

Keep your journal faithfully. It is the story of your business's past, present and future; a crucial element in *"making sure it's deductible!"*

Formalize Your Books and Keep All Receipts

If you're a hopeless bookkeeper, do yourself and CRA a favour by hiring someone to do this job for you, at least monthly. You simply can't afford not to. You'll be busy starting up the business, recruiting the staff, finding the income to cover the costs and managing the distribution of your goods and services. You'll also be responsible for keeping your Daily Business Journal (Figure 3.3), a critical tool in ensuring that your expenditures are deductible during a tax audit. Poor recordkeeping can stall your business, so put this into place. Figure 3.4 outlines the minimum reporting structure you want to see to keep on top of your business activities.

It's important to keep these records right from the start. They will provide you with an ability to compare next year's results with your start-up year, and to budget for and chart the growth of your business.

Figure 3.3	Daily Business Journal

Date:

Time	To Do	Incoming Items	Follow-up	Expense Details
6:00 a.m.	Breakfast			km: 36,544
7:00	e-mail		Meet L. Jones	
8:00	Meeting T. Cook		Prepare Quote	Coffee $5.00
9:00	Prepare Market Plan			
10:00	"			
11:00	Mail/Telephone Calls	See log attached		
12:00 p.m.	Meet Banker @ Tini's			Lunch $35.00 km 36,660 B
1:00				
2:00	L. Jones @ Earl's		Prepare Quote	Coffee $5.00 km 36,670 B
3:00	Market Plan			
4:00	Meet Printer @ shop		Proof designs	km 36,750 B
5:00	Exercise			km 36,780 P
6:00	Supper			km 36,800 P
7:00	Finish Market plan			
8:00	e-mail			
9:00	Family time			

Total Expenses: $45.00   **Total Travel: 256 km**   **Business Travel: 206 km**

Figure 3.4	Required Reports

Daily	Weekly Totals	Monthly	Quarterly
Bank Deposits	Bank Deposits	Income Statement	Income Statement
Dollar volume	Dollar volume	Balance Sheet	Balance Sheet
Units Sold	Units Sold	Sales Statistics	Sales Statistics
Staff hours	Staff hours	Marketing Statistics	Marketing Statistics
	NSF Cheque Records	Payroll Remittances	GST/HST Reporting
	Accounts Payable	Cash Flow Requirements	

Tax Filing Deadlines

Most people know that April 30 is the personal tax filing deadline. Unincorporated proprietors can avoid penalties by filing by midnight June 15. But interest is payable on balances due starting May 1st.

Write It Off, Write It All Off

Look upon every expenditure you make in terms of its potential for reducing your taxes, and keep all the hard copy: receipts, invoices, etc. (see Chapter 9). Ask yourself: "Is this deductible?" Keep the receipt and then ask your tax pro.

Keep Track of Your Automobile Costs and Business Driving

Start an Auto Log immediately. Record all expenses of operating the vehicle, the fair market value of the vehicle at the time you started using it for business activities, and the distance you drive with that car: both personal and business kilometres must be kept, faithfully, to help you claim your auto expenses on your return. A sample format follows in Figure 3.5.

Figure 3.5	Auto Log							
Date	Km Start	Km Finish	Destination	Reason for trip	Gas/Oil	M & R	Wash	Park	Other

Plan How to Take Your Tax-Efficient Profits

Leaving CRA to concentrate on catching the tax cheats, you should now have tax compliance house in order with your set-up of procedures. With those basics out of the way, you can concentrate on setting up your affairs to make and report your profits in the most tax-efficient manner. That's where you should be spending the time and money with your advisors in the first place. Remember the reason why you are in business: to make profits and build equity over the long run to your best advantage. Figure 3.6 provides a few basics on maximizing after-tax profits, by choosing a tax efficient organizational structure.

Figure 3.6	Types of Business Organizations

Unincorporated Proprietor	**Incorporated Business**	**Partnership**
Taxed on Net Profits of the Business; not salary or draws	- Taxed as employee - Taxed on certain benefits - Taxed on dividends received as a shareholder - Taxed on sale of equity	Whether incorporated or not, the profits are split and allocated to partners based on details of the partnership agreement.

A Proprietor Can Reduce Taxable Income by:

- Making maximum RRSP contributions
- Minimizing instalment payments, interest, and penalties
- Reducing net business income with CCA deductions, paying operational expenses before year end, buying capital assets before year end, keeping auto log books to maximize car expenses, paying family members to split income and create RRSP room for them
- Deferring income into the future with timing of contracts, if that otherwise makes good business sense.

An Incorporated Business Owner May Reduce Taxable Income Personally by:

- Setting the level of employment income from the corporation to minimize source deductions, which affect the cash flow needed by the business. Suggestion: set salary level to maximize, RRSP room.
- Mind the top of tax brackets
- Optimize your salary/dividend mix
- Set bonus payments when the corporation makes a profit, especially when this exceeds the Small Business Deduction level. These payments might be taken over two calendar years to minimize personal tax. Or, you can decide to pay the bonuses to your family members who work with you, if by doing so you minimize the family tax liability as a whole, and is otherwise in line with employee compensation programs.
- Set dividend payments. Make these throughout the year if you need the money; but consider making at least one in January of the next tax year. You won't have to pay source deductions in advance through the company, and you'll have use of the money for a full 16 months more: January 1, year 1, to April 30 of the following year for example.
- Consider paying taxable and tax-free benefits to yourself and family members. (This will be discussed in more detail in Chapter 8.)

- Interest on shareholders loans: If you own your own corporation, it is possible for you to take a shareholder's loan. Under general rules, if this amount is not repaid within one year of the end of the tax year in which it was made, the amounts are added to your income. However, loans made to shareholders who are also employees are considered exempt from income inclusion if the loans were made because of the employment conditions (i.e., a loan to acquire a company car), and bona fide repayments were arranged.

Make sure you speak with your tax advisor about structuring compensation packages to take advantage of as many of these perks as possible.

RECAP. YOU NEED TO KNOW:

1. The difference between a hobby and a business
2. What constitutes a reasonable expectation of profit
3. How to determine when a business has started up with the result that income is taxable and expenses are deductible
4. How to establish a fiscal year end
5. What reporting method— cash or accrual— your business should use
6. The difference between operating expenses and capital expenses on a tax return
7. Basic GST/HST collection, reporting and filing requirements
8. Setting up claims for auto and home office expenses when there is "mixed (personal-business) use".
9. How long to retain records and in what format
10. How to think about your options in organizing your business structure: to incorporate or not?

YOU NEED TO ASK: Get Help from Your Tax Advisor in Setting Up Your Tax Efficient Small Business

1. **Acknowledge your new relationship with CRA**. Make a point of understanding your obligations to report income under the law, keep records, make remittances like instalments, source deductions, and GST/HST. Be prepared to open your books to CRA's audit scrutiny, and meet hard and soft copy requirements.
2. **Always document and separate personal-use components of any of your expenditures**, and open separate business bank and business charge card accounts.

3. **Know when your business is considered to have started**. When did it go from being a sideline or hobby to a viable going concern? The key is. . .when was there a reasonable expectation of profit or earning income from the business?

4. **Establish your fiscal year end.** This is normally December 31 for most unincorporated small business organizations; however, speak to your tax advisor if you feel there is a bona fide business reason to choose a non-calendar year end.

5. **Write a formal business start plan**, including a marketing and cash flow analysis plan, a formal budget and set up the ability to make comparative reports in the future. These documents will all go a long way to winning a tax audit.

6. **Start keeping a Daily Business Journal** to document your networking, contacts with suppliers and others who will help you build and grow your business. Keep your auto distance travel logs in here as well.

7. **Classify deductible expenditures properly**, into operational and capital items, to facilitate proper applications and do some long-term tax planning.

8. **Know the value of your tax losses** and how to apply them to other income in the current year and in the carry-over periods in order to Tax Cost Average.

9. **Meet the Onus of Proof** — annually. The ability to defend the "grey areas" is a position of power you do not want to give up to a tax auditor, who doesn't know your business or your business plans as well as you do. You can show reasonable expectation of profit better than the auditor can. . .don't give up your edge by keeping poor records during the year.

10. **Review your business organization structure often**: at least every six months. Is the proprietorship the best format, or should you be considering a partnership or incorporation? Is there a better way to split income with family members or a better compensation structure for the owner-manager? Discuss these items with your advisors.

Write Off More Deductions Without Changing Your Life

"You must first clearly see a thing in your mind before you can do it."
ALEX MORRISON

KEY CONCEPTS

- It's important to prepare your tax return to your family's best benefit
- For the "grey" areas, look to precedent setting court appeals
- Once you meet the REOP test, you've got to know your "deductibles"
- There is a difference in writing off current vs. capital expenses
- Prepaid expenses are treated differently again
- Restricted expense rules are often audited first
- Loss deductibility can be lucrative
- Proration of mixed use expenditures is mandatory—and easy

REAL LIFE: Julie was blessed with a special gift—the ability to express herself in painting beautiful Canadian landscapes for reprint on greeting cards. Her studio was in her home, from where she produced, marketed and distributed the cards nationwide. Her twin sister Janet was a writer, employed by the local paper. Her quick wit and quirky sense of humour landed her the role of feature freelance columnist—a job she enjoyed. She also wrote thoughtful messages for her sister's works, on a contract basis. With the pressure of writing a daily column, she often joined her sister Julie in the beautiful mountains of British Columbia, gaining inspiration and insight for their respective art forms.

The sisters, both earning income in the $75,000 range, found they were paying remarkably dissimilar amounts of tax. This prompted a visit to their tax advisor, who confirmed that both their returns had previously been prepared mathematically correctly—but not to their best overall benefit.

Janet, it appeared, was passive about claiming all the deductions she was entitled to. Julie, who knew more about her rights and obligations, fared better. Their advisor, however, found that they could both be decreasing the amount of taxes they were paying, without dramatically changing their lives. They needed to take a fresh look at the costs of running their respective businesses, tax cost averaging, and to stay on top of change in tax and in their business.

However, like many Canadian taxpayers, the twins were afraid to appear too aggressive, because the last thing they needed was trouble with CRA! They wanted to stay under the radar screen.

THE PROBLEM

Every day Canadian business people are contemplating a variety of business transactions and wondering *"Will it be deductible?"* How does one make the judgement call? This can be a real concern for many taxpayers, and legitimately so.

That is because our Income Tax Act alone does not provide the guidance fully required to assess the way Canadians file their returns. There are, in addition, a number of administrative policies enacted by CRA, and these policies, together with the law itself, are prone to a variety of subjective interpretations by both sides.

What's more, the Income Tax Act grants to CRA a number of arbitrary powers. In fact, under Section 152(7), CRA has the right to change your tax return if they don't agree with the way you've filed it. It can change your income figures, your deductions or your credits prior to the expiration of your normal reassessment period, which is three years. Your tax-filing fate, therefore, can rest with an auditor who perceives your *tax and personal affairs* quite differently than you do. Given this reality, it's often difficult to say in advance whether your business expense will ultimately be deductible or not.

For some, this is scary stuff. These grey areas of interpretation by two opposing parties is somewhat weighted in favour of the taxman, according to the historical win/lose status. It's sort of like playing ball against a team who knows more of the rules and also has all the referees on their side. Does the audit process itself lead to inequality of two taxpayers with like enterprises and income levels? Do those who get audited pay more tax than those who don't?

In auditing the books of business, CRA has been regularly challenging business owners who have claimed business losses over several years to demonstrate profit motive and a REOP (Reasonable Expectation of Profit) as discussed in prior chapters. However, thanks to recent court cases, in which the CRA consistently lost, it can no longer use REOP as a reason to disallow business losses in certain instances.

Remember that a net loss from your business can be applied first against all other income of the year and then against all other income of any of the previous three years, or incurred after tax year 2005, for a period of 20 years.

The courts have pointed out the difference between a "commercial activity" and a "personal activity" in providing direction for audit powers. If the business clearly has a commercial basis, and there is no personal element to the business, the business losses are deductible and the lack of REOP is not a legitimate criterion for disallowing the loss. As long as the business does not have a "hobby" element, CRA cannot deny the loss, even if there has never been a profit or never may be.

However, this does not relieve the business owner from the responsibility of establishing proper documentation and business practices. In fact, quite the opposite—the operation of the small business as a commercial activity will help ensure that it is considered to be a business rather than a hobby.

Following are some interesting results of court challenges.

It's Not Personal

In a landmark case that went to the Supreme Court of Canada (Stewart v. Queen [2002]) the taxpayer claimed losses pursuant to Section 20 of the Income Tax Act, for the costs of interest paid on loans made to purchase four condominium units for rental purposes. CRA denied these expenses because there was no "reasonable expectation of profit". They argued that the taxpayer had not had a profit in several years, and the 10 year projection was that he would not have a profit during that time. They argued that the deductions should not be allowed because the taxpayer was investing in these properties in the hopes that their value at some point in the future would yield a high capital gain.

In rendering its decision The Supreme Court of Canada essentially changed the existing law and its interpretation regarding the "reasonable expectation of profit test". It stated that this test had become a tool used by the CRA and the courts to "second-guess" the legitimate business purposes of taxpayers. It went on to state that the test is vague and arbitrary and sometimes results in unfair treatment of taxpayers. A new test was adopted to determine if a person's activities were a source of income: whether or not the activity is a commercial activity or a personal activity. Where it clearly is a commercial activity, the deduction or loss is allowed.

In this case the taxpayer borrowed heavily to purchase the condos, rented them out to arm's length parties and paid interest on the purchase loans. This was clearly a "commercial activity" as opposed to a "personal activity".

Fuel for the Body

In a 1998 appeal to the Tax Court (Scott, 98), a taxpayer who was a self-employed foot and public transit courier, tried to claim the daily cost of food and water needed to keep up the pace of his work during the day. The Tax Court dismissed his case, stating they found those expenses to be personal in nature. The Federal Court of Appeal disagreed. While food and beverages consumed during a work day are normally considered to be a personal expense, the court found that, in this case, the courier had to eat and drink more than normal; in fact, if fuel for an auto was deductible, so should fuel for the body be. The result? A reasonable amount of the expenses should be allowed as a tax deduction.

Sufficient Start-up Time

In a case involving a rental property (Gideon, 98), a doctor and her husband acquired a rental property that suffered losses when adverse economic factors were encountered. Despite the fact that they charged rent proven to be reasonable, reduced the mortgage quickly to minimize interest payments and that the size of the rental losses were steadily decreasing over time, CRA took a hard-line position and reassessed the couple's tax returns to disallow the rental losses claimed over a period of three years. The Federal Court of Appeal allowed the appeal and scolded CRA for failing to allow the taxpayers a sufficient start-up time in which to make a profit. Given the way in which the taxpayers conducted this venture, it appeared to the judge that there was a reasonable expectation of profit in the future.

Home Sales Produced Profits, Not Capital Gains

Failure to recognize a profitable business can bring dismal tax news. This is exactly what happened when a taxpayer built a series of houses and resold each of them in a short period of time (Mullin, 98). A number of these homes were built in a subdivision owned by the taxpayer's father. In this case, one house was allowed as a tax-exempt principal residence, as the taxpayer and his wife lived in the home. However, the taxpayer had not been able to convince the Judge that the other homes were built for investment purposes, because of the "quick flip" in sales. As a result, 100% of the profits from those sales were included in income.

The Dentist and His Sheep

CRA restricted the farming losses of a dentist who raised cattle for five years and then decided to raise sheep. The good doctor was able to beat the taxman by showing he had spent 60 hours or more each week in pursuit of his farming activities, while he practised dentistry less than 24 hours per week. He was also able to show that his investment in the farm was substantial and that over the years, his chief source of income had changed: now it was from the farming operation (Langtot, 98).

Credibility Wins Over the Judge

The commission sales agent faced the wrath of the taxman when his records and log books were, well, skimpy. The Judge at the Tax Court of Canada found him to be totally credible and allowed him to claim expenses as a deduction as a result. The Model Citizen Factor pays off again (Rusnak, 98).

These cases reinforce what you learned in the last chapter on setting foundations for business start-ups: because you have the ability to tell the story of your business circumstances, your intent now and in the future, your activities in pursuit of future profits, you likely have the components for a successful case. In fact, for some, a tax audit can actually be a profitable experience (see Chapter 10).

THE SOLUTION

If you want to make sure your expenditures are tax deductible, be prepared to prove there is a reasonable expectation of *profit* from the business venture. There must be present an *intent* to produce a viable source of income or a potential for that source sometime in the *foreseeable future*. Many taxpayers and their advisors underdevelop this argument during an appeals process, and lose their case.

This shouldn't be, as no one knows *the potential for future profits* of your business better than you do. The auditor can only make a judgement call on what *is* and what *was* in the reassessment period. You can paint the vision of the potential for income in the future, which is your right and privilege under the Income Tax Act:

> ". . . no deduction shall be made in respect of an outlay or expense except to the extent that it was made or incurred by the taxpayer *for the purpose of gaining or producing income from the business. . ."*
>
> ITA Section 18(1) (a)

"It is not necessary to show that income actually resulted from the particular outlay or expenditure itself. It is sufficient that the outlay or expense was a *part of the income-earning process."*
CRA's Interpretation Bulletin IT 487

"An expense would not be disallowed simply because the income-earning process produced a loss as long as *the intention* in making the expenditure was to produce income. Outlays or expenses made or incurred *to maintain income* or *to reduce other expenses* are also deductible as their purpose would be to increase income, whether or not such an increase resulted."
IT 487

THE PARAMETERS

Let's focus now on the "deductibles". Your "business" expenditures, assuming your reasonable expectation of profit from a viable commercial activity exists, fall into five types:

1. Current
2. Capital
3. Prepaid
4. Restricted
5. Not allowable

Current Expenses: These are used up in the course of earning income from the business. Examples are office supplies, wages, rent and other overhead costs. These costs are usually fully deductible against revenues.

Capital Expenses: These expenditures are for the acquisition of income-producing assets with a useful life of more than one year. This includes cars, buildings, equipment and machinery. These expenses are subject to capital cost allowance rates and classes which allow for a declining balance method of accounting for the cost of wear and tear. More about that in the next chapter.

Prepaid Costs: Most businesses must report income and expenses on the accrual method of accounting. In that case, the prepaid expense is prorated and deductible in the year the benefit is received. Only those on the cash method of accounting may claim the full costs in the year paid. This is generally only farmers, fishers and very small businesses.

Restricted Expenses: This includes the costs of meals and entertainment (50% deductible), and the costs of attending conventions (only 2 per year). Home workspace expenses are restricted to net income from the business.

Non-allowable Expenses: Fines or penalties imposed after March 22, 2004 by any level of government (including foreign governments) will not be tax deductible. However, this will not apply to penalty interest, imposed under the Excise Act, the Air Travellers Security Charge Act and the GST/HST portions of the *Excise Tax Act.* Also not allowable is the cost of golf membership.

Be sure to cover these and other expenses that fall into each category with your tax advisor.

In the case of a proprietorship, your deductible expenses are assembled on a Statement of Business Activities (see Figure 4.1). You'll want to make sure that every number stated on this statement is supported by your retrieval boxes of hard copy.

The Statement of Business Activities

Field codes are given to certain figures on the Business Activities Statement that CRA wants to match and analyze. The first is net sales on Line 8000, which is the total of sales, commissions or other fees earned in your business, net of federal or provincial sales taxes and any returns, allowances or discounts that were included in the gross sales figure. These categories should be discussed with your bookkeeper, who should set up the following accounts:

- Gross Sales (which you can break out into types of sales), before taxes
- GST/HST collected
- Provincial sales taxes collected
- Returns of sold items
- Allowances on sold items
- Discounts included in Gross Sales.

Also set up an account for Other Income sources that are outside the normal sales venues on Line 8230.

Cost of Goods Sold

Those who stock inventory will have to keep meticulous track of opening inventory, purchases, cost of sub-contracting and direct wage costs in producing the inventory. From all of these items the closing inventory value is subtracted to arrive at Cost of Goods Sold. You'll notice that only the business portion of costs are to be included here. This is particularly important for direct sellers in the cleaning, jewelry and other home sales enterprises. Those who use any part of their purchases for personal consumption — grocery items, cleaning supplies, jewelry worn personally, clothing worn personally, etc. — must account for this. You may not write off the costs of any inventory items that are used personally. Make sure you keep a separate log to identify such items and their value and be prepared to show this in a tax audit. In that way the auditor can see you have accounted for personal use.

Gross Profit (Line 8519)

This is a very important point of analysis for CRA. For example, let's say your net sales on Line 8000 were $25,000 during the year, but after computing Cost of Goods Sold, gross profit is only $5,000. From this, all other expenses of running the operation — from marketing costs to professional fees and wage costs — must be paid. You find yourself in the hole by $15,000, on Line 9369 Net income (loss) before adjustments.

Margin Analysis

A close look at line 8000 Sales and Line 8519 tells the story of profit margins in your enterprise. If your retail pricing to the customer is not high enough to cover your operating expenses, there is no reasonable expectation of profit. Fact is, you'll always be in a loss position at Line 9369, even if all your operating expenses are legitimate and documented. Most serious business people would want to reassess time and efforts closely to decide whether or not to continue in the same vein, given those poor showings. Change is necessary to stay afloat. *So, to make sure your expenditures are deductible, and resulting operational losses can be used to offset other income of the year, plan for reasonable profit margins now or in the future.*

Business Expenses Only

You'll notice the Statement of Business Activities (Sample 4.1) calls for the *business portion of expenses only*. All expenditures of the business must be prorated if there is any personal use component. *Adequate documentation is the key*, as you'll need to produce receipts for the amounts claimed on Lines 8521 to 9369. Always document why you made the expenditure in the first place. If you can, get into the habit of writing a note on the back of the receipt or invoice:

- Lunch, James Cook, re quote on supplies
- Gift, L. Smith, re thanks for contract
- Dinner, T. Tromblin, re rental property
- Flyers re Maryville campaign.

Sample 4.1 Statement of Business Activities

■◆■ Canada Customs and Revenue Agency	Agence des douanes et du revenu du Canada	**STATEMENT OF BUSINESS ACTIVITIES**

For more information on how to complete this form, see the *Business and Professional Income* guide. | 2

Identification

Your name	Your social insurance number

| From: | Year | Month | Day | To: | Year | Month | Day | Was 2005 your last year of business? | Yes ☐ | No ☐ |

Business name	Main product or service

Business address	Industry code (see the appendix in the *Business and Professional Income* guide)

City, province or territory	Postal code	Partnership filer identification number

Name and address of person or firm preparing this form	Tax shelter identification number

Business Number	Your percentage of the partnership	%

Income

Sales, commissions, or fees	a
Minus – Goods and services tax/harmonized sales tax (GST/HST) and provincial sales tax (if included in sales above)	
– Returns, allowances, and discounts (if included in sales above)	
Total of the above two lines ▶	b
Net sales, commissions, or fees (line a minus line b)	8000
Reserves deducted last year	8290
Other income	8230
Gross income (total of the above three lines) – Enter on the appropriate line of your income tax return	8299	c

Calculation of cost of goods sold (enter business part only)

Opening inventory (include raw materials, goods in process, and finished goods)	8300
Purchases during the year (net of returns, allowances, and discounts)	8320
Subcontracts	8360
Direct wage costs	8340
Other costs	8450
Total of the above five lines	
Minus – Closing inventory (include raw materials, goods in process, and finished goods)	8500
Cost of goods sold	8518 ▶	d
Gross profit (line c minus line d)	8519	e

Expenses (enter business part only)

Advertising	8521
Bad debts	8590
Business tax, fees, licences, dues, memberships, and subscriptions	8760
Delivery, freight, and express	9275
Fuel costs (except for motor vehicles)	9224
Insurance	8690
Interest	8710
Maintenance and repairs	8960
Management and administration fees	8871
Meals and entertainment (allowable part only)	8523
Motor vehicle expenses (not including CCA) (see Chart A on page 4)	9281
Office expenses	8810
Supplies	8811
Legal, accounting, and other professional fees	8860
Property taxes	9180
Rent	8910
Salaries, wages, and benefits (including employer's contributions)	9060
Travel	9200
Telephone and utilities	9220
Other expenses	9270
Subtotal	
Allowance on eligible capital property	9935
Capital cost allowance (from Area A on page 3)	9936
Total business expenses (total of the above three lines)	9368 ▶	f
Net income (loss) before adjustments (line e minus line f)	9369

T2124 E (05)   (Vous pouvez obtenir ce formulaire en français à www.arc.gc.ca ou au 1 800 959-3376.)   Canadá

Sample 4.1	Statement of Business Activities (Cont'd)

Net income (loss) before adjustments (from line 9369 on page 1) _____ g

Your share of line g above _____ h

Minus - Other amounts deductible from your share of net partnership income (loss) from the chart below | 9943 | i

Net income (loss) after adjustments (line h minus line i) _____ j

Minus - Business-use-of-home expenses (from the chart below) | 9945 |

Your net income (loss) (line j minus line 9945) (enter on the appropriate line of your income tax return) | 9946 |

Other amounts deductible from your share of net partnership income (loss)
Claim expenses you incurred that were not included in the partnership statement of income and expenses, and for which the partnership did not reimburse you.

Total (enter this amount on line i above)

Calculation of business-use-of-home expenses

Heat

Electricity

Insurance

Maintenance

Mortgage interest

Property taxes

Other expenses

Subtotal

Minus – Personal-use part

Subtotal

Plus – Capital cost allowance (business part only)

– Amount carried forward from previous year

Subtotal | 1

Minus – Net income (loss) after adjustments (from line j above) – If negative, enter "0" | 2

Business-use-of-home expenses available to carry forward (line 1 minus line 2) – If negative, enter "0"

Allowable Claim (the lesser of amounts 1 or 2 above) – Enter this amount on line 9945 above

---
Details of other partners

Name and address	Share of net income or (loss) $	Percentage of partnership	%
Name and address	Share of net income or (loss) $	Percentage of partnership	%
Name and address	Share of net income or (loss) $	Percentage of partnership	%

Details of equity

Total business liabilities	9931	
Drawings in 2005	9932	
Capital contributions in 2005	9933	

Avoid Pitfalls Claiming Common Business Expenses

Accounting and Legal Fees   The key pitfall taxpayers run into here is that they write off accounting and legal fees in full in cases where they really relate to capital transactions. CRA has issued IT-99R5 to address certain specific cases when legal or accounting fees will be deductible. They will be 100% deductible when paid in normal business activities like preparing contracts, collecting trade debts, preparing minutes of directors' meetings, conducting appeals for sales or property tax assessments and so on. They may even be deductible in defense of a charge of performance of illegal activities, depending on the relationship of the conduct to the income-earning activities. (Also see comments re Damages.) Fees for preparing income tax returns and assistance in preparing an appeal on assessment of income taxes, interest or penalties, CPP or EI premiums will be deductible, as will the costs of preparing advance tax rulings.

However, when legal and accounting fees are incurred on the acquisition of capital property, they are normally included in the cost of the property, or as an outlay or expense in the case of dispositions of capital property.

Legal fees surrounding successful corporate acquisitions will be treated as capital expenses added to the cost base of the shares acquired. Legal and accounting fees incurred in an abortive attempt to acquire shares would normally not be deductible at all unless the taxpayer can demonstrate that s/he intended to make the business a part of a similar business already operated by the taxpayer. (See IT-143 and IT-259.)

Convention Expenses   This is a real problem area for taxpayers at audit time. First, self-employed taxpayers may claim the costs of *only two conventions* a year provided that they were held by a business or professional organization. While you need not be a member of the organization, you must have had an income-earning purpose related to your business in attending the convention. In addition, IT 131 explains another little-known requirement: that the convention be "held at a location that may reasonably be regarded as consistent with the territorial scope of the organization." An example of this would be an ocean cruise held by a Canadian organization. Therefore taxpayers must be cautioned to choose their convention locations wisely — as only two per year are deductible in the first place — and ensure they can prove that attending a convention in another country is directly related to their business or profession.

Damages and Settlements Paid   If you incur damages resulting from a normal risk of your business operations, a deduction for the costs, including interest payments or wrongful dismissal payments, will normally be allowed as fully deductible, unless the damages are on account of capital, in which case they would be classified as "eligible capital property." In such cases, three-quarters of the value of the damages are scheduled in the Cumulative Eligible Capital account, and may be deducted at a rate of 7% of that value per year.

Non-Competition Agreements   Here's a "dark horse" for any business owner who sells his or her company down the road and agrees to work under an employment contract that includes a non-competition clause. Where the payments form a part of the proceeds of sale of the goodwill of the business or the cost of shares, amounts received in exchange for the agreement not to compete can be classified as an "eligible capital expenditure" or capital gain respectively. See IT 467.

Health Care Premiums

For tax years after 1997, the tax department will allow you to deduct from your business income any premiums paid to a private health plan on behalf of yourself, your employees and your spouse or children. For these premiums to be deductible, you must meet certain criteria:

- your income from the business in the current or preceding year must exceed 50% of your income for the year and your other income must not exceed $10,000
- premiums are paid to a government authorized Private Health Services Plan
- the premiums are not claimed as a medical expense by anyone else and
- the deduction depends on several criteria including how many qualifying (non-family) employees are insured and for what part of the year.

The deduction is either the lowest amount that is or would be paid for non-family members or:

- an annual dollar maximum of $1,500 for yourself and each adult family member covered by the plan plus
- $750 for each family member who is under 18 years of age at the beginning of the fiscal year.

Note: If you do not pay the premiums for any employee covered by the plan, the limit for yourself is zero.

If the period of coverage is for less than one year, the amounts are prorated. Where you have no non-arm's length employees, you are limited to the dollar maximums described above.

Hospitality, Meals and Entertainment

CRA has issued IT 518R to overview their position with regard to the deductibility of food, beverages and entertainment. Reasonable amounts may of course be deducted, if incurred to earn income from a business or property. The total costs must, however, be restricted to 50% of the amounts actually paid or payable. Note this 50% limitation will not apply to the computation of the personal tax liability on the T1 General in the following cases:

- The claiming of moving expenses using Form T1M
- The claiming of child care expenses using Form T778
- The claiming of medical expenses.

However, it is important to know that the 50% limitation does apply to taxes and tips left as well as to restaurant gift certificates purchased as a gift for your client. The small business owner must be aware of several exceptions to the 50% restriction which will result in 100% claims on his/her Statement of Business Activities, as discussed below:

- **The Hospitality Business.** Costs of food, beverages or entertainment provided in the ordinary course of business, which is the business of providing food, beverages or entertainment to others in return for compensation. Restaurants, hotels and airlines, therefore, are all exempt from the 50% restriction on food, beverages or entertainment provided to their customers.
- **The Food & Beverage Business.** If the business you conduct is the business of making food, beverages or entertainment, the cost of promotional samples is 100% deductible. However, any time you take someone out for a business meal, the costs will be subject to the 50% rules.
- **Registered Charities.** The 50% restriction will not apply if the food, beverages or entertainment are for a fund-raising event to primarily benefit a charity. The 50% rule will apply to the price of admission to an event that is part of the regular activities of the charity. For instance, Morena invites her client, Gustav, to the annual fund-raising dinner of the Manitoba Theatre for Young People. The expenses in that case are not subject to the 50% rules. Next week, she will be giving Gustav tickets to the group's five

new plays to be held over the next seven months. The cost of those tickets are subject to the 50% rule.

- **Consultant's Billings.** If you do work for a company that entails travel or work "on location," and if the costs of meals are billed to the client and reimbursed to you, you are able to fully deduct those meal expenses, as the reimbursement would be included in your income.

- **Meals at Conferences.** Where an all-inclusive fee is paid, entitling the participant to food, beverages and/or entertainment, a $50 amount is allocated for each day to be the amount that's subject to the 50% restriction. All other costs will be fully deductible.

- **Beverages en Route.** You can fully deduct the cost of any meals and beverages served or entertainment provided on planes, trains or buses (but not ships, boats or ferries), so keep a log of those expenditures, as receipts are normally not available, and CRA will allow a reasonable amount as your claim.

- **Employer-Sponsored Events.** When you entertain your staff, you'll be able to avoid the 50% limitation on food, beverages and entertainment, provided that these are generally available to all employees at a particular place and enjoyed by them, like a Christmas party. After February 24, 1998, such events are limited to six per year.

- **Employer-Operated Restaurants or Cafeterias.** Costs of food and beverages here are not subject to the 50% rule, but subsidized meals do present a taxable benefit to the employees. Restricted facilities like an executive lounge or dining room are always subject to the 50% limitation.

Note that the following activities will qualify as entertainment subject to the 50% rules:

- Tickets to theatre, concerts, athletic events
- Private boxes at sporting events
- Cost of a cruise
- Admission to a fashion show
- Hospitality suites
- Entertaining at athletic or sporting clubs
- Entertaining while on vacation
- Cost of taxes, gratuities and cover charges
- Cost of security escorts
- Cost of escorts or tour guides.*

* Costs of "escort services" are not deductible at all. So now you know.

Interest Costs

Interest costs on money borrowed at a reasonable interest rate to earn income from a business or property will generally be deductible. Interest expenses will not be deductible in the following cases:

- The loan is interest free or the interest costs payable are not reasonable
- The money is not used directly in the pursuit of income from a business with a reasonable expectation of profit

Note: Income from property does not include capital gains accruals. Therefore income in the form of dividends, rents or interest must be present for interest deductibility on loans used to acquire capital properties to be allowed.

CRA has set out its current interpretations on interest deductibility in IT-533 which business owners should know.

- Tracing/Linking: The onus is on the taxpayer to trace funds to a current and eligible usage. Taxpayers must demonstrate that aggregate eligible expenditures from co-mingled accounts, for example, exceed the amount borrowed and deposited to that account.
- Income-producing Accounts: CRA accepts that the use of borrowed money can be for an ancillary, rather than primary income-producing purpose. This will be determined as a question of fact.
- Borrowing to pay dividends. The interest expense amounts will be deductible.
- Borrowing to make loans to employees and shareholders. Interest will be deductible if there is a reasonable expectation of income. This comes from the effort of the employee and such loans would be therefore viewed as a form of remuneration.
- Borrowing to contribute capital. Interest may be deductible if the borrowed funds can be linked to an income-producing purpose (i.e. the issuing of dividends).
- Borrowing to honor a guarantee. Interest costs are generally not deductible unless it can be shown that the transaction will increase the potential for dividends to be received. If the taxpayer receives consideration of some kind for fair market value, such amounts are a source of income and therefore any interest expense incurred to earn it will be deductible.
- Leveraged buy-outs . Interest on money borrowed to acquire common shares will be deductible. CRA comments further by saying there is no arm's length requirement in this case.

- Limitation on Interest Deduction on Purchase of Undeveloped Land: The deduction for interest and property taxes on land is limited to the net income from the land. These limitations do not apply to land used in the course of business other than land development. Interest and property taxes not deductible may be added to the cost base of the land.
- Interest Paid on Capital Property That is no Longer Owned: When a taxpayer borrows money to acquire a capital property for the purposes of earning income from that property and subsequently disposes of the property for an amount less than the amount borrowed to acquire the property, it is deemed that the taxpayer continues to use the property for the purpose of earning income from property. In other words, if the proceeds of the sale are used to pay back the money borrowed, then the interest payable on any outstanding balance will continue to be deductible.
- Capitalizing Interest. Many business owners are unaware of the election to *capitalize* the cost of borrowed money used to acquire depreciable property. This election can be made for the current year and the three immediately preceding years, and for one, some or all of the properties acquired. It can also be made for all the money borrowed or some of it. An election under Section 21(1) or (3) of the Income Tax Act must be made and submitted with the tax return each year to opt for the treatment. Then the amount of the interest is simply added to the capital cost of the property and written off as part of the CCA claim each year. Using this method, you can effectively move your interest deduction to future years when you have a higher income level. Look to IT 121 for more details.

Training Expenses

How much of your training costs — including travel, food, beverages and lodging paid to attend a training course — can you actually claim as a business deduction? There are several important rules to observe here, as outlined in IT 357R2:

New Skill or Upgrading?   Training costs will not be deductible if they are considered to be "capital" in nature; that is if they result in a lasting benefit to the taxpayer. This could include the acquisition of a new skill or qualification. However, if training is taken to maintain, update or upgrade an existing skill, the costs are 100% deductible. . . that is unless they are also being claimed as a non-refundable tax credit under the tuition fee amount.

Examples of expenses that are 100% deductible are:

- A professional development course taken to maintain professional standards
- A tax course taken by a lawyer or accountant, whether or not such work has been done previously
- A course on modern building materials is taken by an architect.

Therefore, training costs to attend a course which results in a degree, diploma, professional qualification or similar certificate is considered to be "capital" in nature. The costs would be scheduled in the Cumulative Eligible Capital account. Examples of this are the following:

- Training by a medical practitioner to qualify as a specialist
- Lawyer taking an engineering course unrelated to the legal practice
- A professor taking a sideline course to acquire skills in a sideline business.

Personal Portion   Any portion of the costs that are personal in nature cannot be deducted. This is assessed on a case-by-case basis and takes factors like duration and location of the course into account, as well as the number of days in which there was no training. It is also important that the costs not be misclassified. If they are really convention expenses, you could be restricted to the "two per year rule" and "territorial scope" rules identified earlier.

Location and Duration   Deductibility of expenses will be questioned if courses are taken abroad or in a resort, particularly if you follow up the course with a personal holiday. If equivalent training was available locally, your expenses for the trip to study at the exotic location will likely be considered personal. Costs for expenses of food and lodging will not be allowed for any days in which no training was held. CRA will make an exception for arrival and departure dates, as well as week-ends, and allow those costs. Remember that the costs of claiming food and auto are subject to the normal limitations.

Deductibility of Seminars   Are they classified as conventions or training courses? This is a question of fact. Conventions generally include a formal meeting of members of an organization or association. Training courses generally have a classroom format and a formal course of study that results in testing and the possibility of certification. Training courses are treated more favourably in that you can attend more than two in a year, however, Interpretation Bulletin 357R2 makes a noteworthy comment: "the total time taken in attending courses in any one year must not be so great as to interfere with the carrying on of the taxpayer's business. If that happens, expenses will not be deductible."

Stay Informed: Resources are Many, Varied and Often Free

In conclusion, if you are wondering about the deductibility of a specific classification of expenses, don't hesitate to seek guidance from an Interpretation Bulletin or other tax information from CRA. This will give you guidance on the position the agency will likely be taking on the issue, and help you with the peace of mind issue.

Remember, if you decide to take an aggressive stance and claim deductions for items that could be called into question, you want to make sure you have a bona fide business purpose documented for each expenditure, and that your business has a reasonable expectation of profiting from your activities and expenditures. The section following may be of some help in audit-proofing those decisions.

TAX ADVISOR

To audit-proof your expenditures and help you *"Make Sure It's Deductible,"* you may wish to take advantage of some of the checklists in Figures 4.2 and Figure 4.3 to help you make sound judgement calls that ensure your books are prepared in your favour. Consider two compliance standards:

Hard Copy Classification

Before spending the money, take a look at the expense that you are contemplating, classify it as an operating or capital expense and prepare your records as detailed in Figure 4.2.

Figure 4.2	**Classification of Expenses**

Expense: _____ Total $_____ HST/GST $_____ PST$_____

Authorized by: _____ Date Paid: _____

1. What is the classification of the expense?   ☐ Operating   ☐ Capital

2. Will the expense impact future revenues? _____

3. Is the expense reasonable under the circumstances? Why? _____

4. Will the expense reduce costs to improve bottom lines? _____

5. Is there a personal use component? If so what %? _____

Figure 4.3	Business Component of Mixed-Use Expenses

Expense	Do You Have Receipts?		Can You Claim the Expense? Talk to your tax advisor about these grey areas	Can You Use It?	
	Yes	No		Yes	No
A. Personal **Groceries**			Usually no, but entertaining for business purposes is tax deductible (50% usually), so is the expense of feeding children in a babysitting business (100%). Personal use must always be isolated, however.		
Clothing			Usually no, however certain clothing is deductible, provided it is unsuitable for street wear; example, judges' robes; entertainers' costumes. These must be depreciated, rather than written off in full.		
Footware			Usually no, however, employed dancers and certain self-employed taxpayers may make a claim in certain cases if their special footware is "used up" in the pursuit of business income. For example, those who run a winter resort might write off the cost of snowshoes worn by instructors, or ballerinas may write off the cost of their shoes.		
Entertainment			Yes, but generally restricted to 50% of costs; except for events that are staff gatherings — but no more than 6 times a year. If you entertain in your home, keep receipts of food, liquor, etc., specific to the event. Keep entertainment log to record name and address of person being entertained.		
Utilities			Yes, a portion of these expenses are deductible if workspace in home claim is otherwise allowed. Keep total bills, but prorate expenses according to square footage of office space.		
Repairs/ **Maintenance**			Yes, certain employed musicians, other employees, and the self–employed may make this claim for repairs to home office, revenue properties, certain equipment. Personal use must be isolated.		
Mortgage (Home) **Payments**			Yes. But only interest costs (not principal) are deductible by the self-employed, according to the space used for business purposes.		
Insurance **Payments**			Yes, if home office claims, musicians' instrument costs, auto expense claims and insurance for other equipment costs are otherwise allowable.		
Car Payments			Never for personal driving; however, costs of running an auto are deductible, if used for business or employment purposes and written off according to information on distance travelled in auto log.		

Figure 4.3	Business Component of Mixed-Use Expenses (Cont'd)

Expense	Do You Have Receipts?		Can You Claim the Expense? Talk to your tax advisor about these grey areas	Can You Use It?	
	Yes	No		Yes	No
Tuition Fees			Claim as a tax credit rather than a deduction if over $100 and paid to a designated educational institute. Sometimes can be claimed as an expense of business as a training cost, in which case either the credit or the deduction must be chosen. For higher-income earners, the deduction may result in a higher claim.		
Gifts			Personal, no. If made to a client of a self-employed taxpayer, or in some cases, an employed commissioned salesperson, yes. Note gift certificates to restaurants are subject to the 50% restriction on meals.		
Medical/Pharmacy			Claim as a medical expense credit on the return. Group health plan premiums may be a tax deductible business expense starting in 1998.		
B. Employment					
Clothing			No. Not even itemized dry cleaning, cost of special shoes or workboots is allowable, but a new Canada Employment Credit is available to cover these costs.		
Car Expenses			Yes, if Form T2200 is signed and auto log kept up.		
Parking			Yes, if duties include working away from the employer's office to sign contracts on behalf of employer and Form T2200 is available.		
Lunches			Only if away on business for employer for at least 12 hours. Entertainment expenses may be allowed if you are a commission salesperson, for the purposes of entertaining your client .		
Office Supplies			Yes, if used up directly in your job and Form T2200 is signed by the employer.		
Long-Distance Calls			Yes, if made for business or employment purposes. However, monthly rental charges are not deductible unless a separate line is installed.		
Special Clothing			Generally no, unless unsuitable for street wear, as explained above.		
* **Tools & Equipment**			The self-employed may write off the cost of tools and equipment according to special rules; the employed taxpayer may not, with the exception of claims for auto, musical instruments or aircraft; also tradespeople and apprentice vehicle mechanics may claim cost of tools under a new limited deduction starting on or after May 2, 2006.		
Licences & Bonding			Yes, these costs are deductible by both employed and self-employed persons.		

Figure 4.3	Business Component of Mixed-Use Expenses (Cont'd)

Expense	Do You Have Receipts?		Can You Claim the Expense? Talk to your tax advisor about these grey areas	Can You Use It?	
	Yes	No		Yes	No
Computers/Phones			Only the self-employed may write off the costs of these capital assets, including cost of acquisition (usually a capital expense) and interest costs.		
Interest Costs			The self-employed may claim the costs of interest paid on loans to finance their operating costs, equipment purchases and home workspace. Employees may only write off interest costs on auto, aircraft and musical instrument acquisitions, but not mortgage interest or other costs.		
Salary to Assistant			Yes, these costs are deductible by both the employed and self-employed. File form T2200 for the employee.		
Office Rent/ In-Home			These costs are deductible by employed and self-employed. However, for employed taxpayers, there is never an allowable claim for mortgage interest or CCA. Unless you earn commissions you also may not claim property taxes or insurance costs.		
Training Costs			These may be deductible against business income or claimed as a tuition tax credit, if eligible.		
Accounting/Legal Fees			Yes, in certain cases, for employees, the fees must be paid to appeal an assessment of tax; or in cases where you were forced to establish rights to salary, wages or commissions owed to you.		
Income Tax Preparation			Not deductible by employees; however employed commissioned salespeople and the self-employed may make a claim; certain investors also.		
C. Investments **Interest Costs**			Yes, deductible if there is a potential for the earning of rents, interest or dividends. However, this is true only of loans used to acquire non-registered investments.		
Safety Deposit Box			Yes.		
Management Fees			Yes, but not for registered investments.		
Accounting Fees			Only if accounting is a usual part of the operations of your property.		
Investment Counsel			Yes. For details, obtain CRA's IT 238.		
D. Self-Employment **Operating Expenses**			Yes, those expenses "used up" in the running of a business are 100% deductible if reasonable and incurred to earn income from a business with a reasonable expectation of profit. May create loss.		
Capital Expenses			No. Only a percentage of costs, known as Capital Cost Allowance, may be deducted, at the taxpayer's option, to write down a notional amount for wear and tear of the asset.		

Business/Personal-Use Classification

Make a list of all expenditures that have both a personal and business component to determine if any of those items are tax deductible, as shown in Figure 4.2. Chart common expenses of the family, and determine whether any of them should be claimed as a business expense, bearing in mind that they must have a direct bearing on the income-earning activities of the business and reasonable under the circumstances.

Penalties for Tax Evasion, Other Missteps

It can be expensive to break tax law. Income tax evasion—the willful understatement of income or overstatement of expenditures—could result in larger fines and even imprisonment. Talk to your tax advisor about staying onside and see the following resources from CRA for more information: Information Circulars 73-10—*Tax Evasion*, 92-2—*Income Tax Act Guidelines for the Cancellation and Waiver of Interest and Penalties*, and 00-1—*Voluntary Disclosures Program*.

Here is a synopsis of important negative outcomes you'll want to avoid:

1. **Failure to file a return of income**—This results in a penalty equal to 5% of the person's unpaid tax payable plus 1% for each complete month past the filing due date up to a maximum of 12 months.
2. **Repeated failure to file**—10% of the person's unpaid tax payable plus 2% for each complete month past the filing due date up to a maximum of 20 months if the repeated failure happens within 3 years.
3. **False Statements or omissions**—For those persons who knowingly—or under circumstances amounting to gross negligence—make, participate or acquiesce in the filing or representation of a false statement or omission, a penalty equal to the greater of either $100 or 50% of the understated tax is imposed.
4. **Third-party misrepresentation**—Third-party tax or financial advisors that know or ought to reasonably know that a false statement is being used in a return are liable to a penalty equal to the greater of either $1000 or the gross compensation that the person is entitled to receive in respect of their services on the particular tax-planning activity.
5. **Tax evasion**—The penalty for prosecution under summary conviction is a fine of not less than 50% and not more than 200% of the amount sought to be evaded, or both the fine and

imprisonment of up to two years. The penalty for prosecution under indictment is a fine of not less than 100% and not more than 200% of the amount sought to be evaded, and imprisonment up to five years.

6. **GAAR**—General Anti Avoidance Rules—can be imposed in cases where it is considered that the taxpayer circumvented the intent of the law in undertaking a series of transactions that result in a tax benefit. While there are no criminal consequences in this case, the avoided tax plus interest must generally be paid. An avoidance transaction for these purposes is defined as:

   • One that does not have a bona fide business purpose; its primary purpose being to provide, directly or indirectly, in a tax benefit or

   • A transaction that is part of a series of transactions in which the primary purpose is, as a whole, to result directly or indirectly in a tax benefit

Waiving Penalties and Interest

Under the Fairness Provision, CRA can waive penalty and interest if the late filing or nonpayment of an amount is beyond the taxpayer's control, such as natural or human-made disasters, personal hardship or CRA information that misled the public.

Voluntary Disclosures Program (VDP)

CRA encourages taxpayers to come forward and correct past omissions so that the taxpayer can be compliant with their legal obligations. Under the VDP, taxpayers who make a valid and complete voluntary disclosure would still have to pay the tax owing plus interest, however CRA could provide relief from penalties and prosecution.

RECAP. YOU NEED TO KNOW:

1. What to do when business expenses exceed income
2. How to use jurisprudence to receive direction in the "grey areas"
3. How to link intent to earn income in the future with current costs
4. How to classify expenses into proper tax deductibility categories
5. How to read and use the Statement of Business Activities for the unincorporated
6. How to prepare a margin analysis to justify your commercial activities
7. How to audit-proof expenses that may require restriction, application to current or capital uses, or proration for business/personal use
8. The penalties for non-compliance

YOU NEED TO ASK: Your Tax Advisor for Help In Writing Off More of Your Expenditures By:

1. **Establishing intent**. If there is no profit motive, generally no income is reported, no expenses are deductible. Your expenditures will only be deductible if your activities have a viable commercial activity linked to them. You must report your income and expenses in that case. (Otherwise you could face the potential of being charged with gross negligence or tax evasion.)
2. **Documenting profit potential guidelines in assessing REOP**. Put yourself in the tax auditor's shoes. Review the general factors considered by CRA in assessing Reasonable Expectation Of Profit as outlined in IT504:

   • Time devoted to the business
   • Distribution activities: presentation of works, products, services, to the public
   • Time spent in marketing the goods or services of the enterprise
   • Revenues received
   • Historical record of profits
   • Cyclical trends in the business
   • Type of expenses claimed and their relevance to the business
   • Business owner's qualifications to run the business successfully
   • Business owner's membership in professional associations
   • Growth of revenues, taking into account economic conditions, and other market changes.

   All criteria are analyzed together. Make sure your Daily Business Journal addresses these 10 factors. (Refer back to Chapter 3.)

3. **Establishing revenue channels and streams.** Identify your unique product/service and income-earning process, your distribution channels, payment methods, pricing policies and gross margins by preparing detailed budgets and projections.

4. **Knowing your profit margins well**. Ask your tax advisor to discuss this with you.

5. **Understanding expense restrictions**. Don't try to claim more than two conventions per year; or 100% of meals and entertainment costs, or 100% of legal fees paid to acquire your office building. Scan Interpretation Bulletin, Information Circulars and Tax Guides from CRA for important information about claims for your business. Buy a highlighter pen for sections you wish to discuss with your advisors.

6. **Establishing consistent bookkeeping practices** Attach expense classification and verification statements to your hard copy receipts to document intent and proration for personal use. As a minimum:

   • Get receipts/invoices for all expenditures
   • Keep logs for cash expenses like parking and payphones
   • Classify receipts/invoices (current, capital, restricted, prepaid)
   • Enter into bookkeeping system
   • File hard copy in folders/envelopes for retrieval
   • Keep a meticulous auto distance log.

7. **Finding the "low-lying fruit."** Are there expenditures you have made that have a business component? If so, are you claiming the business portion of those expenses on your return? Try to turn every expenditure into a legitimate tax deduction.

8. **Preparing foresight to challenge hindsight.** Before spending another dollar — ever — stop to consider "Is this deductible?" Is there a business purpose attached to the expense? If not, can there be? Document this. Remember, a tax auditor's interpretation about expense reasonableness comes from an unfair advantage: hindsight. The onus of proof rules can actually put the taxpayer in a position of power for two reasons:

   • You have the power of vision on your side: you can outline the potential for profit
   • You have the position of fairness on your side: the courts have ruled it is unfair for an auditor to judge business acumen with hindsight. There aren't too many taxpayers who actually risk their resources to intentionally lose money. Rather, commercial viability must be considered.

For these reasons, therefore, you should pursue your rights under the law to claim every one of the business expenses you are entitled to, even those with mixed components of personal and business use. (Also see comments in Chapter 11.)

9. **Establishing your rights to legitimate business losses, and fight for them.** There is no legislated time limit for a "reasonable expectation of profit." If a tax auditor is looking at a period of two to three years only, it is quite possible it is unreasonable of him/her to expect a profit from your business yet. This is very true of business activities undertaken by songwriters, visual and recording artists, writers, farmers, and others. Some of these taxpayers may take years to reach the critical acclaim to be profitable (and be sure, CRA will be there then to take their share of the profits). Therefore it is most important for you to be able to establish legitimate operating losses that can be carried forward to offset future income. CRA will not take this right away from you if you can show that you have conducted your affairs in legitimate efforts to make profits.

10. **Appealing with proper process.** If you are facing an unfavorable reassessment of tax, know your appeal rights and deadlines. Find out everything you can about the way CRA has taxed those in similar ventures. Ask your advisors for information about recent court cases that deal with the issues you face in growing your business. Be highly proactive.

CHAPTER 5

Simple Rules for Writing Off Asset Purchases

"Talent alone won't make you a success. Neither will being in the right place at the right time. The most important question is: "Are you ready?""
JOHNNY CARSON

KEY CONCEPTS

- Expenses for the cost of an asset with a useful life of more than one year must be "capitalized"
- Assets used to earn income in a business will often lose their value over time
- CRA allows a "permissive deduction" to account for this loss in value
- Capital Cost Allowance (CCA) is a declining balance method of accounting for depreciation due to wear and tear
- Repairs and restoration of an asset to its original condition are 100% deductible as a current expense

REAL LIFE: Jared enjoyed his work as a waiter while he attended university. During his days at The Happy Hunter Inn, he encountered many guests, one of whom was a local businessman, Allan Blair; another was a local business woman, Juanita Carez. The usual chit chat between server and client led to a number of interesting conversations. Jared was a computer whiz who specialized in devising policies and procedures for businesses struggling with the ever-changing world of information and communications technology. Before he knew it, he was subcontracting for Allan's company and Juanita's, and reaping the rewards of a job well done. . .further referrals.

Jared found himself, at year end, clearly in business, and with a major tax problem. . .where to start in gathering information about his income and expenses? After meeting with his accountant, he was surprised to find his income records and deductions for operating expenses were in fairly good order. What he needed to look for to complete his tax return, was the details about the assets he had acquired in his business: his computer, his office furniture, his desk, his car and his professional library.

THE PROBLEM

Jared's accountant was trying to save him tax dollars by scheduling his assets used in the business. Problem was. . .he bought some new, some used; and his parents gave him the rest of it. How to schedule these business assets involved not just receipting, but also looking for Fair Market Valuations. How was he supposed to get that? Also, for what? He wasn't even sure he knew what this CCA was all about!

THE SOLUTION

Jared's accountant did another wise thing: he sat Jared down and gave him a crash course in Capital Cost Allowance. . .the deduction allowed to acknowledge the wear and tear on business assets used to produce income. By knowing how assets are written off for tax purposes, he knew he would help Jared make wise tax-oriented decisions about spending his money in the future.

He also filled him in on some recent tax changes:

Small Tools The May 2, 2006 federal budget increased the cost limit for small tools, kitchen utensils and medical or dental instruments that qualify to be included in Class 12 (eligible for 100% write-off) from $200 to $500 when acquired after May 2, 2006. The definition of "tools" in Class 12 also specifically excludes electronic communication devices and electronic data processing equipment (e.g. cell phones and PDAs).

Computer Equipment Computer equipment purchased after March 2, 2004 may be included in new class 45 with an amortization rate of 45%. Rapidly depreciating office equipment (other than computer equipment) continues to be eligible for the separate class election in class 10.

GST Provisions. The GST rate changed from 7% to 6% effective July 1, 2006.

Jared was anxious to learn more about these terms and the timing of his future asset acquisitions, and the tax consequences of their dispositions, too.

THE PARAMETERS

An income-producing asset used in a business can be "written down" to acknowledge depreciation due to its use. No one really knows for sure what the value of an asset is at any given point in time. This will only be realized upon disposition — when the owner sells the asset, or disposes of it in another way — converting it to personal use or transferring it to a relative, for example.

Therefore, the acknowledgement of the cost of depreciation of assets for tax purposes is really an educated guess. The Department of Finance has done some of that guesswork for you by prescribing special classes for the assets to fall into, and rates of depreciation resulting in a write-off called "Capital Cost Allowance." CCA is a deduction from business income, subject to special rules. The CCA deduction can often be inadequately or incorrectly used by taxpayers, with the result that tax is overpaid in the long run. Some parameters for avoiding this are outlined below.

Accuracy of Claims Is Important

CCA is known as a "permissive deduction." The claim is made at the taxpayer's option; however, there is a special rule the taxpayer must know about to manage the account properly: notify the CRA promptly if an error is made. That's because the adjustment period for permissive deductions like CCA is only 90 days after receipt of the Notice of Assessment or Reassessment. This is shorter than the normal adjustment period, which is ten calendar years for most other federal provisions. (Tax auditors have been known, however, to allow retractive CCA claims when a file is audited.)

Capitalize Expenditures With Life Spans of More Than One Year

Generally, assets with a useful and enduring life such as automobiles, trucks, machinery and buildings are considered capital expenditures, that must be scheduled for CCA purposes. Their costs may not be written off in full in the same way that other operating expenses are. This is where many taxpayers make expensive mistakes. Jared, for example, thought he could write off the full $3,000 he spent on his computer system. Unfortunately only a fraction of the expenditure would be allowed this year.

Capitalize Expenditures With Values Over $500

Even though small equipment and supplies may have a useful life of more than one year, if their value is under $500 they can generally be written off as operating expenses. This includes small tools or office equipment acquired on or after May 2, 2006. (The amount was $200 before this.)

Know When Repairs Are Capitalized

Does the repair of an asset add to its useful life? If so, the amounts are likely added to the capital cost of the asset. Does the repair, on the other hand, simply put the asset back to its original condition? In that case, we generally write off the costs in full. For example, replacing the shingles that blew off the business premises during a windstorm would be fully deductible, whereas replacing the whole roof would be treated as a capital expenditure.

Know Your Basic CCA Rate Structure

CCA is also known as the diminishing-balance method of claiming depreciation. This means that a fixed maximum percentage is applied against the balance of the capital cost of the asset remaining at the end of each year. To arrive at this fixed percentage, assets of a similar type are classified or "pooled" into specific classes for CCA purposes. Your tax advisor will have a complete listing, as will CRA's business guides.

Know About the "Half-Year Rules"

When assets are acquired, the "Cost of Additions," which generally includes both GST/HST and PST, is recorded on the CCA schedule. A "half-year rule" is then applied to most assets. That is, in the year of acquisition, the CCA rate can be applied only to half the cost of the asset.

Certain Assets Are Exempt From the Half-Year Rules

Class 12 assets, other than computer software, a television commercial message, certain assets acquired from related persons and a video cassette acquired after February 15, 1984, for rental to persons for less than seven days a month, are all examples of assets not subject to the half-year rule.

Cost of Additions

The "cost of additions" includes taxes and freight charges. Things are a bit more complicated when the properties are acquired through a "deemed disposition," such as on the death of a taxpayer, or a "change in use" from personal to business use. In that case, deemed dispositions or transfers are valued at **Fair Market Value (FMV);** that is, what a willing buyer would pay a willing seller for the asset on the open market. There are special rules when the amount received for the asset is inadequate, especially between related parties, when trade-in values are below FMV or if assets are disposed of at a superficial loss.

Short Fiscal Years

Here is an important rule for start-up businesses: the CCA claim is generally prorated when there is a short fiscal year. This means that if you started your business on July 1, and had a December 31 fiscal year end, only 50% of the normal available CCA deduction allowed can be claimed. If you started your business on September 1, only one third of the normal CCA deduction is claimable, and so on.

Cost of Borrowing to Buy Assets

Interest costs to buy assets used in a business will be tax deductible as an operating expense of the business. If there is a personal component to the use of the asset, the interest, like other related expenses, must be prorated. Many taxpayers don't know about this little rule: the taxpayer can choose to capitalize any annual financing fees paid for the assets, simply by adding the cost on to the undepreciated capital cost of the asset, in order to preserve more of those costs for future use, when profits are perhaps higher. To do so, the taxpayer must make an election under Subsection 21(3).

Calculating the CCA

Take a look at the CCA Schedule used by the CRA to calculate CCA. (Figure 5.1) It forms a part of the Statement of Business Activities. You can readily see the requirements. It is important that you understand them, even if you won't be filing your own tax return, as you contemplate the timing and consequences of asset acquisitions and dispositions you may be making throughout the year:

Box 1: Enter the right class number

Box 2: Enter the Undepreciated Capital Cost (UCC) balance from last year

Box 3: Record the cost of your capital additions, including taxes and freight, or record the FMV of assets converted to business use or given to you as a gift. Account for any personal use components in detail boxes below.

Box 4: Record your proceeds of disposition, but only up to the original cost noted on your CCA schedule when you acquired the asset, plus any capital improvements over time. Account for any personal use components in detail boxes below.

Box 5: Subtotal

Box 6: This is the adjustment box for your half year rule

Box 7: This is the figure upon which this year's CCA deduction is calculated

Box 8: This is the CCA rate applied to this class of asset

Figure 5.1 Asset Tracking System for Tax Purposes

Area A - Calculation of capital cost allowance (CCA) claim

1 Class number	2 Undepreciated capital cost (UCC) at the start of the year	3 Cost of additions in the year (see Areas B and C below)	4 Proceeds of dispositions in the year (see Areas D and E below)	5 * UCC after additions and dispositions (col. 2 plus col. 3 minus col. 4)	6 Adjustment for current-year additions (1/2 x (col. 3 minus col.4)) If negative, enter "0"	7 Base amount for CCA (col. 5 minus col. 6)	8 Rate %	9 CCA for the year (col. 7 x col. 8 or an adjusted amount)	10 UCC at the end of the year (col. 5 minus col. 9)

Total CCA claim for the year (enter this amount, minus any personal part and any
CCA for business-use-of-home expenses, on line 9936 on page 1**)

* If you have a negative amount in this column, add it to income as a recapture on line 8230, "Other income," on page 1. If no property is left in the class and there is a positive amount in the column, deduct the amount from income as a terminal loss on line 9270, "Other expenses," on page 1. Recapture and terminal loss do not apply to a class 10.1 property. For more information, read Chapter 4 of the *Business and Professional income* guide.

** For information on the CCA for "Calculation of business-use-of-home expenses", read Chapter 4 – Special Situations in the *Business and Professional income* guide.

Area B - Details of equipment additions in the year

1 Class number	2 Property details	3 Total cost	4 Personal part (if applicable)	5 Business part (column 3 minus column 4)

Total equipment additions in the year **9925**

Area C - Details of building additions in the year

1 Class number	2 Property details	3 Total cost	4 Personal part (if applicable)	5 Business part (column 3 minus column 4)

Total building additions in the year **9927**

Area D - Details of equipment dispositions in the year

1 Class number	2 Property details	3 Proceeds of disposition (should not be more than the capital cost)	4 Personal part (if applicable)	5 Business part (column 3 minus column 4)

Note: If you disposed of property from your business in the year, see Chapter 4 in the *Business and Professional income* guide for information about your proceeds of disposition. Total equipment dispositions in the year **9926**

Area E - Details of building dispositions in the year

1 Class number	2 Property details	3 Proceeds of disposition (should not be more than the capital cost)	4 Personal part (if applicable)	5 Business part (column 3 minus column 4)

Note: If you disposed of property from your business in the year, see Chapter 4 in the *Business and Professional income* guide for information about your proceeds of disposition. Total building dispositions in the year **9928**

Area F - Details of land additions and dispositions in the year

Total cost of all land additions in the year	**9923**
Total proceeds from all land dispositions in the year	**9924**

Note: You cannot claim capital cost allowance on land.

Box 9: This is your CCA deduction (remember you can claim any amount up to a maximum of Column 7 × Column 8)

Box 10: This is a very important figure, your UCC balance to be carried forward (Column 5 less Column 9)

Best bet: speak to your tax advisor first and have a Tax Savings Blue print—your "what if scenarios" prepared in advance of taking action.

Handling Dispositions

It is advisable to consult your tax advisor in order to calculate the most advantageous procedure to follow when disposing of assets, depending on the circumstances, as income inclusions or certain deductions can result when all assets of a class are disposed of.

Remember that dispositions could occur due to sale, but also due to other circumstances, such as transfer of assets to another or to personal use, or cessation of business due to death, or emigration. In those latter instances, called "deemed dispositions," FMV of the asset must be determined.

If the proceeds of disposition of any asset *exceed the cost of the asset*, the result is a capital gain. In that case, the gain is reported separately. The proceeds that are subtracted from the adjusted cost base of the class on the Capital Cost Allowance Schedule cannot exceed the original cost of the asset (plus additions and improvements).

Dispositions of All Assets in the Class

While acquisitions and dispositions of assets to an existing pool of assets affect the Undepreciated Capital Cost (UCC), it is only when all assets in a class are disposed of that reconciliation of all the capital cost allowance claims made for the class will be made to reflect the actual increase or decrease in value of the assets in that class over time. When the proceeds of disposition of the last asset are subtracted from the UCC of the class, you may have a positive or a negative result.

If the proceeds of disposition are greater than the UCC of the class, your CCA claim made over the years has exceeded the actual decrease in value of the assets in the class. Therefore, the negative UCC must be added to your business income for the year. This is known as *"recapture."*

If the proceeds of disposition are less than the UCC of the class, your CCA claim was insufficient to account for the actual decrease in value of the assets in the class. In this case, the ending UCC of the class may be taken as a deduction from your business income for the year. This deduction is known as a *"terminal loss."*

This reconciliation, when the last asset in a class is disposed of, applies to all classes except class 10.1 — passenger vehicles. More on this in Chapter 6.

Computer Upgrading Challenges Are Recognized

As mentioned earlier, computer equipment purchased after March 2, 2004 may be included in new class 45 with an amortization rate of 45%. Rapidly depreciating office equipment (other than computer equipment) continues to be eligible for the separate class election in class 10. These rules allow the taxpayer to elect to record their capital acquisitions in a separate class if the asset is worth more than $1000. This allows the taxpayer to write off terminal losses sooner, when this equipment is disposed of. If it is still in use after 5 years, it is merged into the normal Class 10 or Class 8 pools.

Data Network Infrastructure Equipment — equipment that supports advanced telecommunications applications such as e-mail, Web searching and hosting, instant messaging and audio- and video-over-Internet-Protocol (VOIP) includes assets such as switches, multiplexers, routers, hubs, modems and domain name servers that are used to control, transfer, modulate and direct data, but does not include office equipment such as telephones, cell phones or fax machines, equipment such as web servers that are currently considered to be computer equipment, or property such as wires, cables or structures. Prior to the 2004 budget, this equipment is included in class 8. Equipment acquired after March 22, 2004, is included in new class 46 with a CCA rate of 30%.

Computer Software

If you acquire a program that has a lasting and enduring benefit, it will be classified in class 12 — 100% depreciation rate. This software would, however, be subject to the "half-year rule." If there is no lasting and enduring benefit — for example, the software is considered to be an operational expense — a full tax deduction is possible. Systems software is generally classed in class 45 and depreciated at a rate of 45%. Remember, if it costs more than $1,000, it will qualify for inclusion in a separate Class 10.

Patents and Licences

Innovators have some interesting rules to contend with in writing off their patents and licences. These are usually written off on a straight-line basis over the life of the patent or licence. That is, if you paid $15,000 for a patent for a period of 15 years, the depreciation would be $1,000 a year. Licences of an indefinite period are classed as "eligible capital property." Three-quarters of the costs may be written off on a 7% declining balance. For all patents and rights to use patented information acquired after April 26, 1993, a CCA Class 44 is available with a 25% declining-balance rate.

Separate Classes for Certain Autos

Automobiles are generally classified in Class 10, at a CCA rate of 30%. These are usually known as "motor vehicles," and all like assets are pooled together in this class. An exception to the "pooling" rule applies to autos classified to be luxury or "passenger vehicles." Each such vehicle used for business purposes is placed into its own class 10.1, which also features a CCA rate of 30%. However, there are deductibility restrictions on CCA, interest and lease costs. For example, since January 1, 2001, the maximum capital cost has been $30,000 plus taxes.* This means that if you buy a $50,000 car, you can only take a CCA deduction based on a value of $30,000 plus taxes, if it is a passenger vehicle. The half-year rule also applies on acquisition of the vehicle, and in the year of disposition. More on this in Chapter 6.

Separate Classes for Certain Buildings

Pooling is not allowed in cases where a taxpayer owns a number of rental properties, each with a capital cost of $50,000 or more. In such cases, each building is listed in a separate class (usually class 1 — 4%). Where the taxpayer owns a condominium or row-housing structure, the aggregate cost of all the units in a building will become one class for each group of structures that costs $50,000 or more.

Land

Remember that land is not a depreciable asset, so it cannot be scheduled for CCA purposes. That means the value of land must be removed from the purchase price in real estate transactions. Be sure to dig out your property tax assessment for those purposes (or other reasonable valuation). Also be aware there are special rules on accounting for the sale of land and building to ensure valuations are not weighted in favor of more advantageous terminal loss write-offs.

GST/HST Exceptions

The Input Tax Credits (ITCs) received by a business registered to collect the GST/HST will have an impact on the "Cost of Additions." For example,

---

* Current at time of writing.

assets classified as "Capital Personal Properties" for GST/HST purposes (those used 51% or more for business) qualify for a full input tax credit of GST/HST paid. Once received, such an input tax credit must *reduce* the capital cost of the asset used for capital cost allowance purposes. Therefore, it is important to keep track of ITCs received specifically for capital assets.

GST Rate Changes. Specific rules will apply to the acquisition or sale/transfer of property as a result of the GST rate changes in 2006:

- Ownership or Possession Transferred before July 1, 2006:   7%
- Ownership and Possession Transferred on or after July 1, 2006: 6%
- Written Agreement Entered Into on or before May 2, 2006:   7%*

> *Taxpayers may apply to CRA for a transitional adjustment which reduces the effective rate of GST from 7% to 6% if the transfer of ownership and possession both take place after July 1, 2006.

Streamlined Accounting Methods. Small businesses may use the Quick Method or Special Quick Method of remitting GST/HST amounts where they do not track GST paid or received. As a result of the GST rate reduction, the rate used in the calculation of the amount to be remitted is also reduced. The table below shows the old and new rates for businesses using the Quick Method and supplying mainly services. The new rate will apply to reporting periods that begin on or after July 1, 2006. For reporting periods that straddle July 1, 2006, the old rate will apply to consideration that becomes due before July 1, 2006.

| | Supplies Made in | | | |
| | HST Provinces | | Non-HST Provinces | |
Permanent Establishment in:	Old Rate	New Rate	Old Rate	New Rate
Non-HST Provinces	11.6%	11.0%	5.0%	4.3%
HST Provinces	10.0%	9.4%	3.2%	2.6%

TAX ADVISOR

It is very important for small business owners to plan asset acquisitions and dispositions carefully. Set up a tracking system, as shown in Figure 5.1, for your tax records. Notice the important figures: your CCA deduction and the UCC or Undepreciated Capital Cost. This UCC figure is what you'll base next year's CCA deduction on. It will be increased by any future additions, and decreased by future dispositions.

Planning Opportunities Using the CCA Claim

The most important thing to remember about planning with your CCA deduction is that *CCA is always claimed at the taxpayer's option.* This allows you to tax cost average over time to get the best after-tax return for your money.

Ask your tax advisor about options for making a CCA claim in the following circumstances:

- in year of acquisition
- in year of disposition
- when an asset appreciates in value
- when an asset depreciates more than the prescribed rate
- when business income is very low
- when net income is anticipated to be much higher next year
- when it is your goal to increase RRSP contributions.

Buy vs. Lease

Prepare a Tax Savings Blueprint – "what if scenarios" — that give you exact dollar outcomes to determine whether there are any tax benefits of buying an asset vs. leasing it. There are two points to consider:

Your Marginal Tax Rate Not only do you need to know that your income will support the leasing payments or interest costs, but you'll need to know the true dollar value of the deduction. Here's an example, using the acquisition of a motor vehicle, when the marginal tax rate is 26%; assuming 100% business use.

Figure 5.2	Tax Cost Analysis: Motor Vehicles			
How?	**Tax Provision**	**Write-off in Yr. 1**	**Write-off in Yr. 2**	**Dollar Value of Tax Write-off @ 26% MTR**
Buy	CCA on auto total cost of $25,000*	$3,750	$6,375	Yr. 1 = $ 975; Yr. 2 = $1,658
	Interest on car loan @ 6%	$1,500	$1,350	Yr. 1 = $ 390; Yr. 2 = $ 351
Lease	Monthly leasing costs	$6,000	$6,000	Each year $1,560

* *Year 1:* 30% × $25,000 = $7500/ $3750. *Year 2:* ucc is $21,250 × 30% = $6375

So, if this taxpayer bought the car and took out a car loan to do so, his tax write-offs in Year 1 would amount to $3,750 + $1,500 = $5,250 and the real dollar value of those write-offs would be $975 + $390 for a total of $1,365. Leasing the vehicle would bring a real dollar saving of $1,560; so the taxpayer in this case gets a bigger benefit, in the amount of $195, in Year 1 by leasing.

In Year 2, there is no "half-year rule" on the asset acquisition. Therefore the real dollar value of the tax write-offs for CCA and interest is a total of $2,009; of the leased option, it's $1,560, so the CCA/interest claim is better.

One must also take into account, however, the cost and cash flow available under each option, assuming the identical vehicle is purchased. Have your tax advisor prepare a chart that looks like the one in Figure 5.3, to help you make the decision.

Figure 5.3	Before-Tax Earnings Chart

	Year 1	Year 2
Cash to be generated to pay for the car bought with a car loan:		
Interest amounts	$ _____	$ _____
Principal amounts	$ _____	$ _____
Total	$ _____	$ _____
Cash to be generated to pay for the leased car	$ _____	$ _____
Before-tax earnings required	$ _____	$ _____

Which option can you best afford?

Your Balance Sheet   Take into account the effect of asset acquisition methods on your balance sheet, and the overall fiscal health of your business. Will a lender, for example, finance your leasing costs with an operating line? Or is it easier for the lender to provide you with a loan for a specific asset purchase? This will have a bearing on your decision making as well as the tax implications.

RECAP. YOU NEED TO KNOW:

1. When to buy your capital assets to get the best "tax bang" for your buck

2. When to make adjustments for errors or omissions on your CCA claims

3. How to write off small tools and other equipment with costs under $500

4. When to capitalize repairs and maintenance, and when to expense the costs

5. What CCA rate will be applied to your asset acquisitions

6. When the half year rule will be applied, and when it won't

7. What happens to your CCA deduction when you have a short fiscal year

8. When to expense and when to capitalize interest costs on loans for acquiring your assets

9. How to account for any personal use component of asset use

10. Special rules for writing off your computer and communications equipment costs

11. Why certain vehicles are reported in a special CCA class

12. How to account for the cost of land and building

13. Whether it's better to lease or buy your assets

14. How a Tax Savings Blueprint can help you assess your tax efficiencies

YOU NEED TO ASK: Your tax advisor for help in making the right decisions in acquiring and disposing of capital assets by:

1. **Reviewing Notices of Assessment or Reassessment from CRA promptly.** Changes you wish to make to your claims for CCA have a time limit: adjustments can only be made within 90 days of receipt of the Notice of Assessment or Reassessment.

2. **Bringing details of your asset acquisitions and dispositions** to your tax advisor each and every year. This includes what happened during the tax year, as well as previous asset tracking worksheets.

3. **Classifying assets purchased properly.** 100% write-offs are not allowed on the purchase or improvement of assets with a useful life of more than one year. This is an expensive mistake that can generate extra interest costs with CRA.

4. **Scheduling the cost of improvements to assets.** Restoration of the asset to its original condition is expensed (100% deductible). The cost of improving the useful life of the asset is generally capitalized (subject to CCA deduction).

5. **Classifying your assets correctly.** Make sure you know the CCA rate that will be applied to the new asset you are thinking of purchasing, and whether there is an exception for the half-year rule.

6. **Prorating your CCA claim in the first year of business.** CCA rates and the half-year rule apply to businesses that are in existence for a full fiscal year. This means that a business that started mid-way through a fiscal year must prorate the calculated CCA claim by the number of days the business was operating.

7. **Capitalizing interest costs if your business is losing money.** This is a great way to preserve the costs for use in the future when income may be higher, thereby tax cost averaging.

8. **Disposing of all the assets of a class with tax efficiency.** Recapture will increase your net profits; terminal losses will decrease them. Do some tax planning to assess proper tax timing of dispositions, if this makes sense otherwise (i.e., the buyer is co-operative).

9. **Updating for tax incentives.** The government often provides tax incentives for those who invest in new assets in their business. Check out the latest interpretations of recent federal and provincial budget provisions with your tax advisor before purchasing new assets.

10. **Tracking GST/HST paid carefully.** If you are a GST/HST registrant, you'll be able to claim back the cost of your taxes paid on the asset against your GST/HST remittances. This can give your cash flow an important boost. Complete the CCA tracking system suggested in Figure 5.1 to make sure all the information you need to properly file your income tax return as well as your GST/HST return is available.

11. **Prorating your maximum CCA deduction for any personal use of the asset.**

12. **Preparing a tax and cash-flow comparison** of the costs before you make the decision to buy or lease an asset...your Tax Savings Blueprint!

....

CHAPTER 6

Maximize Home Office and Auto Expense Benefits

"The person who makes no mistakes, does not usually make anything."
WILLIAM CONNOR MAGEE

KEY CONCEPTS

- Common costs like operating your auto and home office may be deductible
- In each case, allocation must be made for a personal use component
- Auto expenses break down into "fixed" and "operating" costs
- Autos are classified as either "motor vehicles" or "passenger vehicles" for CCA purposes, depending on their cost
- To satisfy a tax auditor, auto distance logs are required
- Home offices must be exclusively set aside from the rest of the home; their size recorded
- Your home office must be your principal place of business or used regularly to see your customers
- Home workspace costs cannot be used to increase or create a business loss

REAL LIFE: Tom, a high school teacher, taught art and woodworking during the day, and built beautiful furniture in his spare time. Over the years, as he perfected his craft, people would marvel at the beautiful pieces in his home and beg him to consider designing and crafting something special for them too. Tom's hobby quickly flourished into a business with a potential for profit. In fact, he had visions of opening a furniture store one day, specializing in California-style pieces.

THE PROBLEM

At tax-filing time Tom wondered about the $3,500 he had received for making a piece of furniture for his neighbours, the Smiths. Should he report the income? If so, are there expenses he can claim to offset his income? For example, can he claim the costs of setting up his workshop, his tools and the varnish he uses to finish the furniture? What about the trips back and forth to pick up supplies. Are they deductible?

THE SOLUTION

As you know from prior chapters, tax deductions are legitimized by virtue of the fact that they are (a) reasonable and (b) incurred in a commercial activity that has a reasonable expectation of profit. In Tom's case we need to first assure ourselves that his enterprise is not a hobby. CRA's IT334 explains:

> "In order for any activity or pursuit to be regarded as a source of income, there must be a reasonable expectation of profit.
>
> Where such an expectation does not exist (as is the case with most hobbies), neither amounts received nor expenses incurred are included in the income computation for tax purposes and any excess of expenses over receipts is a personal or living expense, the deduction of which is denied. . .
>
> On the other hand, if the hobby or pastime results in receipts of revenue in excess of expenses, that fact is a strong indication that the hobby is a venture with an expectation of profit."

Tom therefore begins by computing whether there is indeed an excess of income over expenses. Gathering receipts for operating expenses, like the varnish, paint, paint remover, brushes, etc. is easy. However claiming his auto expenses and his home office expenses is trickier. Tom needs to know how to legitimize those real costs of doing business.

THE PARAMETERS

The specific deductions that any business may take should be made in the following order:

- Costs of goods sold
- Operating expenses
- Auto expenses
- Capital Cost Allowance
- Home office expenses.

Cost of goods sold reduces gross profits on the Statement of Business Activities to account for purchases of goods that will be resold.

Other operating expenses come next. This is for things that are "used up" in the business: advertising, supplies, rents, salaries, and so on. These amounts are 100% deductible and can be used to offset other income of the year if the operating expenses exceed revenues for the year. Capital cost allowance is next in line, claimed at the taxpayer's option, depending on the results desired in the current year.

In the case of a car, a separate worksheet is first prepared. See Figures 6.1, 6.1.2, 6.2, and 6.3 to compute fixed and operating costs based on the business use of the car. The owner can now decide, based on whether or not an operating loss already exists, whether to claim the deduction for CCA.

Next, one takes a close look at other assets. Should the deduction for CCA be taken for these assets? It is possible that the owner may wish to create a larger tax loss, if other income sources of the year, like pension or interest income, for example, are high, or if the owner wants to carry excess losses back to any one of the prior three taxation years. This is a way to recover previously paid taxes. Or the owner may wish to save the CCA deduction for a future date, when income is higher.

Finally, one comes to the deduction of the home workspace expenses. There is an important rule to remember in claiming these amounts, which warrant their ordering position at the end of the process: *you may not increase or create an operating loss by taking a deduction for home workspace expenses.*

TAX ADVISOR

There are special requirements to be met when claiming common business expenses like the costs of running your car and the costs of keeping a workspace in the home. It is most important that they are observed, as the deductions are both lucrative and frequently audited.

Automobile Expenses

Almost every small business owner claims auto expenses against the revenues of the business. However, this line is also the subject of more failures than any other on a tax audit. The main tax-filing traps are ones taxpayers must assume responsibility for. They fail to keep receipts and a record of their travels.

Managing Your Auto Log

An "auto log" cannot just record business driving. Be prepared to show the auditor how many kilometres were driven in the entire year for personal and business purposes. Many, no most, taxpayers have trouble keeping this log. Yet it's mandatory and will cause your claims to be reduced or disallowed completely if you don't have one.

For this reason, it's a good idea to keep your business kilometres driven in your Daily Business Journal. Before you leave your home office (see Figure 6.1), make sure you record the kilometres when you start.

Then make a point of charting your business driving during the day. Often that means that the full day of driving is technically deductible.

What's not allowed is the distances you drive to pick up milk on the way home. That's "personal" driving as is driving to and from work, unless of course, the post-office where you pick up your business mail is in the grocery store in which you buy the milk, or you see a client on the way.

So it's important to isolate the personal portions of any of your driving in order to give the auditor an accurate picture of the business use of your auto.

Also allowed is a reasonable estimation of coin car washes and coin telephone calls. When people log these actual amounts, usually they find they are underestimating their expenses.

Figure 6.1	Auto Log Summary										
Month	Km Bus	Km Pers	Km Total	Gas	M & R	Park	Wash	Ins.	Int.	Other: (Explain)	$
Jan											
Feb											
Mar											
Apr											
May											
Jun											
Jul											
Aug											
Sep											
Oct											
Nov											
Dec											
Total											

Figure 6.1.2   From CRA Worksheets:

Chart A – Motor vehicle expenses

Enter the kilometres you drove in the tax year to earn business income	_____	1
Enter the total kilometres you drove in the tax year	_____	2
Fuel and oil	_____	3
Interest (see Chart B below)	_____	4
Insurance	_____	5
Licence and registration	_____	6
Maintenance and repairs	_____	7
Leasing (see Chart C below)	_____	8
Other expenses (please specify)	_____	9
	_____	10
Total motor vehicle expenses: Add lines 3 to 10	_____	11

Business-use part: $\left(\dfrac{\text{line1}}{\text{line2}} \right)$ X line 11 _____ = $ _____   12

Business parking fees	_____	13
Supplementary business insurance	_____	14
Add lines 12, 13, and 14	_____	15

Allowable motor vehicle expenses: Enter the amount of line 15 at line 9281 on page 1

Note: You can claim CCA on motor vehicles in Area A on page 3.

Chart B – Available interest expenses for passenger vehicles

Total interest payable (accrual method) or paid (cash method) in the fiscal period	_____	A
$_____ * x the number of days in the fiscal period for which interest was payable (accrual method) or paid (cash method)	_____	B

Available interest expense: amount A or B, whichever is less (enter this amount on line 4 of Chart A) $ _____

*For passenger vehicles bought: *from September 1, 1989, to December 31, 1996, and from 2001 to 2005, use $ 10
*from 1997 to 2000, use **$8.33**

Chart C – Eligible leasing costs for passenger vehicles

Total lease charges incurred in your 2005 fiscal period for the vehicle	_____	1
Total lease payments deducted before your 2005 fiscal period for the vehicle	_____	2
Total number of days the vehicle was leased in your 2005 and previous fiscal periods	_____	3
Manufacturer's list price	_____	4

The amount on line 4 or ($35,294* + GST and PST, or HST on $35,294), whichever is more

$_____ * x 85% = ... _____   5

[($800*+GST and PST, or HST on $800) x line 3] ▶ _____ – line 2: _____ . . . . = _____   6
30

[($30,00*+GST and PST, or HST on $30,00) x line 1] . . . . = _____   7
line 5

Eligible leasing cost: line 6 or 7, whichever is less . . . . $ _____

(Enter this amount on line 8 of Chart A above)

* If you entered into a lease agreement before January 1, 2001, make the following changes to the chart:

	After 1990 and before 1997	1997	1998 and 1999	2000
* for line 5, replace $35,294 with:	$28,235	$29,412	$30,588	$31,765
* for line 6, replace $800 with:	650	550	650	700
* for line 7, replace $30,000 with:	24,000	25,000	26,000	27,000

Figure 6.2	Maximum Deductible Costs of Passenger Vehicle*		
Date	**Interest Costs**	**Leasing Costs**	**CCA**
After June 17, 1987 and before Sept. 1, 1989	$8.33 a day	$600 a month	$20,000
After Aug. 31, 1989 and before 1997	$10.00 a day	$650 a month plus taxes	$24,000 plus taxes
Jan. 1 to Dec. 31, 1997	$8.33 a day	$550 a month plus taxes	$25,000 plus taxes
Jan. 1, 1998 to Dec. 31, 1999	$8.33 a day	$650 a month plus taxes	$26,000 plus taxes
Jan. 1 to Dec. 31, 2000	$8.33 a day	$700 a month plus taxes	$27,000 plus taxes
Jan. 1 to Dec. 31, 2006	$10.00 a day	$800 a month plus taxes	$30,000 plus taxes

* Notices for changes in maximum deduction ceilings are usually announced for the next tax year in December.

REAL LIFE: Assume Guam, who is a self-employed hairdresser, drove 15,000 km this year for business purposes, out of 20,000 km driven in total. His total expenses for the car were $7,500. Using the following formula, Guam would compute the tax-deductible portion of his expenses:

$$\frac{\text{Total Business Kilometres}}{\text{Total Kilometres Driven in Year}} \times \text{Total Expenses} = \text{Deductible Expenses}$$

$$\frac{15,000}{20,000} \times \$7,500 = \$5,625$$

The deductible amount is therefore $5,625.

The actual expenditures that you have for your car during the year are classified into two groups:

Operating Expenses
- Gas and Oil
- Maintenance and repairs
- Tire purchases
- Insurance and Licence Fees
- Auto club premiums
- Car washes

Fixed Expenses
- Interest costs
- Leasing costs
- Capital cost allowances

The operating expenses are straightforward: keep the receipts, total them and claim a portion of them according to the business-use fraction determined by your travel log.

The fixed expenses will be subject to the proration as well; however, they are separated because there have been certain restrictions attached to them over the past several years. As you can see, there was a significant development in tax law on June 17, 1987. That was the day the

Finance Minister announced the concept of "Passenger Vehicles." A passenger vehicle, in tax jargon, is also considered to be a "luxury vehicle." That is, tax write-offs for the fixed costs of passenger vehicles are limited to certain ceiling levels, as outlined in Figure 6.2.

So, if for example, you buy a new car for a total of $40,000 plus taxes, your capital cost would be limited to a total of $30,000 plus federal and provincial sales taxes.

If you leased a vehicle for, say $900 a month, the most you could write off for tax purposes was $800 a month plus federal and provincial taxes.

And if you paid the bank an interest charge on the loan you took to buy your car, your maximum interest expense deduction was limited to $10 a day or about $300 a month. Take these restrictions into account before making your buying decisions.

In fact, you might ask yourself whether paying $40,000 for a car is really worth it, if *it's not deductible!*

*To take that thought one step further. . .*does it make sense to buy a new car at all? If, for example, a new car costs $40,000, but the same model, two years old, costs $25,000, what's the better decision? From a tax viewpoint, it's the $25,000 car (but ask them to throw in a bumper-to-bumper three year warranty!).

If your car is not classified a "passenger vehicle," it will be called a "motor vehicle" for tax purposes. That means the car is not subject to the passenger vehicle restrictions. A vehicle is either below the cost factors outlined above or it may be a motor vehicle-automobile. In this sub-category, the value may exceed the cost limits but have an allowable "use factor." For example, you can avoid the "passenger vehicle" restrictions with:

- A pick-up truck that seats one to three people used more than 50% of the time to transport goods or equipment
- A pick-up truck, sport utility or other van that seats four to nine people used 90% of the time or more to transport goods, equipment or passengers
- A farm truck used primarily (more than 50% of the time) to transport goods or equipment, or more than 90% of the time to transfer goods, equipment or people for the purposes of earning income.
- A clearly marked police and fire response vehicle.

Claiming Capital Cost Allowances (CCA)   The CCA classification used for a motor vehicle or a motor vehicle-automobile is Class 10, featuring a rate of 30%. You may have many different vehicles in this class, providing they each fall under the restricted values defined above.

Acquisitions increase the value of the CCA pool, dispositions decrease the pool, and only when all the assets of the class are disposed of are there recapture or terminal loss consequences. See Chapter 5 for explanations of these terms.

A passenger vehicle is classified in Class 10.1, which also has a CCA rate of 30%. However, all Class 10.1 assets must be listed separately, rather than pooled together in one class. In the year of acquisition, the normal "half-year rules" apply to both Class 10 and Class 10.1. That is, only 50% of the normal capital cost allowance is claimed in the year of acquisition.

As mentioned earlier, your CCA deduction is always claimed at your option, so if your other business expenses are already high enough to reduce income to the desired level, you can choose to "save" the higher Undepreciated Capital Cost to another year.

Dispositions   Here are two more points to remember regarding passenger vehicles:

- there is a "half-year rule on disposition" of a passenger vehicle. That is, you will be able to claim 50% of the capital cost allowance that would be normally allowed if you owned the vehicle at the end of the year.
- terminal loss is not deductible and recapture is not reportable on Class 10.1 vehicles. This means you should keep a close eye on the value of your luxury vehicle, and consider whether it makes sense to trade it in, if it drops too far below your allowable depreciated value.

In the case of Class 10 vehicles, there is no half-year rule on disposition of all the vehicles in the class. That is, the normal terminal loss and recapture rules apply to the self-employed. This is not the case for employees who write off the cost of their vehicles. These taxpayers may not claim a deduction for terminal loss when they dispose of their Class 10 assets.

More Than One Vehicle   Things can get somewhat complicated if you use more than one vehicle in the business. For example, let's say you own a florist business, have a delivery van, but also use your personal vehicle to give quotes and make supply runs. In that case, the costs of the van would not normally be subject to prorations or restrictions if it was used full-time for delivery of flowers. The driving with the personal car would obviously have a business component, which could be deductible if you kept the distance records.

In fact if you use your spouse's car occasionally for your business affairs, keep track of the distance driven. Use those distance points to reduce your overall expenses. To be completely accurate, you can keep separate distance logs for each vehicle. This would enable you to claim a portion of annual costs, like insurance, for example, on both vehicles, as long as you don't claim more than one full claim on each vehicle.

Figure 6.3 shows what a typical auto expense worksheet would look like for filing purposes, with information taken from the distance log and saved receipts.

Figure 6.3	Worksheet for Deductible Auto Expenses

Distance Log:

Total kilometres driven to earn income	15,896
Total kilometres driven in the year	22,554

Operating Expenses		**Fixed Costs**	
Gas and Oil	$1,527.00	Insurance	$1,250.00
Repairs/Maintenance	2,456.00	License	48.00
Car Washes	150.00	Interest	3,000.00
Motor League Auto Club	65.25	CCA from schedule	3,750.00*
Total	$5,496.25	Total	$6,750.00

Total Auto Expenses	Operating Expenses	$5,496.25	
	Fixed Costs	6,750.00	* This can be claimed in any amount up to $3750 at your option.
	Total	$12,246.25	
Personal Use Component		(3,615.13)	
Deductible Auto Expenses		$ 8,631.12	

Home Workspace Expenses

It is relatively easy to make the claim for home workspace expenses on the tax return. Whether you have a workshop in which you build furniture or a showroom for your Christmas wreathes and candles, keep all of your receipts for all utilities, mortgage interest, property taxes, insurance, maintenance and repairs for the whole home. Then prorate these by the fraction that you obtain with the following information:

$$\frac{\text{Square footage of home workspace}}{\text{Square footage of entire living area}} \times \frac{\text{Total Expenditures}}{\text{Allowed}} = \frac{\text{Deductible}}{\text{Portion}}$$

When computing the entire living area of the home, it is usual to exclude bathrooms and closets. When allocating areas for home with an unfinished or partially finished basement, only include the square footage of the areas that constitute "living area." That would usually include the area in which the wash is done, but not unfinished areas or storage space.

If part of the home was used for storage of business items, like lumber in a carpentry business or boxes of goods for resale, this area would be added both to the home workspace area and to the entire square footage of the home. Where someone uses a garage as a workshop, the square footage of the garage is added to both the numerator and the denominator, and so on.

Total expenditures can include the following:

- Heating costs
- Electricity
- Insurance
- Maintenance

- Mortgage interest
- Property taxes
- Cleaning costs

These items are totalled for the year, and then prorated according to the home workspace ratio. See Figure 6.4 for an example.

Figure 6.4	Worksheet for Deductible Home Workspace Expenses

Home workspace ratio:

Home workspace area	250 sq. ft.
Living area of the home	2,400 sq. ft.

Operating Expenses:

Heating costs	$ 1,632
Electricity	1,245
Insurance	895
Maintenance	1,496
Mortgage interest	8,479
Property taxes	4,532
Total	$18,279

Calculation of Allowable Claim:

Total	$18,279	
Less personal portion	16,375	(2,150/2,400 × $18,279)
Allowable Claim	$ 1,904	

There are three more things you need to know to claim home workspace costs properly:

1. You may only claim home workspace expenses if the space is used as follows:

- exclusively to earn business income on a regular and continuous basis for meeting clients, customers or patients; or
- as the principal place of business of the individual.

To clarify, under the first criteria, one or more rooms are set aside solely or exclusively for income-producing purposes. This means, it can't be your living room, or a desk in your bedroom, without a specifically defined, partitioned-off area.

As well, the space must be used to regularly meet customers at some level of frequency, which will be determined according to the type of business and individual facts of each taxpayer upon audit. Therefore, it would be most important to keep a log of appointments to justify these claims.

So for example, a chiropractor who has an office downtown where she sees patients, as well as one at home, would have to justify the home workspace claim by showing that clients regularly attended the home office for treatment. This is best done with a home workspace appointment log.

Another business person, a self-employed editor, for example, would not normally see clients in her home, but would still be entitled to make a claim as it is her primary place of business.

Meeting this second criteria may be more difficult for some. For example, a plumber may make a legitimate claim for home workspace expenses despite the fact that he usually works away from the home workspace. This claim will be allowed if there is no other principal place of business to prepare books, take appointments, prepare quotations, and so on.

2. You do not use the claim to increase or create an operating loss in the business.

Example 1:	Operating profit before home workspace	=	$3,500
	Home workspace expenses		$2,000
	Net profit		$1,500

This claim is OK as a loss is neither created or increased.

Example 2:	Operating profit before home workspace	=	$1,000
	Home workspace expenses		$2,000
	Net profit		($1,000)

This claim is not OK as a loss was created using home workspace expenses. The claim must be adjusted as follows:

Operating profit before home workspace	=	$1,000
Allowable Claim for home workspace		$1,000 only
Adjusted net profit		Nil
Carry-forward of home workspace expenses		$1,000

The carry-forward amount can be used to offset business income next year, so be sure to review your tax records for this amount next year, and use it up.

3. You can and should audit-proof your home workspace claim.   Sketch out the office area and its relationship to the living area in the rest of the house. Keep this in your tax files in case of a tax audit, to be used to justify the percentage of tax deductible expenditures that you have claimed. In all cases, expenses claimed as deductions must be reasonable.

RECAP. YOU NEED TO KNOW:

1. When a hobby becomes a business, so that home workspace and a portion of auto costs can be claimed on the tax return

2. Why it is important to claim operating expenses before making a CCA claim

3. How to keep a proper auto distance log for tax purposes

4. Which trips are deductible and which trips are considered personal in nature

5. How to track unreceipted costs like coin parking and car washes

6. Why your vehicle's fixed and operating costs are separated for tax purposes

7. The difference between a motor vehicle, automobile and passenger vehicle for tax purposes

8. How tax deductions differ for Class 10.1 assets on acquisition and disposition

9. How to claim expenses when you and your spouse have joint use of the car

10. The restrictions surrounding home workspace expense deductibility

YOU NEED TO ASK: Your Tax Advisor to help you compute car and home workspace claims to your best advantage by:

1. **Preparing a preliminary Business Statement.** If a profit motive is found to exist — i.e., income has the potential to exceed expenses — your hobby could very well be a viable business income source, against which you can claim a series of deductions.

2. **Knowing how to order your deductions**. On your preliminary Business Statement for tax purposes, claim cost of goods sold first,

then operating expenses, auto expenses, other capital cost allowances and finally home office expenses. That's because CCA is claimed at your option, and home office expenses can be carried forward for use in offsetting business profits next year. Then, once you know your net income level, you may wish to reduce your CCA deduction, to use up your home workspace deduction first, particularly if you suspect you may be subject to recapture on your CCA claims in the future.

3. **Keeping an Auto Log.** It's mandatory during a tax audit.

4. **Keeping a log of cash expenditures for your car.** This includes coin car washes, parking meters. CRA allows a reasonable estimate, but a log will likely produce higher claims.

5. **Knowing your auto expense restrictions.** Fixed expenses like interest costs, leasing costs and capital cost allowances on your vehicle will be subject to restrictions if you exceed certain value limits. Check these out before making the decision to buy or lease.

6. **Sketching out your home office.** Make sure you can justify your home office claims by drawing a sketch of the office and how it relates in size to the rest of the living area of the home.

7. **Keeping an Appointment Log for your home office.** This is particularly important if you also have an office downtown, for example. You must use the home workspace either as the principal place of business, or exclusively to earn business income on a regular and continuous basis for meeting clients, customers or patients.

8. **Remembering never to increase or create an operating loss from the business with home office claims.** They will be disallowed and you could forget to claim the carry-forward of these expenses to income in future years.

CHAPTER 7

Profiles of the Self-Employed

*"I do the very best I know how — the very best I can; and
I mean to keep on doing so until the end."*
ABRAHAM LINCOLN

KEY CONCEPTS

- Industry profiling is used by CRA to detect commonalities and differences in small business reporting
- Examining the latest tax proposals in the context of annual business planning is important.
- Spousal RRSP contributions are an important component of income splitting in retirement for self employed couples
- Profile-unique tax provisions can be identified using a common tax filing framework based on the Business Activities Statement
- Members of partnerships have unique filing consequences on their personal returns, and special rules must be observed by those who are also spouses
- Artists and writers have unique time-specific tax consequences
- Child care providers can claim more of home and food costs
- Farmers benefit from unique averaging provisions

REAL LIFE: Marcie runs a babysitting enterprise out of her home. Her husband Jim, is a full-time farmer. Between the two of them, keeping up with the changing tax rules has been a challenge. They each use their cars in business; to pick up supplies, meet prospective clients and conduct the affairs of their respective operations.

Marcie is a multi-faceted individual. She helps out where she can: daily she works in Jim's business as the bookkeeper, where she is paid a salary as an employee. She is also an accomplished singer/song-writer. One of her pieces is being reviewed by a major record company and a television network, as her specialty is writing children's songs.

Jim's affairs are such that his start-up years were very lean. He is carrying forward unused losses of $38,000. This year was a banner year;

unfortunately world market activities have reduced pricing to such an extent, Jim is worried he won't be able to meet his commitments. He is now contemplating a partnership with a neighbour and/or the possibility of selling the farmland, which is extremely valuable, just to make ends meet.

THE PROBLEM

This couple already has an interesting tax situation. With change on the horizon, there may be a few more tax twists. Marcie is an employee, but also runs two businesses of her own. In the meantime, Jim needs to maximize his tax write-offs for today and the future, to pull out of his farming enterprise with the greatest success over the long run.

THE SOLUTION

This couple should get some advice from a qualified tax professional who can look not only at the current year results, but the carry-over years — three years back and up to 20 years forward — in assessing future business decisions, as special tax rules exist, for both the earning of profits and the appreciation of equity.

THE PARAMETERS

CRA's audit activities involve audit projects which test compliance for different groups of tax filers. This "profile approach" brings non-compliance to light by highlighting differences in filing patterns, and targets areas where income appears under-reported or expenses overstated.

CRA also asks you to identify your "Industry Code" for these reasons right on your business statement. These codes are broken down into professions, services, sales, wholesales, construction, manufacturing and natural resource industries.

Therefore, it's important that you and your advisor identify the taxpayer profile that you and your business fit into, and discuss what basic and industry-specific reporting rules you'll be required to follow, based on special provisions outlined in the Income Tax Act, the latest budget proposals, as well as CRA's forms and Interpretation Bulletins or Information Circulars.

Next, it is important to flesh out your tax-filing profile with the circumstances specific to the way you run your business. For example, a self-employed editor would spend more on couriers or communications costs, while an in-home footcare specialist would likely claim larger amounts for auto expenses and medical supplies. Both these taxpayers would likely file similar home office claims, though, and be subject to maximum fixed cost ceilings on their automobile values.

Both these taxpayers would also want to overview their current tax-filing obligations in order to properly assess their RRSP contribution limits; and other investment opportunities. They should discuss opportunities to split income in retirement by making spousal RRSP contributions.

Because entrepreneurs must be visionary and forward-looking in planning for their next income sources, it makes sense for them to anticipate changes within their ventures. For this reason, the self-employed taxpayer is in an excellent position to explore and define potential tax results before making any financial moves as a regular part of business planning. To gather the right information to do so, ask intelligent questions of professional advisors about tax change and present business budgets and cash flows in a logical orderly way, so that the advisor can do a better job, quicker.

Following is an overview of taxation profiles for five different tax-filing profiles: the one-person operation or sole proprietorship, the business partnership, the self-employed artist/writer, the self-employed babysitter and the farming proprietorship. You will notice that each business has specific tax rules designed to address the nature of the different enterprises. In addition, you'll see certain similarities in the tax-filing framework for the unincorporated:

- Methods of Reporting Income
- Deduction of Operating Expenses
- Computation of Capital Cost Allowances
- Computation of Auto Expenses
- Computation of Home Workspace Costs
- Personal Use Allocation.

Sole Proprietorship

The buck stops here...so does all liability for business performance results and costs. Unincorporated small business owners file personal tax returns (T1's) to report their business income before June 16 to avoid late filing penalties. From landing the first contract to buying the new computer, or hiring the first employee, these small businesses have true grit. . .and true tax audit problems, if they don't conform to the rules. Income must be reported and deductions calculated on the Business Activities Statement before subtracting home office and

personal use to arrive at Net Income. Consider the tips listed in Figure 7.1
as you get started, and remember:

- **Keep an eye on gross revenues.**   If your gross revenues exceed
  $30,000 you'll need to register to collect and remit GST/HST in
  most industries. Speak to your tax advisor about the details of this
  obligation.
- **Time Capital Asset Transactions Carefully.**   When you acquire
  assets with a useful life of more than one year, that generally cost
  $500 or more, you must schedule them and claim CCA to account
  for depreciation for tax purposes. Also remember that consequences
  of disposition—terminal loss, recapture and capital gains—are all
  reported in the calendar year in which the transaction occurs.
  Timing your acquisitions and dispositions carefully allows you to
  tax cost average over time.
- **Keep an Eye on Tax Changes.**   Every federal budget introduces
  new nuggets of tax gold for the alert taxpayer and advisors. Be
  sure to discuss the following recent changes and develop Tax
  Savings Blueprints to anticipate the effects on your family's after
  tax results:
  - Tax brackets and most personal non-refundable tax credits are
    indexed to inflation every year. How much can you pay yourself
    and your family members on a tax free basis every month?
    (discussed further in the next chapter).
  - RRSP contribution maximums are rising. Is everyone in the
    family utilizing their RRSP contribution room to reduce taxes,
    clawback zones used to calculate refundable and non-refundable
    tax credits, and take advantage of investment earnings that
    compound on a tax deferred basis within the plan?
  - Changes have been made to the taxation of dividends from
    large public corporations and highly profitable small business
    corporations. Are you aware of how to take advantage of these
    lower marginal tax rates on this income source?
  - Certain business expenses have been recently restricted—the
    cost of fines and penalties unless part of a prescribed list is a
    good example, as is the restriction of tax adjustments to a
    10 year period.
  - Other provisions have been expanded—CCA rules for computer
    write-offs, for example, and the extension of the non capital loss
    carry forward period to 20 years.

What other tax changes affect spending decisions in your proprietorship?

Figure 7.1	The Tax-Filing Framework of the Self-Employed

Transaction	Tax Tip
Income Reporting	Report income on the "accrual" basis. That is, include it in the taxation year in which it is earned. You will likely conform to a fiscal year ending December 31, unless there is a bona fide non-tax reason to have a non-calendar year end. In that case you can make a special election with CRA. In the first year of business, you could have a "short year": September 1 to December 31, for example. In that case, you'll need to prorate your deduction for capital cost allowance, and allocate expenses incurred during the time of business only (e.g., mortgage interest, property taxes and other annualized expenses).
Purchases of Goods for Resale	Keep opening inventory valuations handy, add purchases and deduct closing valuation balances to arrive at Cost of Goods Sold.
Operations	Classify all expenditures into either capital or operational groupings.
Entertainment and Meal Expenses	Mark reason for meeting, name of client on back of all receipts or on invoices. Most of these costs will be restricted to 50% deductibility.
Promotional Expenses	100% deductible. Any portion that qualifies for a charitable donation may be written off as a non-refundable tax credit or carried forward.
Communication Costs	Put assets with a useful life of more than one year into CCA classes, do not claim full costs of monthly phone rental unless you have separate business line installed. Long-distance business calls are deductible in full. The portion of air-time for cell phone, personal devices, or on-line time for internet use that relates to business income may be deducted.
Leasing, Equipment Repairs and Maintenance	All deductible in current fiscal year; year end is a good time for maintenance and repairs to reap tax rewards sooner.
Sub-Contracting	Deduct as fees 100%; ensure you can prove this is not an employer-employee relationship that should have been subject to source deductions.
Salaries, Wages, Bonuses, Vacation Pay	All deductible, as are employer's portions of CPP and EI. Make sure you make source remittances to CRA on time to avoid penalties.
Professional Fees	Fully deductible in the year incurred, except if on account of capital transactions, in which case they are deductible outlays on Schedule 3 when the capital asset is disposed of.
Home Office Set-Up	Separate it out from the rest of the house. Measure the square footage of the office and compare to the total square footage of the living area. Acquire Furniture (Class 8 @ 20% rate), Supplies (100% deductible) and Equipment (Class 8, 10 or 45). Keep all receipts for interest, utilities, etc.
Business Vehicle	Convert to business use by finding the Fair Market Value, if the vehicle was previously in use. Or, if new vehicle is acquired, determine the capital cost from the bill of sale. Start keeping a distance log. Save all receipts for operating/fixed costs.

Partnerships

Partnerships involve a particular form of business organization that differs from a sole proprietorship in several ways. To begin, tax calculations are unique:

- One Statement of Business Activities is prepared for the partnership itself, as it is treated as a separate entity for tax surpluses.
- The individual partners, who are allocated a share of the partnership income or losses, attach a copy of the partnership statements to their own personal returns (assuming partnership is unincorporated), and can make an adjustment for individual expenses of the business incurred outside of the partnership.
- Partnerships follow the same rules for claiming income and expenses that proprietorships do (although some professional partnerships can account differently for Work in Progress). However, unlike a proprietorship, the partner's interest in the partnership is itself a capital property which can be bought or sold, and the adjusted cost base of this interest must be recorded and tracked. The adjusted cost base is increased by income earned and capital contributed and decreased by losses incurred and cash draws. Because a partnership itself does not pay tax, most tax preferences—such as donations, resource expenditures and investment tax credits—are allocated from the partnership to the partners for claim on the partners' returns. Although no cash is involved, these allocations are treated as draws for tax purposes and also reduce the adjusted cost base of the partnership interest.

Partnership Assets   In general, capital cost allowance is claimed on partnership assets on the partnership's statements, so assets used should be scheduled by the partnership itself. Certain assets not owned by the partnership, such as an individual's vehicle, can be written off on each individual's income tax return. Capital gains or losses on the disposition of the partnership's assets are calculated by the partnership, and allowances are taken at the partnership level for eligible capital property.

Adjustments for Individual Expenditures   Certain computations must be made at the *individual* rather than the partnership level:

- Charitable donations and political contributions made by the partnership must be claimed by the individual partner who made them. An adjustment is made to the adjusted cost base of the partnership interest in these cases.

- The individual partner's expenses for advertising, entertainment or expenses for the individual's auto, for example, can be used to reduce the partner's net income from the business on the personal tax return.
- Any GST/HST paid on such income-tax deductible individual expenses qualifies for the GST/HST rebate on Line 457 of the tax return, provided that the partnership is a GST/HST registrant.
- Interest expenses paid on money borrowed to acquire an interest in the partnership or for additional equity contributions must be deducted on a calendar-year basis; other expenses may be deducted either on a calendar year or in the fiscal period ending in a calendar year, depending on the fiscal year end choice made for the business.

Property that is transferred from an individual to the partnership may be transferred at FMV at the time of transfer, or at certain agreed upon amounts, by special election on Form T2059, *Election on Acquisition of Property by a Canadian Partnership*. However, where a transferor holds a right to acquire certain non-depreciable capital property whose tax cost is greater than its FMV, within 30 days after disposition, no loss may be recognized on the transfer. This must be deferred until the earliest of:

- a subsequent disposition of property to a person that is neither the transferor nor a person affiliated with the transferor;
- a change in the property's use from income-producing to non-income producing;
- a "deemed disposition" due to a change of residence or change of taxable status.

Generally speaking, if the partnership acquires the property at less than its capital cost, it is deemed to have acquired it at the capital cost. The partnership is deemed to have taken capital cost allowance equal to the difference.

Be sure you discuss with your tax advisor any transfers of assets from one business organization to another before the transfer, so that you fully understand the tax consequences. This should also hold true when you enter into or leave partnership arrangements.

Partnerships Between Spouses   Where there is a bona fide partnership between spouses, the Attribution Rules* should not apply either on the business income or any subsequent capital gain. Each partner would report his or her share of the partnership income and any

*Attribution Rules apply when an individual (usually the higher earner) transfers or loans property, directly or indirectly to a spouse, common law partner or minor child for that person's benefit. Resulting income is usually taxable to the transferor.

subsequent gain or loss on disposition of the business, according to their partnership agreements.

However, CRA can and will adjust the partners' share of income, if they are not dealing at arm's length, to an amount the department deems "reasonable" under individual circumstances. This is outlined in the Department's Interpretation Bulletin IT 231. Also note that income earned from funds transferred to a limited partner or a partner who is not actively engaged in the partnership will be considered income from "property" rather than business income, which would then be attributable back to the transferor.

To avoid the discretionary power of the Attribution Rules one or all of the following conditions should be met:

- Both spouses are actively engaged in the business (time expended and expertise provided are taken into consideration).
- One spouse is actively engaged in the business, while the other invests his or her property in the business (except as discussed under limited partnerships above).
- Each spouse has invested his or her own property in the business, and the profits or losses are apportioned to these investments.

Before embarking on a family business, it is a good idea to discuss with an accountant or lawyer what form of business organization the venture should take and to draw up specific agreements relating to ownership, remuneration, share of profits, etc. This will not only clarify the effect of attribution rules on your business, but will also help you reap the highest after-tax return for your efforts. At very least, establish firm agreements before starting. This is necessary for tax purposes and is in accordance with prudent business practice. You may wish to:

- Draw up a legal business or partnership agreement between husband and wife showing how annual profits and losses are to be split and how assets are to be shared on terminating the partnership or unincorporated business.
- Itemize which assets will be used in the business.
- Keep separate bank accounts for the business (never mix business funds with personal bank accounts).
- Keep strict and accurate records of all inventory.
- Allocate auto expenses between personal and business use.
- Accurate record-keeping of all income and expenses is essential.

Probably the leading cause of partnership dissolution is the inability for partners to get along. Whether you partner with your spouse, a neighbour, or a colleague, it's most important to document your entry and exit clauses in such a manner so as not to disturb the business enterprise.

Artists and Writers

Tax returns prepared for artists are also unique. The work of artists and writers may require much more time to generate a profit than ordinary businesses. As a result of significant losses in court, CRA has agreed that continuous losses for many years alone would not be sufficient to establish that there is no reasonable expectation of profit in such ventures.

As a result, a broader application of the tests for profit motive have been established to give direction not only to artists and writers, but other small businesses who need more time to establish profitability. Many of these creative entrepreneurs must also work at other jobs to finance their investment in their businesses in the meantime. CRA has recognized that other factors must be considered before ruling that the venture is a "hobby" or "sideline" only. Relevant factors include:

- the time devoted to the activity
- the extent to which the taxpayer has exhibited his/her work both in group and private exhibitions or the extent and nature of works published
- the extent to which the taxpayer is represented by private art galleries or art dealers or by publishers or the degree to which bona fide efforts have been made to have works published
- planned or intended course of action, including recent sales of significance, plans for exhibitions, efforts to increase representation by galleries and dealers, recent commissions for work, work in progress, anticipated revenue for royalties and sale of book rights for movies, TV, etc., and receipt of government grants
- the taxpayer's efforts to promote the sale of his/her works
- type of expenditures (i.e., whether a substantial portion of expenses is applicable to research, promotion and direct cost of works or, alternatively, whether the expenses are primarily those that would be expended irrespective of the taxpayer's art activities; for example, office-in-home and auto expenses)
- the increase, if any, in the value of the artist's works as he or she progresses
- the taxpayer's qualifications (i.e., educational background, honours, awards, grants, etc.)
- the significance and growth of gross revenue, as well as the risk of loss
- external factors that may be affecting sales (e.g., economic conditions, change in the public mood, and bankruptcy of art galleries or publishers)
- profit in prior years or continuous losses.

When it comes to claiming specific operational expenses, CRA has also shown tolerance for the specific circumstances of the artistic community. For example, CRA has agreed that self-employed performing artists may deduct the cost of music, acting or other lessons to develop their talent. Examples of other deductible expenses for those artists and writers who are self-employed include:

- accounting and legal fees
- agents' commissions
- cost of transportation, including board and lodging if the engagement is out of town, or the costs of transporting a large instrument or equipment
- insurance premiums and repairs to instruments and equipment
- cost of special make-up
- cost of publicity photos
- cost of video-taping or recording performances used for preparation or presentation
- cost of repairs, alterations, and cleaning of clothes used specifically in self-employment
- cost of music, acting or other lessons for a role or part or for general self-improvement in the field
- capital cost allowance on instruments, sheet music, scores, scripts, transcriptions, arrangements, equipment, and wardrobe
- office-in-the-home expenses
- cost of industry-related periodicals
- motor vehicle expenses.

Where an artist is both an employed artist and a self-employed artist for part of the year, expenses must be allocated as follows:

$$\text{Total Allowable Expenses} \quad \times \quad \frac{\text{Time Worked as Self-Employed}}{\text{Total Time Worked}}$$

or any other reasonable allocation.

Visual artists will be allowed to exclude the value of inventory in computing income. Costs will be written off in the year they are incurred rather than apportioning such costs to particular works and claiming them when the works are sold. An artist is also allowed to take a work of art from inventory and, without taking an income inclusion, claim a tax credit for donations if the price qualifies as a certified cultural gift.

As well, artists who donate their works to charities may value such a gift at any amount not exceeding its fair market value, but not less than inventory cost. This has the effect of creating income from which the charitable donations can be deducted but may affect other credits.

The value of workshops, seminars and other training programs provided to an artist who belongs to a national arts service organization will be taxable, as will prizes and awards received as a benefit from employment or in connection with a business. These amounts are not eligible for the scholarship exemption.

Artists who receive a project grant that is considered neither business nor employment income may be eligible to claim offsetting expenses in one of two ways. They can choose to deduct reasonable expenses incurred to fulfil the conditions of the grant, supported by receipts, or they can claim the scholarship exemption*, but not both. In the later instance, you'll note that the normal scholarship exemption provided for students who qualify for the education amount is not allowed unless the artist too qualifies for the amount.

Note: Certain "prescribed prizes" received by an artist are not included in income at all. This includes prizes recognized by the general public and received after 1982 for meritorious achievement, like the Nobel Prize or Governor General's Literary Award.

Child Care Providers

This business profile is also an interesting one, because it sets an example for the self-employed who may have a number of otherwise personal expenditures that have a primarily business component. We are speaking here of the claim for home workspace, food and toy costs.

A self-employed baby-sitter may deduct various business expenses against income earned from the baby-sitting enterprise, including government grants. To report income earned and deductible expenses on the tax return, the self-employed baby-sitter must keep a record of all income received; therefore, a separate bank account for such deposits would be a good idea. Like other small business owners, she should begin keeping receipts of items purchased and used in the baby-sitting business.

The dilemma often faced is this: "I use my whole home for the business when the children are here. How do I properly allocate the personal portion?" If there is no one area set aside exclusively for the business, portions of rent, mortgage interest, property taxes, utilities and repairs would be deductible, according to the amount of floor space used in the baby-sitting

---

*Scholarship exemptions were previously set at $500 and $3000. For 2006 and subsequent years the full amount of scholarships, fellowships and bursaries are excluded from income if an education tax credit is claimable.

business and *the number of hours the daycare centre is open,* as illustrated below:

$$\text{Total Operating Expenses of the home} \times \frac{\text{Square footage of home workspace}}{\text{Total square footage}} \times \frac{\text{No. of hours daycare is open in the year}}{\text{Total hours in the year}}$$

The result of this equation is the total deductible home workspace expenses. These claims must follow normal rules; that is, home workspace costs must not increase or create a loss.

Additional deductions for food, toys and supplies related to the business would also be deductible. As well, a claim for capital cost allowance could be made for assets such as furniture, office equipment or a vehicle used in the enterprise.

Deductible Child Care Expenses:

- Accounting Costs
- Advertising
- Art & Craft Supplies
- Auto Expenses
- Bank Charges
- Blankets
- Books
- Capital Cost Allowances
- Diapers
- Employee Expenses
- Entrance Fees to Parks, etc.
- Cost of Field Trips
- Food
- Household Costs
- Insurance
- Postage
- Repairs
- Soap and Shampoo
- Telephone/Communications*
- Towels and Toothbrushes
- Toys for the Children
- Training Courses
- Travel Costs**

* Note, unless a separate business line is installed, the monthly rental on the personal phone will not be deductible.

** Per trip expenses may be claimed instead of keeping a detailed auto log if you only use a vehicle occasionally for business purposes.

Food costs may prove to be a problem to track. If all food consumed by the children could be purchased separately, the full food bills could be deducted. However, in most cases, food is purchased at the same time for both family and business consumption. Therefore, in a separate book of account, the baby-sitter should keep a record of food items to feed the children and then prorate the total food bill accordingly.

Once all the applicable deductions are taken from baby-sitting income, it is possible that the baby-sitter's net income, which is used in computing the Spousal Amount, is low enough for a full or partial claim by the higher-earning spouse. If net income is just over the threshold limits, a Registered Retirement Savings Plan could be purchased for the self-employed spouse, if she reported earned income last year. The results would be a reduced net income, possibly Spousal Amount Claim for the higher-income earner, and increased refundable tax credits such as the Canada Child Tax Benefit.*

Like other self-employed persons, the baby-sitter can begin making contributions on her own behalf to the Canada Pension Plan based on net income from her business.

When issuing receipts, the baby-sitter should break down how much money the parents paid for children under seven and those over six, so that parents can take advantage of higher allowable deduction limits for preschoolers.

Farmers

The income from farming is considered to be business income that is subject to the same tax-filing provisions applicable to other businesses. That is, a Statement of Business Activities must be filed with the tax return. Farmers who are not CAIS (Canadian Agriculture Income Stabilization) participants will use Form T2042, *Statement of Farming Income and Expenses*, to report income and expenses from farming activities. Those who are CAIS participants will use Form T1163 and possibly T1164.

Most of us think of farmers as those who raise cattle or other domestic animals, or as those who grow grain. However, other activities that are considered "farming enterprises" include the tillage of soil, maintenance of race horses, bee-keeping, operation of a wild game reserve, nursery or greenhouse businesses, fruit growing, raising poultry, fur farming, growing Christmas trees or even raising fish. Here's what you need to know to make sure your offsetting expenses are deductible.

Filing Methods   Persons who are in the business of farming or fishing may use the cash method of accounting to compute their income. This method calculates income actually received during the year that is reduced by expenses actually paid during the year. They also have the option of reporting income using the accrual method; income is calculated as it becomes receivable and expenses are deducted as they become payable.

The farmer may elect to use the cash method by filing a tax return using the cash method. Once this is done, all subsequent returns must be filed in a similar manner, and a formal request to change must be made to the Director of the local Tax Services Office. In the case of a partnership,

---

* This RRSP contribution should be made in addition to a contribution by the higher earning spouse, who will reap a higher marginal return from his/her contributions due to income level.

each partner must elect to have the income from the farming or fishing business reported using the cash method. This means that all partners must file a tax return in the year of election.

Instalment Payments   Farmers are required to remit tax in instalments, but only once a year, on or before December 31, based on two-thirds of estimated tax for the current year. Canada Pension Plan contributions are also required on net farming income and should be factored into the instalment payments.

Reporting Farm Expenses   Farm expenses are reported on Form T2042/ T1163, and can include the following:

- building and fence repairs
- capital cost allowance on assets owned, claimed at your option
- cleaning, levelling and draining land
- crop insurance, GRIP and stabilization premiums, as well as NISA administration fees
- interest on farm loans, mortgages and vehicles
- insurance on farm buildings, and in certain cases, life insurance policy premiums (that is, only if the policy was used as collateral for a business loan. For more details, see IT 309R2)
- machinery expenses including gas, diesel fuel and oil, repairs, licences and insurance
- mandatory inventory adjustments included in income last year
- memberships and subscription fees
- motor vehicle costs, prorated for any personal-use component
- livestock purchased
- professional fees
- property taxes
- office supply costs
- optional inventory adjustments included in income last year
- rent for land buildings or pastures
- salaries, wages and benefits, including employer's contributions, for family members
- small tools that cost less than $500
- utility bills for farm buildings
- seeds, plants, feed, supplements, straw and bedding, pesticides, veterinary fees and breeding fees
- 50% of meals and entertainment costs.

Home Workspace Expenses   Certain household expenses can be claimed as a business expense on the tax return under the general pro-visions for home workspace expenses. This includes heat, electricity, insurance, maintenance, mortgage interest, property taxes and other expenses, prorated for the business/personal-use portions and subject to the restrictions that no loss can be increased or created using the home office expenses.

Communication Costs   Long-distance calls that are personal in nature may not be deducted. Circle all personal calls on every monthly phone bill and use the rest of the bill as a deduction, if you have a separate business phone. If there is no separate phone, the monthly rental charge is usually considered a personal expense. You can also deduct the portion of your air-time costs of a cellular telephone or on-line charges for internet access that reasonably relate to operation of the farm.

Deductible Wages for Spouse   Salaries paid to a spouse or common law spouse in a family business are fully deductible, provided the following factors are in place:

- the work was required to be done, was actually done and would otherwise have required the hiring of a stranger
- wages were reasonable and actually paid and documented.

All persons employed by spouses must have Employment Insurance premiums withheld and remitted, as well as Canada Pension Plan premiums and Income Taxes. A T4 Slip must be issued under normal rules. Employment by a person who controls 40% or more of the issued voting shares is not insurable; neither is employment of a spouse unless the remuneration is tax deductible under the Income Tax Act (see comments below), nor is a salary level that is unreasonably high. These tax provisions can make a considerable impact on the incomes of farmers and owners of small businesses. In effect, both spouses can earn income in their own right, allowing for legitimate income splitting within the family.

Wages Paid to Children   The same general rules apply to children's wages (that is, reasonable wages must be actually paid for services that were necessary in producing income and that would have required the services of outside help). The employer must also contribute a portion of the premiums paid by the child to Employment Insurance (and Canada Pension Plan if child is 18 or over) on the source deductions remittance form. The employer's portion is a deductible expense.*

*In some cases EI premiums are not payable for family members. To determine whether you should deduct these premiums Form **CPT1**, *Request for a Ruling as the Status of a Worker under the Canada Pension Plan* or *Employment Insurance Act* is available. Those who deduct premiums by mistake can recover overpayments for only 12 months in retrospect

There are some important points to remember when paying your children:

- If you pay your children by cheque, the CRA will accept your cancelled cheque as a legitimate receipt.
- Receipts signed by the child are required if you pay cash.
- If you give your child livestock or grain in lieu of money for the payment of wages, the child must report the value of this livestock or grain on his/her tax return as income. In order to claim the wage expenses, you will be required to include in your gross sales income the value of this property given to your child.
- The value of board may not be claimed as an expense if this is supplied to any child who is dependent upon you for support.

Source Deduction Remittances for Small Business   Those employers with average monthly withholding amounts of less than $1,000 for the second preceding calendar year and who have no compliance problems in either their withholding account or GST/HST account, for the preceding 12 months, may choose to remit their source deductions withheld from employees on a quarterly rather than a monthly basis. These remittances would be required on March 31, June 30, September 30 and December 31. The remittances are due the 15th of the month following the end of each quarter.

Vehicle Costs   As you have learned, the most important part of claiming any vehicle expenses is to keep a distance log, which can record your total business driving for the year, if your vehicle was used both for personal and business driving. The size of deductible expenditures for your vehicles depends on how many you have and what they are used for. Restrictions on certain expenses apply to passenger vehicles.

Farm trucks or vans, on the other hand, are "motor vehicles-automobiles" that will be exempt from these restrictions if they are designed to carry the driver and two passengers and are used primarily (which means more than 50% of the time) to transport equipment or goods, or if the motor vehicle is used 90% or more of the time to transfer equipment, goods or passengers for the purpose of earning income.

Group receipts in categories before you compute deductible totals. All of the following expenses are deductible: gas and oil; interest on loans (subject to restrictions for passenger vehicles); insurance; licence renewal costs; tires and repairs; lease payments (again, restrictions may apply to passenger vehicles); auto club premiums; car washes; parking and tolls. By keeping all receipts in order and faithfully maintaining a distance log, you will maximize your tax deductions and minimize the time required to file your tax return. Joint owners of a motor vehicle cannot deduct more than one owner could deduct.

Ineligible Expenses　Expenses not allowable include:

- replacement or improvement of assets (these must be capitalized)
- principal payments on borrowed money, including repayments of a loan for tile drainage
- the value of animals that have died during the year (when they are purchased, the cost is written off as an expense)
- expenses for a personal garden or upkeep of livestock gifted to children.

Inventory Valuations　To combat the fluctuations in income that a farmer may experience, the role of his/her inventory is an important one in determining the net income each year. That is because CRA wishes to avoid tax loss reporting in cases where expenditures have been made to increase inventory size. There are two inventory provisions for the farmer. One is optional, the other mandatory.

MIA　CRA won't just let you write off operational losses from a farm, if you have purchased inventory on hand. A Mandatory Inventory Adjustment must be made. The effect of this provision is to reduce the amount of the cash loss a farmer may have in one tax year, by adding in the market value of inventory on hand at year end. Amounts included in income must be deducted the following year, thereby reducing income earned from operations in that year.

OIA　A farmer has a further opportunity to average income and losses over the years, by electing to make an Optional Inventory Adjustment. Such an adjustment, which adds the Fair Market Value of all remaining inventory (less the MIA provision) to a farmer's income will further reduce a farmer's remaining cash loss in one year, and then be deducted from income the next. The definition of inventory for these purposes may include all inventory on hand including livestock owned, cash crops, fertilizer, chemicals, feed, seed, fuel, etc. Proper management of this provision can save the farmer thousands of dollars over the years.

Certain Prepayments　Under the cash method of reporting income, amounts are generally deducted when paid. However, a deduction for prepaid expenses can be made in advance, but only for the current year and one more year. The portion of amounts paid for tax years that are two or more years after the actual payment must be deferred and deducted in those future years.

For example, if $5,000 was prepaid in 2001 for five consecutive years of insurance coverage, $2,000 could be deducted in this and then $1,000 in each following year.

To be deductible, the amount is required to have been paid in a preceding tax year and cannot be deductible in computing income of the business for any other year.

Land Improvement Costs Expenditures, such as clearing land and constructing unpaved roads, are deducted as a current expense by farmers. A farmer may claim less than the full cost of these expenses in the year they are incurred. He or she will be allowed to carry forward and use the remaining undeducted amounts in a subsequent year. This is significant to farmers who have little or no net income in the year the expenditure is made, because it allows the deferral of the write-off to a year when there is taxable income. As well, the cost of laying or installing a land drainage system will be deductible, whether it is composed of tile or other materials.

Livestock Income Tax-Deferral Program Here's a little known tax saver. A tax-deferral program exists for farmers who had to deplete their breeding herds of grazing livestock because of drought conditions. Farmers will be required to include the proceeds received for the forced destruction or sale of breeding animals in income. However, an offsetting deduction may be taken to defer tax on such proceeds to the next tax year. Qualifying areas will be determined every year upon recommendation by the Minister of Agriculture and Agri-Food. Ask your tax advisor to brief you on this year's prescribed areas.

Loss Deductibility

CRA groups farm losses into three categories:

- Losses from a full-scale farming operation (the taxpayer spends all of his/her time and effort in the operation of the farm and farming is the chief source of income). These losses are deductible in full against other income the taxpayer may have.
- Farm losses claimed against other income when it is clear that the taxpayer's chief source of income is not farming.
- Farm losses claimed against other income when it is questionable whether a business actually exists. (These losses are not deductible at all, because the activities are considered to be a hobby.)

The tax department will look at a number of conditions as proof that a viable operation exists. These guidelines are also useful in determining whether other business ventures have a reasonable expectation of profit.

- **Gross and Net Income From the Farming Operation.** This includes the amount of capital invested, and a close look at the cash flow of the business.

- **The Size of the Property Used for Farming.** Your losses may be disallowed if:
  - Your property is too small to project any hope of profit.
  - You have made no attempt at farming or developing your land.
  - You have no intention of using more than a fraction of the land over a period of years. There must be potential for profit that you can document and justify with cash flow statements and budgets for the future.

- **Qualifications of the Taxpayer.** Losses will generally be allowed if:
  - You have farming background experience and spend most of your time on the operation during the busy months.
  - You make commitments for the future expansion of the farm.
  - You qualify for some type of provincial assistance.
  - You personally are involved to a large degree in the operations.

- **Other Sources of Income.** Generally speaking, if your chief source of income is from other sources, losses may be restricted or disallowed. If forced to earn income elsewhere in a bad year, full losses may be allowed if it can be proven that farming is still your chief source of income and that it is your intention to continue spending most of your time and money on the future of the farm.

- **Future Business Plans.** Be prepared to show how your farm will be maintained and developed in future years.

Also be aware that if you have a capital gain, perhaps from farmland sold during the year, interest or property taxes that were included in any restricted farm losses of prior years that have not yet been deducted may be used to reduce the capital gain, but not to create or increase a capital loss on the sale of the farmland.

Restricted Farm Losses   Farmers whose chief source of income is not from farming are currently restricted to a maximum farm loss write-off of $2,500 plus one-half of the next $12,500 for a maximum of $8,750. This means that a loss of $15,000 or more will qualify for a write-off of $8,750.

This provision of the Act is the subject of numerous court cases. Farmers argue that they are in the full time business of farming and therefore should be allowed full loss deductibility; while CRA argues that the chief source of income is not from farming and therefore losses should be restricted.

Value of Accounts Receivable   A taxpayer is required to include the value of accounts receivable in income in cases where (1) a Canadian resident ceases to carry on the business of farming and becomes a non-resident; (2) a Canadian resident ceases to carry on a farming business in another country and becomes a non-resident; and (3) a non-resident ceases to carry on a Canadian farming business after July 13, 1990. In such cases, inventory will be considered disposed of at its fair market value.

Farmers and the GST/HST   Most farmers should enquire about becoming GST/HST registrants when speaking to their accountants, or to CRA directly. This is because most supplies produced by farmers are zero-rated; that is, no GST/HST is charged by the farmer on the sale of supplies, but a GST/HST input tax credit can be claimed to recover GST/HST paid on purchases incurred in producing supplies. Examples of zero-rated supplies are livestock used to produce wool or food, grains, seeds (not garden seeds) and fodder crops, share cropping and unprocessed fish.

Special Capital Cost Allowances Classes and Rates for Farmers   Most items of farm equipment can be considered as depreciable assets, subject to a variety of prescribed classes and rates. Generally, they fall into Class 1 (4% Building), Class 8 (20% for non-motorized equipment), and Class 10 (30% for motorized equipment), or Class 45 (45% for computer equipment).

For a complete list, see CRA's Farming Income Guide. Farmers who buy certain pollution-control manure-handling equipment, including pads, liquid manure tanks, pumps and spreaders may qualify for special accelerated CCA rates. Contact the Minister of the Environment for more details.

Also note that the cost of paving roads must be added to Class 17, which has an 8% rate. Casing and cribwork for a waterwell as well as the cost of the system that distributes water, such as the pump, pipes and trenches, will all be capitalized in Class 8, which has a 20% rate.

Eligible Capital Properties   Farmers who own milk and egg quotas have what is known as an "eligible capital property," which is a property that has a lasting economic value and therefore must be written off over time. To do so, a special account is set up — the cumulative eligible capital account — and 3/4 of the value of the quota is recorded here. The annual allowance that is claimed against other income is 7% of this amount. However, a CEC allowance deduction will only be allowed if there is a positive balance in the account. Any negative balance would have to be reported as income, consistent with the capital gains inclusion rate.* If the property is qualified farm property eligible for the $500,000 Capital Gains Exemption, qualifying income amounts will be reported on Schedule 3, Capital Gains and Losses, to enable the deduction.

Capital Gains Exemption

The $500,000 Lifetime Capital Gains Exemption may be used on the gains generated by the disposal of shares of the capital stock of a small business corporation owned by the individual or partnership related to him or her. A small business corporation is a Canadian-controlled private corporation in which all or substantially all of the assets are used in an active business carried on primarily in Canada. The shares must be owned by such an individual through the 24 months immediately prior to the disposition. During the holding period, more than 50% of the FMV of the corporation's assets must have been used in an active business.

Those who own qualifying farm property, may also make the claim for farm property acquired after June 17, 1987, including real property owned by the taxpayer, spouse or child for at least 24 months immediately before sale. A gross revenue test must be met; that is, in at least two years prior to disposition, gross income earned by the individual by active farming operations must exceed net income from all other sources. Second, all or substantially all of the fair value of the farm assets must be used in active business operations for at least 24 months prior to disposition.

On farms acquired before June 17, 1987, the $500,000 Capital Gains Exemption will be allowed if the farmland and buildings were used in an active farming business in Canada in the year of sale, and at least five years prior to the disposition.

Consult your tax advisor about meeting the qualifications to enable a future tax-free gain of farming property held by your family.

Family Farm Rollovers A tax-free rollover of farm assets, including the farmland, depreciable properties and eligible capital properties, will be allowed on transfers to the spouse, children or grandchildren. This means that no capital gain or loss, terminal loss or recapture will generally arise on the tax return of the transferor. However, to qualify, the property must have

---

* For business years ending after October 17, 2000, 2/3 of the gain is included in income. The original purchase of ECP was originally factored by 3/4 for determination of the pool addition (2/3 times 3/4 is 1/2).

| Figure 7.2 | Transfer of Farm Assets | | |

Asset	While Living	At Death		Transfers to Spouse or Child
Equipment	At any amount between FMV and transferor's undepreciated capital cost	$\dfrac{\text{FMV of asset}}{\substack{\text{FMV of all}\\\text{assets in}\\\text{that class}}}$	$\times$ UCC of all assets in that class	Special Election: The lower of Capital Cost Or $\dfrac{\text{Capital Cost of Asset}}{\substack{\text{Capital Cost}\\\text{of all property}\\\text{in same class}}} \times \substack{\text{UCC of all}\\\text{in same}\\\text{class}}$ Or FMV if transferred to spouse, Or an amount between FMV and special election for transfer to child
Land	At an amount between the fair market value and the transferor's ACB	At the adjusted cost base immediately before death, or any amount between ACB and FMV		

Note: The deceased's legal representative may choose to transfer property at any amount between its FMV and ACB or UCC before death, if this is to the advantage of the estate. The property must have vested indefeasibly within 36 months of date of death.

been used principally in an active farming business, and the child must have been a resident of Canada immediately before the transfer.

The meaning of "child" has been extended to include persons who, before reaching age 19, were under the control and custody of the taxpayer and dependent upon him. This could include nephews, nieces and in-laws. The cost of acquisition of the property is equal to the deceased's deemed proceeds of disposition.

When transfers occur due to death, the property must be transferred to the child within 36 months. In either case, transfers can be valued at an amount between ACB (adjusted cost base) and FMV (Fair Market Value). Also see Figure 7.2 for rules surrounding depreciable property.

As well, farm rollovers from a child to a parent would be allowed in cases in which the child dies leaving a surviving parent.

Property eligible for such transfers includes property leased by a taxpayer to the family farm corporation. A special election is available to transfer depreciable property on death (including buildings, equipment or other depreciable property used in business). This may be done in any amount between the fair market value of the property and its undepreciated capital cost at the time of transfer. Eligible capital property (ECP) can be transferred at any amount between FMV and:

$$^4/_3 \times \text{Cumulative Eligible Capital*} \quad \times \quad \frac{\text{FMV of Property}}{\text{FMV of all Eligible Capital Property}}$$

Careful planning of disposition and acquisition cost values would allow the farm family to maximize use of the capital gains exemption on transfer and capital and non-capital loss provisions to minimize tax now and in the future.

Note: A farmer who transfers shares of a family farm corporation or interests in a family farm partnership at fair market value to his/ her child who then disposes of it before attaining age 18 will be subject to the attribution rules on farm income earned. The same attribution rules would hold true in cases where a spouse disposes of the property during the farmer's lifetime except this time attribution applies to the capital gain or loss.

Fishers: Also note that these rollover rules apply to fishers on or after May 2, 2006, as does the Capital Gains Exemptions on dispositions of qualifying property.

Construction Industry

As of January 1, 1999, businesses whose principal activity is construction must ensure they record the name, the amount paid, and the identifier number (Business Number or Social Insurance Number) of their subcontractors. The due date for reporting this information is 6 months from the end of your reporting period of the year following the end of fiscal year of the business.

Contractors who pay subcontractors must file Form T5018 Summary of Contract Payments. They are also encouraged to send a T5018 Information Slip to each subcontractor. Alternatively, the information may be reported on a line-by-line basis in a column format with the appropriate summary information.

Only payments for services in excess of $500 per year need be reported. Payments primarily for goods need not be reported unless there is a total annual service component of $500 or more.

---

* Only on the sale of assets are adjustments made to income in order to adjust for the capital gains inclusion rate in effect at the time of sale.

Figure 7.3	Tax Action Planner

Month	Week 1	Week 2	Week 3: 15th	Week 4	Week 5: 30th
January	RRSP contr. Mo. end review	Payroll Accts. Payable	Remit Source Deductions, GST for Dec.	Payroll	Final Quarter Review
February	RRSP Contr. Overview T4s, T5s, T3s Mo. end review	Payroll Accts. Payable	Remit Source Deductions, Prepare to remit tax return	Payroll, Mail or Distribute T4 Slips	
March	RRSP Contr. Mo. end review	Payroll, Accts. Payable	Remit Source Deductions, Instalments	Payroll	**Appointment with Tax Advisor re tax return**
April	RRSP Contr. Mo. End review	Payroll, Accts. Payable	Remit Source Deductions, GST for 1st quarter	Payroll	1st Quarter **Review; File tax return if you owe money**

Continue planner for the months of May through December

THE TAX ADVISOR

It is important to communicate effectively with your tax advisor throughout the year. Work with a **Tax Action Planner,** which records tax-filing milestones throughout the year on your Daily Business Journal. The key—know your tax filing compliance milestones.

RECAP. YOU NEED TO KNOW:

1. What industry profile your business falls into for audit purposes
2. When a small supplier for GST purposes is required to register to collect the tax
3. What the latest tax changes are regarding tax brackets, rates, RRSP contribution room, and business expenses
4. How partners are taxed in the partnership and on the personal return
5. How partnerships between spouses are affected by Attribution Rules
6. What specific rules apply to artists and writers when claiming expenses and losses
7. New rules surrounding scholarship exemptions
8. The nuances surrounding home workspace claims for babysitters
9. How loss deductibility and the requirement for tax installments differ for farmers
10. How losses are averaged and assets are transferred in family farm or fishing enterprises

YOU NEED TO ASK: Your Tax Advisor for Help In Setting Up Your Industry Filing Profile By:

1. **Summarizing your business activities.** Develop a business plan. This will help you and your advisor make decisions about your form of business organization and family income splitting opportunities, while meeting audit requirements surrounding REOP. See Figure 7.4.

2. **Choosing the right method of reporting income.** Make sure you choose the correct reporting method when you start your business, and that you know the exceptions to the rules. Farmers and very small businesses may use the "cash method" of reporting income, for example. Most other businesses, though, must report their income on the "accrual basis." Special provisions may be available for certain professionals, and those who qualify for a variety of reserving provisions. Discuss this concept with your tax advisor.

3. **Planning the deduction of operating expenses.** Remember that most operating expenses are 100% deductible against revenues of the business. In the case of husband and wife teams, it is most important to show that personal living expenses are not claimed against business income. (Farmers should allow for food taken for personal consumption if costs are written off.)

4. **Planning to write off tax losses.** CRA has made a practice of scrutinizing certain industries more thoroughly than others when it comes to writing off tax losses. This is particularly true of the farming community and the construction industry. Discuss the loss-filing rules applicable to your industry with your tax advisor.

5. **Knowing why you could be chosen for audit.** CRA has profiled certain industries due to their work with Statistics Canada, who have identified the skimming of receipts by certain small businesses as a major component of the Underground Economy. Special investigative projects have been identified in the following areas:

   - independent couriers
   - subcontractors in construction and home building
   - unregistered car salespeople
   - carpet installers
   - direct sellers
   - mechanics
   - auto body repairers

   If you are in a high-risk group, be sure to put your affairs in order, as the probability of audit is higher in those identified industries.

Figure 7.4	Business Profile Overview

Business Name: _____

Type Of Business:

Proprietorship   Owner: _____

Partnership   Partners: _____

_____

_____

Corporation _____ Date of Incorporation _____ Costs: _____

Business Plan:

Source of Revenue:	Year 1	Year 2	Year 3	Year 4	Year 5
Total					

Operating Expenses:	Year 1	Year 2	Year 3	Year 4	Year 5
Total					
% Of Income					

Profits	Year 1	Year 2	Year 3	Year 4	Year 5
Total					
% Of Income					

Obstacles Forecast: _____

_____

_____

_____

How to Put Your Family to Work and Write It Off!

"See it big, and keep it simple."
WILFRED PETERSON

KEY CONCEPTS

- You can hire your family members to work in your business and it's deductible
- Amounts must be paid for work actually completed
- Payments must be reasonable and in line with what you would pay a non-related person
- Hiring should be formal, with contracts in place
- Proper payroll procedures must be in place including T4 slip processing
- Remittances of statutory deductions must be made
- Taxable and tax free perks add value to employment contracts
- Tax withholdings should be minimized to avoid tax refunds, maximize savings
- It is important to know the difference between an employee and a contractor

REAL LIFE: Raj and his wife Vasi were happy to live in Canada. They had immigrated from their native India last year, and in January of the new year opened their own business in Canada—an Indian restaurant. Vasi did the cooking, with her sous-chef, daughter Tara, while Raj and his son Ram, played host and waiter respectively. After their first quarter in business, their books showed a small operating profit. However, the proprietorship showed no deductions for wages for the family members, and Raj wondered if he could reduce his tax liability any further by paying his family members. Was this possible? How would he justify payment of wages and the work of the family retroactively?

THE PROBLEM

Most new businesses in Canada have something in common: usually the whole family pitches in to get the business established profitably. While it is legally possible to pay your family members to work in your small business, and deduct the amounts from the profits of your business, be careful not to make the common mistake that Raj has made: he didn't keep the documentation required to show that the family members were actually working in the business, and, worse, he didn't actually pay them the money. Therefore at tax time, he'll be unable to write off any salary or wage expenses retroactively. However, for the future, Raj and his family are poised for some significant tax savings solutions.

THE SOLUTION

Family members can be hired as hourly employees, wage earners, sub-contractors, commission salespeople, or any other position you would hire a stranger for. You can pay them salary, wages, gratuities, overtime, premium hours, banked time, retroactive earnings, salary, bonuses, commissions, advances, draws, gifts, severance, sick leave, vacation pay, wages in lieu of notice or a number of taxable or tax-free benefits.

However a simple rule must be followed in hiring and remunerating your family members: *treat the process of hiring and paying your family members in the same manner as if you were hiring a stranger.* All the paperwork must be in place, including the signing of employment contracts or sub-contracts, or the keeping of time cards to support hours worked. Without the paperwork, not only will it be impossible to write off the amounts paid to your family members, but you'll also miss out on an important tax saver: the ability to legitimately split income amongst family members.

The establishment of formal payroll records, however, can only happen once you have determined whether you have an employer-employee relationship with your family members who work in your business. If you do, certain statutory source deductions must be made from gross pay and remitted to the government on a regular basis.

You should also know that there are a number of important tax-savings tips that you can utilize in designing compensation packages for your employees, including family members. For example, consider the following a primary goal in negotiating employment contracts: *Put as many after-tax dollars in your employee's pockets, as soon as possible.* There are many ways to do this, including the minimization of taxes withheld at source.

THE PARAMETERS

The following parameters should be observed in order to deduct amounts paid to family members for working in your small business:

Formalize Hiring Practices

When a business hires an employee, generally the employee is given a role description, a rate of pay or salary level, and a series of expectations that can include termination, confidentiality and non-compete clauses. When a business hires a sub-contractor, the self-employed person generally submits a proposal to the business to perform a certain task that has a start and end period and an agreed-upon invoice price.

In a family business, such formalities are often dropped or forgotten about. However, they are just as important, and certainly, from a tax point of view, even more important, as CRA will scrutinize these "non-arm's length" transactions even more closely. (A non-arm's length relationship generally exists when one deals with someone related by blood, marriage or adoption.)

To legitimize your deduction for amounts paid to family members, CRA will want to know that the following criteria are met:

- The work actually has to have been done by your relative
- The work was necessary and would have otherwise required the hiring of a stranger
- The amounts paid are compared to what would have been paid to a stranger for the same work
- The amounts paid were reasonable in relation to the relative's age and experience
- The amounts were paid in pursuit of profits from the business.

It is a very good idea to establish a Human Resource Guide or Policies and Procedures Manual in which your human resource policies are outlined. This can include things like job descriptions, job postings, employer-paid training, sick leave and vacation policies, sexual harassment and bereavement policies, and so on. This will also show to CRA that you are running a serious, for-profit business with a future orientation for earning profits.

Employed or Self-Employed?

This is an important question, as the business owner will have certain obligations to meet by law, if the relationship is one of "master-servant."

CRA defines an employer-employee relationship as follows:

> "a verbal or written agreement in which an employee agrees to work on a full-time or part-time basis for a specified or indeterminate period of time, in return for salary or wages. The employer has the right to decide where, when and how the work will be done. In this type of relationship a *contract of service* exists."*

When a family member works in the business, the owner must do the following:

• Make statutory deductions from gross pay for contributions to Canada Pension Plan, Employment Insurance and Income Taxes. These must be remitted usually once a month, although very small businesses have the option to remit each quarter. Children under 18 need not contribute to the Canada Pension Plan; while those over 70 (except in Quebec) or in receipt of CPP benefits need not contribute at all.
• Prepare a T4 slip for each employee and issue it by the end of February each year.

Where a family member works as a subcontractor to the business, a "business relationship" is said to exist. CRA defines a business relationship to be the following:

> "a verbal or written agreement in which a self-employed individual agrees to perform specific work for a payer in return for payment. There is no employer or employee. The self-employed individual generally does not have to carry out all or even part of the work himself. In this type of relationship, a *contract for service* exists."*

The amounts invoiced to the business must be paid in a timely fashion to the sub-contractor (usually within 30 days). By the way, the invoiced amount is fully deductible by the business owner.

The subcontractor who is unincorporated must then remit CPP premiums via the income tax return at year end, and in some cases, tax instalment payments, quarterly.

In addition, if the subcontractor earns more than $30,000 in gross fees billed, GST/HST registration may be required. This should be

---

* CRA publication: *Employee or Self-Employed?*

taken into consideration before deciding on what status your family member prefers to have in working within your business.

Therefore, you will need to know whether the relationship you have is a contract *of* service or a contract *for* service. There are four basic factors CRA will look at if the determination is borderline:

1. **Control.** The degree of control exercised by the payer will help to define the relationship with the person doing the work. If the payer has the right to hire or fire, controls the payments of wages and how much is to be paid, and decides on the time, place and manner in which the work should be done, including hours of work, and the assessment of quality of work, generally there is a strong indication of an employer-employee relationship. Additional factors include control of the list of clients of the business and the territory covered, as well as training and development.

2. **Ownership of Assets and Tools.** If the payer supplies the equipment and tools required to perform the tasks of the job and pays for repairs, insurance, rental, fuel or other costs of operation, generally an employer-employee relationship is considered to exist.

3. **Risk of Loss.** The payer is generally considered to be the employer if s/he assumes the financial risk for the company including the responsibility for covering operating costs like office expenses, salaries, insurance coverage, freight and delivery, rent, bad debts, damage and promotional expenses. Those who receive remuneration without financial risk — that is salary is paid in full regardless of the health of the business — would generally be considered to be an employee.

4. **Integration.** This final factor is considered from the worker's viewpoint. If the worker is not dependent on the payer, and simply integrates the job done for the payer into his own business activities, the worker is likely self-employed. It would be important to show that the self-employed person has other jobs lined up with other suppliers, for example, to consolidate this position. However, if the job done for the payer is actually integrated into the payer's commercial activities, to the extent that the worker is connected with the employer's business and dependent on it, likely an employer-employee relationship exists.

Taken all together, the circumstances surrounding these four criteria will generally help you to determine whether an employer-employee relationship exists.

REAL LIFE: Marina works in her husband Paul's construction business, doing the books. She has a home office, she answers the phone for the business from there and prepares the books on the computer that Paul bought for her. He has asked her to be in the office available for calls from 9 until 2 every day, but Marina often spends all day there to finish correspondence, invoicing and other odds and ends. Paul is her only payer.

In this case there is a very strong likelihood that Marina will be considered to be Paul's employee. He has acquired and written off the equipment she needs to do her job; he controls the place and the time she works and she has no other clients. She should be filling in a time card to post her hours worked; or he should have Marina on an employment contract if salary is being paid. He should issue a T4 slip at year end, and make periodic source remittances for CPP, EI and Income Tax.

If Paul was one of a series of clients for whom Marina was doing the books, if she purchased her own equipment and tools, if it could be shown that Marina took on the risk of paying overhead and responsibility for the contracts she bid and won, there would be an indication that Marina, in fact, was self-employed. Marina would then become a supplier of Paul's and submit invoices to be paid within usually a 30-day period.

In that case, Marina would have to do at least four things from CRA's perspective:

- self-report her income on her income tax return
- make CPP premium contributions via the tax return at the end of the tax year when she files her return
- pay tax instalment payments if she owed CRA more than $2,000 in the current tax year and the immediately preceding year and
- register to collect the GST/HST if her gross earnings exceeded $30,000.

Payroll Procedures

Once you have determined the relationship you have with your family members is actually an employer-employee relationship, you'll have to put payroll procedures in place. The basic payroll equation you must follow when preparing payroll for your family business is shown in Figure 8.1.

As you can see, Gross Pay can comprise three remuneration types: cash, and taxable benefits, which are reported on the T4 slip, and tax-free benefits, which are not. From this Gross Pay, the employer may take one of two types of deductions:

Figure 8.1 The Basic Payroll Equation

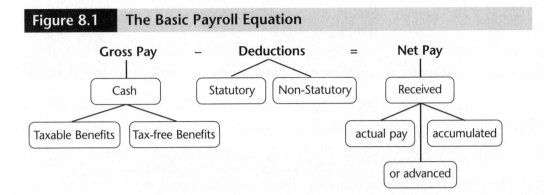

- Statutory deductions—those required by law—which are CPP, EI and Income Tax deductions
- Non-Statutory deductions, which can include deductions for union dues, registered pension plans, charities, and other deductions at the option of the workplace.

Finally, the net pay is arrived at. This can be given to the employee in cash or by cheque, deposited directly to the employee's bank account, or held or advanced.

10 Steps in the Payroll Cycle

1. Collect information about the employees' gross pay for the period on the Payroll Journal.
2. Determine the CPP and EI premiums payable by looking up the gross earnings in the CRA Guide Books or on CRA's Tables on Diskette (TOD).
3. Determine the amount of taxes to be withheld based on CRA's Form TD1 or other specialized forms filed with you by the employee.
4. Calculate Net Pay on the Payroll Journal and double-check all figures.
5. Calculate the Employer's Portion of CPP and EI.
6. Calculate the Total Employer CRA Remittance Required for the current period for total Income Taxes withheld, CPP premiums withheld plus Employer's Portion, EI premiums withheld plus Employer's Portion.
7. Total the CRA remittance for the period. Write the cheque for the remittance.
8. Prepare the bookkeeping journal entries for the payroll:
   - to record the payment of the payroll
   - to record the withholding amounts as a liability.

9. Write the payroll cheques and double-check all to the Payroll Journal before distributing the cheques to the employees.

10. Prepare a new payroll Journal for the next pay period, carrying forward all year-to-date accumulated figures.

Employer's Obligations for the CPP

Hiring an employee can be a costly undertaking for a small business. That's because the employer must make additional contributions to the Canada Pension Plan and Employment Insurance, besides the deductions that are taken for the employee's contributions.

In the case of the Canada Pension Plan, the employer must match the employee's contributions. CPP premiums do not have to be deducted from those who make less than $250 a year in agriculture, forestry, trapping, fishing, hunting, horticulture or lumbering employment, and work less then 25 days in the same year, employment of a child under 18, casual employment for purposes other than normal trade or business, residence benefits of clergy, severance pay or death benefits. For a complete list check CRA's *Employer's Guide to Payroll Deductions*.

A $3,500 basic exemption is allowed before CPP premiums are payable. That is, if your employee earns less than $3,500 for the year, no CPP premiums are payable. Or, in an another example, if your employee earns $6,500 in the year, and is over the age of 18, CPP premiums must be contributed on earnings of $3,000 ($6,500 – $3,500). You should also know that in the following circumstances, CPP premiums will be prorated:

1. The employee is under the age of 18
2. The employee is over the age of 70 (except in Quebec)
3. The employee has started to receive a retirement or disability benefit from the CPP
4. The employee is deceased.

In the last three instances, CPP premiums are payable until the month of the event. CPP is remitted for teenagers in the month after they turn 18.

Employer's Obligations for the Employment Insurance (EI) Fund

As with the CPP, both the employer and the employee must contribute EI premiums to the fund. However, there are certain exceptions to the rules for remittance, according to the Employer's Guide for Payroll Deductions, which is a document employers and their bookkeepers should review at least annually or whenever there is a change in income tax rate or bracket structure. It states that "even if there is a contract of service, employment is **not insurable** and therefore not subject to El premiums in the case of:

- casual employment that is not expended for your usual trade or business;
- employment when you and your employee do **not** deal with each other at arm's length. Two categories are addressed here:
  - ◦ Related persons: those connected by blood relationship, marriage, common-law relationship, or adoption. Where the employer is a corporation, the employee will be related to the corporation when s/he is related to a person who either controls the corporation or is a member of a related group that controls the corporation.
  - ◦ Non-related persons: an employment can be non-insurable if it is apparent from the circumstances of employment that the parties were not dealing with each other in the way arm's length parties normally would;
- when a corporation employs a person who controls more than 40% of the corporation's voting shares;
- employment by an employer in agriculture, in an agricultural enterprise, or in horticulture when:
  - ◦ the person receives no cash remuneration; **or**
  - ◦ works less than seven days with the same employer during the year;
- employment of a person connected with a circus, fair, parade, carnival, exposition, exhibition, or other similar activity, **except** for entertainers, if that person:
  - ◦ is not your regular employee; and
  - ◦ works for less than seven days in the year"

It is wise to request a ruling when there are any doubts about the requirement to deduct El premiums for family members or other non-related employees whose circumstances of employment are unusual. Do so by completing form **CPT1,** *Request for a Ruling as the Status of a Worker under the Canada Pension Plan or Employment Insurance Act.* Avoid overpaying El premiums, as they are expensive (1.4% times the employee's contribution) and recoverable for only 12 months in retrospect if paid in error.

Overpayments that are made because an employee works for several employers during the year will be recoverable by filing an income tax return at year end. However, the employer gets stung here: there are no refunds for you, even if your employee has already maxed out contributory earnings with another employer. You also do not have the choice to stop contributing to the fund because the maximum was already reached for the employee with another employer.

Reduce Tax Withholding—File TD Forms

As an employer, always be vigilant about designing compensation packages that are tax efficient. That begins by helping your employee invest more of the first dollar earned— before tax withholding—rather than the last. To ensure that only the correct amount of tax is withheld, your employee must complete Form TD1 *Personal Tax Credit Return,* one for the federal government and the province of residence to report personal tax credit entitlements. Employees who are paid commissions and who claim tax deductible expenses against these may choose to complete Form **TD1X,** *Statement of Commission Income and Expenses for Payroll Tax Deductions,* instead of Form TD1. Also, note that fishers complete Form **TD3F,** *Fisher's Election to Have Tax Deducted at Source.*

In some cases, tax withholding can be reduced further by filing *Form T1213 Request for Reduction in Tax Withholding.* This should be initiated by your employee when there are additional deductible expenditures during the year that do not show up on the *TD1 Form.* This would include RRSP contributions not deducted from pay by the employer, child care expenses, tax deductible support payments, employment expenses on *Form T777 Statement of Employment Expenses,* carrying charges and interest expenses on investment loans, loss carry overs, allowable business investment losses, or other items like significant charitable donations or rental losses. Supporting documentation must be attached.

Form T1213, which results in a Letter of Authority permitting you to withhold less tax, is not required—that is, you can reduce tax withholding without formal permission—if you are otherwise making tax withholdings for the following amounts which are tax deductible to your employee:

- employees' contributions to a registered pension plan (RPP)
- union dues;
- contributions to a retirement compensation arrangement (RCA) or certain pension plans; or
- contributions to a registered retirement savings plan (RRSP) provided you have reasonable grounds to believe the contribution can be deducted by the employee for the year

File the Letter of Authority with your payroll records. This is a great way to bring the benefits of a tax refund directly into your employees' pocket books every two weeks. It can help them save on a tax-deferred

Figure 8.2	How to Reduce Tax Withholding at Source

Canada Revenue   Agence du revenu
Agency   du Canada

REQUEST TO REDUCE TAX DEDUCTIONS AT SOURCE FOR YEAR(S) ————

- Use this form to ask for reduced tax deductions at source for any deductions or non-refundable tax credits that are not part of the Form TD1, *Personal Tax Credits Return.*
- All your income tax returns that are due have to be filed and amounts paid in full before you send us this form.
- You usually have to file this request every year. However, if you have deductible support payments that are the same or greater for more than one year, you can make this request for two years.
- Send the completed form with all supporting documents to the Client Services Division of your tax services office. You can find the addresses on our Web site at www.cra.gc.ca/tso or by calling us at 1-800-959-8281.
- We will notify you in writing within four to eight weeks whether or not we approve your request.

Identification

First name	Last name	Social Insurance Number

Address

City	Province or territory	Postal code	Residence	Telephone / Business

Employer Name	Contact person	Telephone and fax numbers

Address

Request to reduce tax on

☐ Salary
☐ Lump sum (indicate the amount and payment type; for example, a bonus or vacation pay)
  $ _____ and _____

Deductions and non-refundable tax credits

Registered retirement savings plan (RRSP) contributions .... $ _____
- Give details or a copy of the payment arrangement contract
- Do not include contributions deducted from your pay by your employer.

Child care expenses .... $ _____
- Give details on a separate sheet.

Support payments .... $ _____
- Attach a copy of your court order or written agreement and Form T1158, *Registration of Family Support Payments* (if not previously filed).
- Recipient's name and social insurance number.
  _____ | | | | | | | | | |

Employment expenses .... $ _____
- Attach a completed Form T2200, *Declaration of Conditions of Employment,* and Form T777, *Statement of Employment Expenses.*

Carrying charges and interest expenses on Investment loans ...... $ _____
- Attach a copy of statements from the lender confirming the purpose and amount of loan(s) and the interest payments to be made in the year.

Other (for example, charitable donations or rental losses) .... $ _____
- Attach all supporting documents. Use a separate sheet to give details if necessary.

  Specify: _____

                    Total amounts to be deducted from income $ _____

Subtract income not subject to tax deductions at source (interest, net rental or self-employed income) $ _____

Registered retirement savings plan (RRSP) contributions   Net amount requested for **tax waiver** $ _____

Certification

I request authorization for my employer to reduce my tax deductions at source based on the information given. I certify that the information given is, to the best of my knowledge, correct and complete.

_____   _____
         Signature   Date

T1213(04)   (Français au verso)   **Canada** basis by investing the freed-up tax withholdings into an RRSP, thereby building wealth faster in a tax-deferred manner, while averaging into the marketplace all year long.

Remember, a tax refund is a bad thing. . .don't overpay taxes within the family. . .make that money work for you all year long. You are only required to pay the correct amount of tax, and not one cent more.

Pay Tax-Free Perks to Your Family Members

A host of tax-free benefits can be paid to your family members. Figure 8.3 provides a checklist of benefits common to small businesses for you to choose from:

Figure 8.3	Tax-Free Perks for Employees and Family

Tax-Free Benefits	**Description**
Wedding or Christmas Gifts that do not exceed $500	Not taxable, as long as the gift is not in cash or near-cash. Maximum of two non-cash gifts and two non-cash awards.
Discounts on Merchandise	This status will not extend to cases where the merchandise is purchased below the merchant's cost. A commission received by a sales employee on merchandise acquired for the employee's personal use is not taxable, nor is a commission received by a life insurance salesperson for the acquisition of his/her own policy.
Subsidized Meals	Not taxable if the employee is charged a reasonable amount that covers the cost of food, its preparation and service.
Uniforms and Special Clothing	Payments made by an employer for laundering special uniforms or for reimbursement of the employee's expenses in laundering uniforms will not be taxable to the employee.
Recreational Facilities, including memberships to social or athletic clubs	Pools, gym, exercise rooms or fees paid to be members of a social or athletic club qualify as a tax-free benefit to the employee, if it can be shown such a membership is primarily to the advantage of the employer. See IT148 and IT470.
Moving Expenses if the move was required by the employer	• Cost of movers to move and store household effects • Cost of moving the family including all travelling expenses • Cost to move personal items such as a car or trailer • Reasonable temporary living accommodations in the new work location if the new residence is not ready • Charges for alterations to furniture and fixtures that were part of the old home • Costs of cancelling a lease

Figure 8.3	Tax-Free Perks for Employees and Family (Cont'd)

- Costs of discharging a mortgage
- Legal fees and transfer taxes to buy a new home
- Long-distance charges incurred to sell the former residence plus costs of keeping up the old residence after move if efforts to sell are not successful
- Costs of house-hunting trips to new location
- Charges and fees to disconnect telephone, TV aerials, water, etc.
- Costs to connect and install utilities, appliances, and fixtures from old home
- Costs of auto licences, inspections and drivers' permit fees if owned at former residence
- Costs to revise wills, or other legal documents if necessary because of move
- Certain losses on selling of home: The first $15,000 plus one-half the amount over $15,000.

Premiums Paid under a private health services plan.	See IT339, which describes private health services plans. Premiums paid to private health services plans are not taxable to the employee. Also be aware that premiums paid by proprietors now qualify as a tax deduction, provided certain conditions are met. The proprietor must be actively engaged in the business; self-employment income must comprise at least 50% of the individual's total income for the year or the individual's income from other sources may not exceed $10,000. As well, a maximum deduction of $1,500 for each individual and his/her spouse and $750 per child will be allowed, unless there is at least one qualifying non-related employee. In that case, amounts are based on the lowest cost of equivalent coverage for non-family members.
Employer's Required Contribution to Provincial Health and Medical Plans	Remittances to certain provincial Health Insurance Plans are considered to be employer levies and so are not taxable.
Attendant Costs	For the assistance of a mentally or physically challenged employee who works in your business. This provision, together with the next one, can go a long way in helping families who support employment of a disabled relative in the family business, on a tax-assisted basis.
Transportation to and from work of blind or severely impaired employees	Also includes costs of parking near the work location. A great way to help your disabled relative find a rewarding and productive work position and absorb the costs of attending the jobsite as well.
Employee Counselling Services	Not taxable if for mental or physical health or for re-employment or retirement. Therefore you can have your company pay for your relative's re-employment services once it's time for the person to move on.
Employer-Paid Training	Courses taken by the employee which enhance the employer's business activities will be received by the employee tax-free. This is a great way to have the government pay to enhance your child's resumé.

Figure 8.3	Tax-Free Perks for Employees and Family (Cont'd)
Board and Lodging at a Remote Work Site	See Form TD4 to establish tax-free status on employer-paid board and lodging and transportation at a special work site.
Subsidized School Services in remote areas	If employer provides free or subsidized school services. This tax-free benefit will not extend to a payment of an educational allowance made directly to the employee, unless the allowance covers away-from-home education of a child who is in full-time attendance at a school using one of Canada's official languages. The school must be only as far away as the nearest community to the remote worksite in which there is a suitable school.

Note: Employers may be required to remit GST/HST on certain taxable benefits.

So, as you can see, you can arrange your family's remuneration in such a way that much of it is tax-free, by maximizing opportunities to use RRSP deductions, and making a point of paying at least a portion of your family's remuneration with tax-free perks. Speak to your tax advisor about the possibilities for the coming year.

TAX ADVISOR

When hiring any employees, including relatives and family members, do the following:

Set up an employment contract   This will help you determine factors of remuneration. Make sure it has the following components:

- Identifies the parties to the agreement
- Outlines the duties of the employee
- Outlines the remuneration
- Outlines vacation pay and sick leave policies
- Outlines how changes to the contract will be recorded
- Outlines non-competition agreement
- Outlines confidentiality agreement
- Outlines termination procedures
- Outlines how notices are to be given to each party
- Outlines the binding effect of the contract
- Some contracts also outline arbitration procedures.

Your legal representative may suggest other standard clauses to include in all employment contracts. It is important to put your family members on the same legal footing as others hired in your business. For this reason it is a good idea to have every employee sign a contract.

Keep Time Cards for Hourly Staff   You may wish to devise a time card that looks something like the one in Figure 8.4, and then have your bookkeeper summarize the hours.

Keep Formal Payroll Records   These should be summarized in a payroll register with the following components for hourly wage-earners:

- Regular hours, rate of pay, total pay for this period and cumulative
- Overtime hours, rate of pay, total pay for this period and cumulative
- CPP, EI and tax deductions for this period and cumulative
- Total deductions for this period and cumulative
- Net pay for this period and cumulative
- Cheque number.

Prepare Payroll Source Remittances   These should generally be monthly, but quarterly if the source deductions owed are less than $1,000 a month. These remittances are made on a special form which will be forwarded to you regularly by CRA.

Figure 8.4	Sample Time Card

Employee Name _____   Emp. No. _____

Week of _____

Day	Time		Tot Time	Time		Tot Time	Time		Tot Time	Time		Tot Time	Tot Reg hrs	Other Tot hrs	Total Time
	In	Out		In	Out		In	Out		In	Out				
Sun															
Mon															
Tue															
Wed															
Thu															
Fri															
Sat															
Total															

Prepare a T4 Slip One should be prepared for each family member, by February 28, for the prior calendar year.

Preparing the Income Tax Return Write off the gross wage expenses, and the employer's portion of CPP and EI premiums paid for employees during the year.

Proprietors remember: one-half of the CPP/QPP payable on the self employment earnings will be a deduction in the calculation of Net Income on the tax return (line 222). The remainder will still be written off as a non-refundable credit.

RECAP. YOU NEED TO KNOW:

- How to employ family members on a tax compliance basis: document need, actual performance and reasonableness of the remuneration paid
- How to assess the difference between an employee and a contractor
- What the filing deadlines are for source remittances and T4 slip preparation
- When to deduct and pay CPP and Employment Insurance premiums
- How to reduce tax withholding payments to account for your employee's tax deductible expenses, refundable and non-refundable tax credits
- How to provide tax free benefits to your staff; and manage perks that are taxable

YOU NEED TO ASK: Your Tax Advisor for help in setting up your simple steps to making family payroll costs deductible by:

1. **Paying your family members as you would a stranger.** Put them on the payroll, make sure the work is actually done, and that you pay the relative the same as you would pay a stranger for the same work.

2. **Discussing the difference between a sub-contractor and an employee.** Do you have a contract of service, or a contract for service? In the former case, you have an employer-employee relationship. Take stock of who has control of the relationship, who owns assets and tools, who bears the risk of financial loss for non-performance, and how the job the worker does integrates with the business itself.

3. **Understanding the basic payroll equation.** Gross pay, which can include cash and/or taxable benefits should be clearly defined on each employment contract and thought through with the help of a tax and a legal advisor.

4. **Making compensation tax-efficient.** You can do this by minimizing withholding taxes on RRSP contributions, or by adjusting for child care deductions, moving expenses, loss carry-forwards or other deductions or credits the employee may have. You can also endeavour to pay the employee as many tax-free perks as possible.

5. **Making statutory deductions.** You'll be helping to create a tax-assisted pension income source in retirement, when you contribute to the CPP. EI contributions need careful consideration—will benefits be payable? Remember, the employer's portion of CPP/EI premiums is tax deductible to you. Be sure to make those contributions on time to avoid interest and penalties.

6. **Contributing to private health insurance plans for family members.** Here's a tax-free perk for the family that's deductible to the business owner, provided that certain conditions are met. For example, there are maximum deduction limits if your workforce is comprised primarily of family members.

7. **Subsidizing your employees' meals, giving discounts on merchandise, paying for athletic club memberships, and employee training.** These are great tax-free perks you can give to family members to improve their lifestyle and career paths.

8. **Making sure the young contribute to an RRSP as early as possible, with 18% of the earnings they make in your business.** This is a great way to build long-term, tax-assisted wealth quickly for your teenager.

9. **Giving the whole family a raise with income splitting.** Make sure you calculate the tax benefits of formalizing the work your family does to help grow your small business.

CHAPTER 9

Often-Missed and Little-Known Family Tax Deductions

"The only true failure lies in failure to start."
HAROLD BLAKE WALKER

KEY CONCEPTS

- Take a team approach: family tax planning strategies can reduce taxes
- Each family member has a "tax free zone" that family business owners can maximize
- Start with the lower income earner and work your way up the income scale, transferring deductions and credits along the way.
- Build wealth as a family unit by being as tax efficient as possible
- Invest the first rather than the last dollar earned: never overpay source deductions
- Brush up on the many new family tax deductions and credits this year
- Invest as a family: start with maximum individual RRSP contributions, then split income carefully to avoid Attribution Rules

REAL LIFE: The Hamptons of Elm Street are a typical Canadian family. Husband Tom works as an employee for a computer consulting firm. He earns $85,000 a year plus the benefits of having a company car at his disposal. This adds a taxable benefit of $5,000 to his income every year. Wife Helen stays home with her family, but has a part-time craft business she runs out of her home, grossing $25,000 annually. Daughter Suzanne, a happy 14-year-old (yes, that is a bit unusual), babysits every afternoon for the neighbours. She earns $3,500 annually. Son Cal, a 16-year-old volleyball star at his high school, has a part-time job at the local hamburger joint on weekends. His gross earnings are $8,200 annually.

149

There are numerous changes about to happen in the Hampton house-hold. Tom is considering one of two career moves. He can take a management promotion within his company, and renegotiate his contract for cash and/or benefits. Helen is on the verge of a major expansion in her business. She needs help in production and distribution, and is just about ready for a bookkeeper as well. She estimates her gross revenues next year could jump to over $50,000.

Suzanne has just received word of a remarkable opportunity. She is an up-and-coming young pianist. She has been asked to tour with a professional production company over the summertime. She would be earning $3,000 a month and living with a chaperone. Her living expenses would be covered.

Cal, showing signs of young entrepreneurship, has decided to take some extra courses after school to shore up his computer skills. He wants to get a car (doesn't every 16-year-old?) and has been looking for a few more hours at work.

This is one productive family, with all kinds of potential for tax deferral and income splitting. The problem is they don't know it, and as a result, overpay their taxes every year.

THE PROBLEM

If the Hamptons in our scenario above could get together, and plan their tax affairs to minimize taxes paid as a family, chances are their combined productivity would reap extra tax rewards now and in the future.

Suzanne and Cal should be as aware as their parents of current tax brackets, in order to make the most of every productive hour they work, and to know how to work their time and money around this information, now and in the future.

THE SOLUTION

Have you ever wondered how many millionaires are created in Canada? Recent statistics, based on a report by Capgemini SA and Merrill Lynch & Company (National Post June 21, 2006), reveal that as the baby boom generation reaches its peak earning years, the largest source of wealth for millionaires will shift from employment (32%) to inheritances (16%). Business ownership is the source of 26% of millionaires' wealth in Canada, although globally, it is the single largest source of wealth at 37%. Of Canada's 230,000 millionaires (a 7.2% increase in numbers over the year before), 70% are over the age of 50 and one third are over 70, and so they will be transferring their primary source of wealth to the next generation shortly—an estimated $1.2 trillion in assets are expected to change hands. Millionaire investors today tend to hold 30% of their assets in equities, 20% in alternative investments, and 21% in fixed income.

Will your family be among those who become millionaires in the next several years? Remember, it takes just as much time and effort to think big as it does to think small. When you think big, on tax savings, that is, you will have a very good chance of joining the ranks of Canada's top earners, and wealth creators.

To become wealthy, one must accumulate capital. Many Canadians begin this process with a tax exempt principal residence. While interest costs are not deductible, future capital gains are tax exempt. As children grow up, each adult in the family should focus on owning a tax exempt principal residence. To save enough money for this to be affordable, future family residence owners should leverage their before tax earnings with their RRSP contributions. The principal residence, if properly capitalized, can in fact become an anchor of opportunity for later investments.

Capital accumulation also results when more of the first dollars earned go into your family's collective pockets, rather than the government's. That's where vigilance over withholding taxes—and the size of your tax refund (a bad thing, by the way)—is important.

Finally, taxes are only paid when income is "realized" or generated for tax purposes. Those who are asset-rich can often choose when that realization will occur and if astute, will do so when it makes tax sense. That means you should be considering the tax consequences of your decisions all year long and discussing them with your tax and financial advisors.

Tax planning, therefore, is for everyone at every income level. Your goal is to plan tax minimization, over a period of years with individual tax cost averaging, but also for the team: each family member and the unit as a whole.

Family tax-planning activities should include the following:

- Income creation to maximize the use of each family member's Tax Free Zone
- Income diversification to reduce family tax rates
- Income splitting to leverage tax free zones and tax rates
- Minimizing "Realized Income for Tax Purposes"
- Timing income strategies to defer taxes to the future

- Tax sheltering in registered and non-registered investments
- Maximization of all tax credits and deductions available
- Utilization of the Capital Gains Deduction within the family.

THE PARAMETERS

Following are some basic tax-planning parameters the Hamptons could discuss with their tax advisors to take advantage of the 8 steps above.

Create Income to Maximize Family Member's Tax-Free Zone

Tax-Free Zones are levels of income Canadian taxpayers can make without paying any taxes at all. This includes a calculation of total deductions and are credits available for each family member and the family unit as a whole:

Basic Personal Amounts   Those with taxable incomes under the Basic Personal Amount (BPA) will pay no taxes (however, proprietors may be liable for their portion of CPP premiums). This annually-indexed amount will rise to $10,000 per person by 2009*. This means that a four member family can earn $40,000 tax free, soon.

RRSP Room   A taxpayer who earns $10,000 in qualifying "earned income" and accumulates $1800 in RRSP contribution room. So, there are two things you need to note here:

- Family members who are not taxable by virtue of the Tax-Free Zone, must still file a tax return to accumulate RRSP Contribution Room.
- In the following year, the Tax-Free Zone will be increased by the amount of the RRSP Room earned in the year before, provided that an RRSP contribution is in fact made. In our example, then, the family member could make about $11,800, using the RRSP opportunity, and still pay absolutely no taxes.

Other Deductions and Non-Refundable Tax Credits   Every taxpayer, including the low-income earners of the family, should strive to maximize allowable tax deductions and non-refundable tax credits, all of which will increase the Tax-Free Zone, and/or reduce net income (Line 236) to a level in which transferrable provisions can be used.

Check out the new tax provisions introduced with the May 2, 2006 federal budget, to help increase your family's tax free zones this year:

- **Exemption for Scholarship and Bursary Income** — starting in 2006, this income is fully exempt and extends also to fellowships. However, students must be eligible for the education tax credit to qualify.

* For current BPA see www.knowledgebureau.com, and later pages in this chapter.

- **Tradespeople's Tool Expenses** — up to $1000 of costs of new tools will be deductible starting in 2006 (bought after May 2) to a maximum of $500. Apprentice vehicle mechanics can claim this in addition to their existing deduction, based on costs that exceed the greater of $1000 and 5% of apprenticeship income. For 2007, the deduction will be linked to calculations of the Canada Employment Credit.
- **The Canada Employment Credit** — recognizes the costs of work-related expenses such as driving to and from work, lunch and dry cleaning. It begins on July 1, 2006 with a $250 maximum credit but is in full force starting in 2007 and future years at $1000. It will be indexed to inflation in subsequent years.
- **Children's Fitness Tax Credit** — up to $500 in eligible fees paid for children under 16 to participate in eligible sports and physical activity programs will be available starting in 2007.
- **Pension Income Credit**—starting in 2006, for those eligible private pension recipients age 65 (or those under 65 receiving eligible pension income) a tax credit of up to $2000 is possible.
- **Amount for Public Transit Passes** — starting in 2006 families can claim a credit for monthly or annual public transit passes on the tax return of each individual who purchased one. After July 1, 2006 receipts are required.
- **Tuition, Education and Textbook Tax Credit** — recognizes the costs of textbooks for post-secondary students and is claimed, starting in 2006, as part of the tuition and education credit, based on a monthly allocation, depending on whether the student is in full time or part time attendance.

Other changes are discussed later in the book and should be discussed in detail with your tax advisor. For a complete budget summary see www.knowledgebureau.com. It's free, and a good starter script for your discussions.

Diversify Income to Increase Tax-Free Zones and Reduce Tax Rates

The type of income your family members earn can also have an effect on their tax-free zone, as shown below:

Tax-Free Dividend Income Zones   Depending on where you live in Canada, the earning of dividend income can provide a substantial Tax-Free Zone. The actual amount varies depending on the dividend tax credit rate for your province and the nature of your other income sources, but in many cases significant savings are possible. Discuss these with your tax accountant in light of recent tax changes.

Tax-Free Capital Gains Income Zones   To earn a taxable capital gain, the taxpayer must dispose of an asset in one of the following ways:

- Through the actual sale of the asset
- Through a "deemed disposition," which can occur:
  - When one asset is exchanged for another
  - When assets are given as gifts
  - When property is stolen, destroyed, expropriated or damaged
  - When shares held by a taxpayer are converted, redeemed or cancelled
  - When an option to acquire or dispose of property expires
  - When a debt owed is settled or cancelled
  - When property is transferred to an RRSP or other trust
  - When the owner of the property emigrates
  - When the owner of the property changes the asset's use from business to personal
  - When the owner of the property dies.

If our taxpayer's only income of the year is from a capital gains disposition, the capital gain could be twice the Tax-Free Zone (that is, if the Basic Personal Amount grows to $10,000, Capital Gains of $20,000 will be tax free).

Split Income Earned by the Family

With an understanding of how to build income within Tax-Free Zones, comes another problem. How do I actually put taxable income into the hands of my family members? There are a number of ways that you can split the income earned within the family unit as a whole to accomplish the lowest overall household tax cost over a period of time. To do so, though, you must be well versed in the Attribution Rules, which generally prohibit taxpayers from transferring income from the higher earner to the lower earners in order to reduce or avoid taxation. An exception to this rule is the money earned by family members who work in a family business.

For example, if Tom reported all the money in the family ($126,700 in this instance), the family tax liability would be just over $40,000.* Assume, however, that $25,000 of this is earned by wife Helen and $8,200 by son Cal, both of whom work in the family business. In that case, the actual family liability is under $30,000 — a difference of over $11,000. . .a year. Multiply this by Tom and Helen's approximately

* will vary by province of residence

40 productive working years, and you have tax savings of over $450,000, assuming no changes in earnings or tax structure.

As you can see, family income splitting is a very important life skill. In fact, when you couple income splitting with wise use of RRSP contribution room, many families could be earning part-time income completely tax-free, investment earnings on a tax-deferred basis, and paying down non-deductible debt with the resulting savings, faster. If your family is going to be working and earning money anyway, it's worth it to take a closer look at some tax-free and tax-deferred income-earning opportunities.

Stay Onside With the Attribution Rules

Money transfered by one spouse (the higher earner) to another (the lower earner), who then invests the sums in a non-registered account and earns interest, dividends or capital gains, will result in attribution of earnings back to the higher earner for tax purposes. In the case of minor children (those under 18) gifts or transfers of money will generally be attributed back to the transferor, if the resulting investment earnings are interest or dividend bearing. Resulting capital gains remain taxable in the minor's hands. There are other exceptions to the Attribution Rules, and some precautions to be aware of.

Caution — Tax on Split Income Income splitting by paying dividends or management fees to minor children, either directly or through a trust from a corporation owned by a parent, are to be taxed at the highest marginal rate on the return of the recipient. Talk to your tax advisor about this "kiddie tax."

Beware — New Definition of Spouse Also, beware of the definition for "spouse" and "common law partner" for those who live common law with partners of the same or opposite sex.
- *A spouse* is a person of the opposite sex who cohabits with the taxpayer in a conjugal relationship.
- *A common law partner* (same or opposite sex) is someone who cohabits with the taxpayer in a conjugal relationship for at least 12 months or partners who live together and have a child in common.

Since January 1, 2001, the following rules have existed:
- "Spouse" will refer to those legally married only.
- A retroactive election is possible for 1998, 1999, 2000 for same sex couples to be considered common law partners if this is to the couple's advantage.

Managing Joint Accounts   *Always document income in joint accounts and from the sale of principal residences.* The interest earnings generated from money held in a joint account will be taxed according to the ownership of the principal. That is, if the husband earned 90% of the principal, he would report 90% of the earnings. If 100% of the money in that account comes from the wife's inheritance, however, 100% of the earnings will be reported by her.

Let's say husband and wife married in their early twenties. The wife worked for a couple of years before staying home to raise a family. She contributed $5,000 to the down-payment of their first home which was 50% of the equity. On the sale of that home, the family made a $25,000 tax-free gain (gains on the principal residence are tax exempt). This money was reinvested in a larger principal residence, that was later sold for a $50,000 tax-free gain. This happened two more times during this couple's marriage. Today, they have sold their last home and moved into a rented condo to maximize their travel opportunities. They have $250,000 in a joint account; the accumulated principal and gains from the tax-free appreciation of their various principal residences. In this case, subsequent investment earnings can be properly split between husband and wife, because the wife's participation in the original transaction can be traced.

Invest Tax-Exempt Sources   We listed in earlier chapters several tax-exempt income sources that, if invested by the recipient, will generate investment earnings in that person's hands. That's why it makes sense, for example, that a low-income earner who receives proceeds from a life insurance policy, an inheritance, a GST/HST Credit or tax refund, for example, should invest those sums to generate future investment earnings, which will be taxed at a low rate, if at all. Don't forget to buy those lottery tickets jointly, too. Earnings on the resulting investment of your tax free windfall could then be split in the future between the winners.

Invest in Spousal RRSPs   One way you can avoid the Attribution Rules now, and split income with your spouse in retirement, is by investing in an RRSP for your spouse. To do so, you must have actively earned income in a prior year, and resulting RRSP Contribution Room. You can find out what your RRSP Contribution Room is by looking at last year's Notice of Assessment. Earnings within the Spousal RRSP will not be taxable until there is a withdrawal.

But, be careful. If the withdrawal is made within three years of the last contribution to any Spousal RRSP, the principal will be taxable to the contributor. Beyond this, withdrawals are taxed to the Spouse. A little loophole can be used when the RRSP accumulations are transferred to a RRIF (Registered Retirement Income Fund). In that case, minimum withdrawals in a Spousal Plan will not be subject to the Attribution Rules.

Grant Interest-Bearing Loans to Family Members   Spouses can loan money to each other, use the funds to generate investment earnings, and have those earnings reported for tax purposes on the return of the debtor provided that the loan bears a commercial rate of interest, and that the interest is paid at least once a year, no later than 30 days (January 30) after the end of the calendar year. The higher earner must report that interest on his/her return.

Create Income From a Spouse's Business   If you loan your spouse the money needed to start a small business, subsequent profits and losses are taxed in the hands of your spouse. Capital dispositions, however, would be taxed in your hands.

Pay a Wage or Salary to Your Spouse or Children Who Work in Your Business   They report the income on their tax returns, and create resulting RRSP room; you report the amounts paid as a legitimate deduction from your business income.

Transfer Dividends to Spouse   If your spouse's income is so low that s/he is not taxable, but has earned dividend income (and the offsetting dividend tax credit, which now is going to go to waste), the higher earner can elect to transfer that dividend income and the dividend tax credit to his/her return, if a tax advantage results. The catch is that the transfer must create or increase the Spousal Amount claimable for the Spouse. The benefits, if any, will depend on the size of the transferor's income.

Invest Child Tax Benefits Received   The Canada Child Tax Benefits, the new Universal Child Care Benefit ($100 a month for each child under age 6) and provincial Child Tax Benefits received for the child may be invested in an account held in trust for that child. If the money is untainted by birthday money or money that should be attributed to another adult, resulting interest, dividends or capital gains will be taxed in the child's hands. These benefits are discussed later in more detail.

Invest in an RESP for the Child   Starting in 1998, an investment in a Registered Education Savings Plan for a child under 18 will generate a new Canada Education Savings Grant from the federal government. Twenty percent of your contribution to a maximum of $400 will be granted each year.

The maximum CESG is usually achieved when you put away $2000, however, there is also a "sweetener" for those with lower incomes:

- For families with qualifying net income of $35,000 (indexed after 2004) or less the rate will be 40% of the first $500 and 20% of the remainder (maximum $100 enhanced grant + $400 normal grant)
- For families with qualifying net income between $35,000 and $70,000 (indexed after 2004) the rate will be 30% of the first $500 and 20% of the remainder (maximum $50 enhanced grant + $400 normal grant)

Earnings within the RESP accumulate tax-free, and if the child chooses to withdraw the funds later to go to a designated educational institute, the earnings and CESG grant will be taxable in his/her hands. Often that means tax-free distributions to the student. Speak to your tax and financial advisor about the immediate return you'll reap on your investment via the CESG and then try to make a contribution *at the end of every year* to maximize savings opportunities with the CESG.

Invest in a Child's RRSP   You can gift your child money to invest in his/her own RRSP. Resulting investment earnings will be tax-sheltered until the child withdraws the money from the plan. However, the child must have "earned income" which creates RRSP Contribution Room. To register this with CRA, the child must have actively earned income sources, and file a tax return to report them every year. Be sure to report all earnings from part-time work like babysitting, lawn care, snow shovelling, etc.

Invest Gifts From Grandparents Who Live Offshore   The Attribution Rules can be avoided on money received from non-resident grandparents or other relatives, provided the money is held in trust for the child and not used by adults for any other reason.

Accumulate Tax-Free and Tax-Deferred Income Within Life Insurance Policies   Usually it costs little to invest in a child's life insurance policy, and this can grow to a lucrative tax-free pension or estate in some cases. Speak to your insurance advisor about this.

Know the Taxation of Income and Assets on Death of a Spouse   While the Attribution Rules can create hurdles for you during your lifetime, CRA does show a bit of consideration, at time of death. For example, life insurance policy proceeds are received by beneficiaries on a completely tax-free basis. (The time to arrange to pay for such a policy. . .is when you are healthy. Look into it now.)

In addition, taxable assets can be transferred to your spouse on a tax-free basis. This includes accumulations within an RRSP, RRIF, other annuities, as well as the transfer of assets held outside a registered plan. In the latter case, the assets may be transferred to the spouse at the adjusted cost base calculated for the deceased, or at Fair Market Value (which means the capital gain, if any, is reported on the final return of the deceased, if this is advantageous), or at any amount in between. Be sure to maximize use of any available capital losses on the final return.

Transfers of assets to children are usually at fair market value in death as in life, with the exception of certain farming assets. Transfers of RRSP/RRIFs to dependent children may also qualify for a tax free rollover even if there is a surviving spouse. But you should receive tax advice before filing the final returns of a deceased taxpayer and, better still, in anticipation of your tax status, well before death.

Minimize Income Realized for Tax Purposes

Another basic taxation concept you should keep in mind as you plan your family's financial affairs now and into the future is how much tax you'll pay on the next dollar of income that's earned and when. This is important, as the next dollar could push you or your family members into a new tax bracket, subject to a higher tax rate. Using a knowledge of marginal tax rates and what you know of the tax benefits of income splitting and diversification, you'll be able to make tax-wise decisions on future investments together with your advisor. This can be as important as asset allocation within an investment portfolio.

In earlier chapters we urged you to consider a Tax Savings Blue-print—a series of "what if" scenarios to calculate your tax efficiencies annually. We are now suggesting that you expand that opportunity within the family unit as a whole.

Because of the progressive nature of our tax system (every person benefits from the basic personal amount and is subject to increasingly higher rates as incomes rise) and the ability to transfer certain family tax deduction and credits, it pays to think tax savings as a family. When analyzing current or potential tax results, begin with the lower income earners and work your way up to the higher earners. Then determine just how much income is required to be "realized" for tax purposes, and how much can be deferred into the future. If you have the option to "realize income" in the hands of each family member and within the lower tax brackets, the family unit as a whole will pay less tax. Here are some suggestions as to how this might be accomplished first by each individual in the family:

- Split individual income sources receivable over two tax years: e.g., severance, bonuses, RRSP withdrawal, sale of capital assets. (Example: dispose of one-half of a duplex owned in each of two tax years.)

- Offset capital gains generated in the year with prior year capital losses incurred by each investor.
- Create future wealth by investing in capital assets: increasing values are never taxed until disposition of the asset. Then plan dispositions strategically around capital loss availability, and income inclusion over a period of years.
- Optimize opportunities to reduce tax rates with special tax provisions applied to dividends, certain foreign pensions (U.S. Social Security; German Pensions), scholarship and bursary income, and small business corporations/qualifying farm or fisher's properties.
- Utilize tax-exempt income planning opportunities (e.g., estate planning with life insurance policy proceeds; tax-free retirement pension income creation through investments in universal life insurance policies, RESP enhancements through the Canada Education Savings Grant, etc.).
- Always look closely at your "income mix" for tax purposes. Use of corporate class mutual funds may be helpful in non-registered accounts.

Income Timing Strategies

Canada is undergoing a mini tax reform relating to its business taxation at the moment. Specifically, the taxation of dividends and capital gains, as well as corporate tax rates are going down. Recent proposals of interest to those who invest in small businesses are:

- **Advantageous Taxation of Dividend Income**: For "eligible" dividends paid after 2005, a new dividend gross up and dividend tax credit mechanism applies. Most dividends paid by public corporations resident in Canada will be eligible under this new scheme, as will certain dividends from Canadian Controlled Private Corporations (CCPCs), when the income from which the dividend is paid has not been subject to the Small Business Deduction and has not generated refundable tax. Where the dividend is eligible, the gross up is 145% of the actual dividends and the dividend tax credit is 19% of the grossed up amount. The result is that the marginal tax rate on such dividends is substantially lower.

Assuming income of $125,000 marginal tax rates are as follows:

	Federal	Federal and Provincial (approximate: varies with province)
Ordinary Income	29%	46.4%
Ineligible Dividends	19.58%	35.25%
Eligible Dividends	14.49%	23.78%
Capital Gains	14.5%	23.2%

- **Capital Gains Exemption on Donations of Publicly Listed Securities:** Gifts of publicly listed securities and donations of ecologically sensitive land will be exempt from tax when donated to public charities on or after May 2, 2006. At the time of writing, consultations were also taking place to discuss the potential of extending this capital gains exemption to donations of listed securities to private foundations.

- **Capital Gains Exemption for Fishers' Property:** Effective on or after May 2, 2006 fishers may transfer fishing property including fishing licenses and shares of a family fishing corporation to their spouse or common-law partner, or children, through a tax free rollover. In addition, qualified fishing property will be eligible for the $500,000 capital gains exemption.

In addition, the following provisions should be taken into account in planning compensation for family members (salary, dividends, bonus, perks) or the acquisition or disposition of business assets held by the family:

1. **Tax Brackets and Tax Rates**: Stay on top of the tax brackets and rates of tax to which your income is subject. Federal tax brackets are indexed to inflation (this is not always true provincially however). At the time of writing, the following brackets and rates were in effect:

2005 Brackets	2005 Rate	2006 Brackets	2006 Rate	2007 Rate
Up to $8,648	0%	Up to $8,839	0%	0%
Up to $35,595	15%	Up to $36,378	15.25%	15.5%
$35,596 to $71,190	22%	$36,378 to $72,756	22%	22%
$71,1901 to $115,739	26%	$72,757 to $118,285	26%	26%
Over $115,739	29%	Over $118,285	29%	29%

Tax brackets are indexed according to increases in the consumer price index. For 2006, the indexation rate was 2.2%. The 2007 brackets had not yet been announced.

2. **Changes in Your Personal Amounts (Non-Refundable Tax Credits):** The May 2, 2006 federal budget proposed to increase the basic personal amount in defined increments to at least $10,000 by 2009, but decreased it by $400 on July 1, 2006 effectively removing any increment for 2006, setting the tax-free zone at $8839 for year. The increments in 2007, 2008, and 2009 are $100, $200, and the greater of $600 and the amount required to increase the basic personal amount to $10,000.

   Every one in the family is entitled to one basic personal amount every year. For 2006, it was possible to earn approximately $737 each month on a tax free basis. This is important if you are paying family members in your small business. By the year 2009, the Basic Personal Amount will increase to $10,000 allowing for the first $833.33 per month to be earned tax free.

Note that the Spousal Amount will also be rising to $8500 by the year 2009. Those over the age of 64 also qualify for the Age Amount, although this amount is reduced when net income is over certain income thresholds. A summary of personal amounts follows:

Summary of Personal Amounts for 2005 to 2007

Personal Amounts		2005	2006	2007
Basic Personal Amount	Maximum Claim	$8,648	$8,839	*
Age Amount	Maximum Claim	$3,979	$4,066	*
	Base Amount	$29,619	$30,270	*
Spouse or Common-Law Partner Amount	Maximum Claim	$7,344	$,7,505	*
	Reduced by Net Inc. over	$735	$751	
Amount for Eligible Departments	Maximum Claim	$7,344	$7,505	*
	Reduced by Net Inc. over	$735	$751	
Amount for Infirm Dependants	Maximum Claim	$3,848	$3,933	*
	Maximum Income	$9,308	$10,446	*
Pension Income Amount	Maximum Claim	$1,000	$2,000	$2,000
Adoption Expenses	Maximum Claim	$10,000	$10,220	*
Caregiver Amount	Maximum Claim	$3,848	$3,933	*
	Maximum Income	$16,989	$17,363	*
Disability Amount	Basic Amount	$6,596	$6,741	*
	Supplementary Amount	$3,848	$3,933	*
	Base Child Care Amount	$2,254	$2,303	*
Tuition, Education and Textbook Amount	Minimum Tuition	$100	$100	$100
	Full-time Education Amount (per month)	$400	$400 +$65	$400 +$65
	Part-time Education Amount (per month)	$120	$120 +$20	$120 +$20
Medical Expenses	3% limitation	$1,844	$1,884	*
Refundable Medical Expense Credit	Maximum	$750	$1,000	*
	Base Family Income	$21,663	$22,140	*
Canada Employment Amount	Maximum	N/A	$250	$1000
Children's Fitness Amount	Maximum	N/A	N/A	$500
Amount for Public Transit Passes	Maximum	N/A	None	None

*These amounts are indexed (and some adjusted per legislation); 2007 amounts unavailable.

Note: it is important to time income inclusions to take into account the top of various tax brackets and the changes in personal amounts. More on this later.

Maximizing Tax-Deferred Investment Vehicles

In anticipation of future tax reductions, as explained earlier, you want to maximize your tax-deferred registered accounts and tax efficient non-registered accounts.

Registered Accounts:
- Shelter as much of your taxable income as possible with RRSPs, RESPs, and RRIFs.

Non-Registered Accounts:
- Plan your realized taxable income and offsetting deductions and tax credits wisely. In the case of dividend income, remember that the gross up will affect net income on Line 236—the figure upon which other refundable and non-refundable tax credits are based. It could also artificially increase "off return" fees like nursing home per diem rates, or other user fees based on the federal tax return.
- Split capital receipts over two tax years or defer to next year.
- Acquire appreciating assets, holding them outside your RRSP. Those appreciating assets will build real dollar value for the future on a tax-deferred basis.
- If you are comfortable with borrowing money to invest in assets held outside your registered accounts, do so after tax analysis, writing off interest expenses today in return for wealth accumulation tomorrow. It is worthwhile discussing such investments with your tax advisor, as interest costs can offset all other income of the year.
- Look into the acquisition of tax-exempt life insurance policies as soon as possible.

Look at every tax dollar saved today as a bonus paid to you and your family.

Find and Maximize Deductions and Credits

Try to arrange your tax affairs to minimize non-deductible expenditures (like credit card debit) and maximize deductions and credits. This should be discussed with your tax advisor and/or financial planner.

There are two types of tax reducers available on your tax return and you should know the value of each to better plan tax timing for your income sources:

- tax deductions
- tax credits.

Tax Deductions   There are three types of deductions to look out for. The first are deductions that reduce your gross income sources, to arrive at Total Income (see figure 9.2 for a list of these). The second grouping is deductions that reduce Total Income, used in determining Net Income on Line 236. These are described below.

Deductions That Reduce Total Income to Arrive at Net Income

- Registered Pension Plan deductions from Box 20 of T4 slips or Box 32 of T4As
- Registered Retirement Savings Plan deductions
- Saskatchewan Pension Plan deductions
- Union, Professional or like dues
- Child care expenses, as computed on Form T778
- Disability supports deduction
- Business investment losses
- Moving expenses, as computed on Form T1-M
- Deductible Child/Spousal support payments
- Carrying charges on your investments, like interest and safety-deposit box fees
- Exploration and development expenses
- Deductions for one-half of CPP contributions for a self-employed taxpayer
- Other employment expenses, as computed on Form T777 or TL2, including artist's and musician's expenses
- Clerics Residence Deduction on Line 231, Form T1223
- Other deductions on Line 232, including legal fees incurred to collect salary and wages owed to the employee, establish a right to a retiring allowance, enforce payment of maintenance amounts previously established as payable, to appeal an assessment of tax, interest or penalties under the Income Tax Act, Employment Insurance or Canada Pension Plan
- Clawback calculation of Employment Insurance or Old Age Security.

The third grouping of deductions reduces Net Income to arrive at Taxable Income.

Deductions that Reduce Net Income to Arrive at Taxable Income

- Employee home relocation loan deduction per your T4 Slips
- Securities options deduction as itemized on your T4 slips
- Other payments deduction for social assistance, worker's compensation or federal supplements
- Limited partnership losses of other years

Figure 9.2	Deductions that Reduce Total Income on Line 150	
Income Source	**Deductions Allowed**	**Documentation Required**
Employment Income on Line 101	Up to $1,000 received by volunteer emergency services personnel is tax-exempt.	None, except a properly completed T4 slip.
Net Research Grants on Line 104	The cost of out-of-pocket expenses incurred in the research process.	A statement itemizing list of expenses.
Wage Loss Replacement Benefits	The cost of premiums paid by the employee since 1968 can offset this income.	Obtain a statement from your employer to verify this amount.
Rental Income	Operating expenses of running the revenue property, including capital cost allowance. Some restrictions apply.	Records of all income receipts, operating expenses, auto logs, and capital acquisitions and dispositions, mortgage fees and payments, etc.
Taxable Capital Gains	Costs of outlays and expenses including brokerage fees and appraisal fees.	All income reports from brokerage houses, and sale of other properties including cost of improvements; expense receipts.
Support Payments	Total amount is reduced for child maintenance if pursuant to agreement made after April 1997.	Court order or written agreement or election to consider child support non-taxable.
Other Income	The first $500 of income from scholarships, fellowships, bursaries is tax-exempt; however it is 100% exempt if the student qualifies for the education credit; also the first $10,000 of death benefits received from a deceased's employer recognizing the deceased's contributions or unused sick benefits. In the case of retiring allowances, rollovers into an RRSP qualify for an RRSP deduction; sometimes a deduction for legal fees is allowed if the taxpayer had to fight to establish rights to the severance.	Keep all supporting documentation for any income sources reported here, including payments for serving on a jury, RESP distributions, payments out of a retirement compensation arrangement, interest earned on loans made for investment purposes to lower-earning family members, annuity payments not reported as pension income.
Self-Employment Income from unincorporated small businesses, professional practices, commission sales agents, farmers or fishermen.	All reasonable operating expenses incurred to earn income from a business with a reasonable expectation of profit, including a deduction for Capital Cost Allowance on business assets.	All supporting income deposit records, receipts and logs for all business expenditures and asset acquisitions and dispositions.

*Note the new Canada Employment Amount will also be available to address the costs of employment, as will the Amount for Public Transit Passes, starting in 2006. Check this one on Schedule 1.

- Non-capital losses of other years
- Net capital losses of other years
- Capital gains deduction
- Northern residents deductions
- Additional deductions for vows of perpetual poverty, net employment income from the United Nations and its agencies, income exempt under tax treaty, alimony or child support received from a U.S. resident.

The value of a tax deduction is directly proportionate to your marginal tax rate. If your marginal tax rate on income is 22%, each tax deduction you can find will reap a tax saving of 22 cents on the dollar. If your marginal tax rate is 45%, each deduction is worth 45 cents on the dollar as well. So, the higher your income, the greater the value of a tax deduction.

Tax Credits

There are two types of tax credits:

Refundable ones like the Canada Child Tax Benefit, the Goods and Services Tax Credit, and a host of provincial refundable tax credits. Both spouses must file a tax return to receive these amounts, as the credits are dependent on your net family income. Those age 19 and over should file to recoup their own Goods and Services Tax Credit.

Non-Refundable Tax Credits, on the other hand, are the allowances the government makes for personal circumstances that warrant consideration under the tax system. These were discussed earlier when we introduced tax brackets and rates.

The federal amounts are found on Schedule 1 of the T1 General Return, and provide the same benefit to all taxpayers, regardless of income level. Similarly, the provincial amounts found on the individual provincial tax calculation forms yield the same benefit for all taxpayers.

However, be aware that tax credits are often "income-tested" and can be "clawed back".

Clawback Zones

For taxpayers in income ranges between approximately $9,000 and $100,000, a variety of "clawback" provisions exist to return the benefits of certain tax preferences to government, as income rises. The effect of this is that low to middle income earners often have a higher marginal tax rate when compared to those at top income levels, who do not qualify for these social benefits. It is therefore most important that those family members, who find their income within a clawback zone, work every legal angle to reduce net income. Top choice is the RRSP, if you are age eligible. Discuss these clawback zones with your tax and financial advisors to see if you can reduce them within the family unit to increase your tax efficiencies and your social benefits. For recent clawback zones visit www.knowledgebureau.com

Universal Child Care Benefits

Starting in July 2006, $100 per month for each child under the age of 6 years are paid to the parents for the purposes of reducing child care costs. **This benefit is taxable** but must be reported by the lower-income spouse or common-law partner. This means that if both spouses work, the income will be taxable at the marginal rate of the lower-income spouse. If one spouse does not work, then a portion of the UCCB may be received tax-free (to the extent that it does not increase the lower-income spouse's income over the tax-free zone governing the spousal amount calculations). For families where the higher-income spouse claims a partial amount for the lower-income spouse, the UCCB will effectively be taxed at the marginal tax rate of the higher-income spouse.

It is important that families maximize the income splitting opportunities available. For example, the person with the lower income in this case should invest the UCCB, thereby generating "own source" investment income properly taxable in that person's hands.

Better still is the opportunity to invest the funds in an untainted trust account in the child's hands; in this way, resulting earnings are generally not taxable nor will they affect the Spousal Amount. More on this later.

Changes to the *Income Tax Act* have been implemented which alter the definition of income for the purposes of repaying EI Benefits, OAS Benefits, Child Tax Credits and GST Credits to ensure that the UCCB is not included in income for these purposes.

THE TAX ADVISOR

Having understood the basic parameters surrounding the claiming of tax deductions and credits, you will now want to know and implement a few strategic tax plans with your professional advisors:

Create New Capital Monthly   If you or any member of your family earns employment income from a source other than your family business be sure to complete Form T1213 to request that a Letter of Authority be forwarded to the employer to reduce tax withheld from your employment income. If possible, have your employer make RRSP contributions directly to your RRSPs and not deduct taxes from the amounts transferred. Also, if you pay tax by instalments, minimize your prepayments in light of anticipated tax reductions. As discussed in earlier chapters, be sure to do the same in the family business.

Pay Off Non-Deductible Debt   Credit card balances attract very high interest rates. A smart way reduce these costs is to make an RRSP contribution (monthly or annually), reap your tax savings and then pay off your personal credit cards and their non-deductible interest costs.

Turn Non-Deductible Debt Into Deductible Debt   Borrow for investments placed in non-registered accounts; the interest on such loans will be deductible. (Please note that the interest paid on money borrowed to invest in RRSP/RESP accounts will not be). Opening a home-based business and claiming home office expenses will make your mortgage interest costs partially deductible; or you can borrow against the equity in the home, place investments in non-registered accounts and then write off the interest on the loan. Discuss these options with your tax advisor.

Maximize RRSP Room for All Family Members   The first way to do this is to file a tax return each and every year in which there is "earned income." This includes the following sources earned by each taxpayer:

- Salary or wages before the deduction of Employment Insurance, Canada Pension Plan or RPP contributions, employee contributions to a retirement compensation arrangement or the cleric's residence deduction.

PLUS:

- Income from royalties from a work or invention of which the taxpayer was the author or inventor
- Net research grants
- Supplemental unemployment insurance benefits
- Employee profit-sharing plan allocations
- Net rental income
- Taxable support payments or repayments included in income, including support payments received by a common-law spouse

- Net income from carrying on a business where the taxpayer is actively engaged in the daily operations, either alone or as a partner
- After 1990, income received from a CPP/QPP Disability Benefit

LESS:

- Refunds of salary, wages or research grants
- Union dues or professional dues paid
- Other employment expenses
- Current-year losses from carrying on an active business
- Current-year net rental losses
- Support payments deducted or repaid
- Any amount included in business income that represents the excess negative balance from dispositions of eligible capital property over and above recaptured deductions previously taken.

Once earned income is known, the figure is multiplied by 18%. The result is then compared to the maximum dollar limits for the tax year. The lesser of the two is used in the calculation of the RRSP deduction claimable on Line 208.

Note: To maximize your annual RRSP contribution consider the following chart:

RRSPs: annual contribution limit: 18% of earned income in the prior year to a maximum dollar limit of:

	2005	2006	2007	2008	2009	2010	2011
Maximum	$16,500	$18,000	$19,000	$20,000	$21,000	$22,000	indexed
Prior year Earned Income	$91,667	$100,000	$105,556	$111,111	$116,667	$122,222	

Tax Planning Strategies for Minors

- Save income attributed to the child (like Child Tax Benefits or the Universal Child Care Benefits) in a separate bank account, untainted by gifts or other transferred funds from adult relatives. Resulting earning are taxed in the hands of the child.
- Invest a child's employment or self-employment earnings; then have the higher-income earner in the family pay for consumer goods. Resulting investment income is either not taxed at all (if income falls under the Tax-Free Zones) or taxed at low rates.

- Make sure the minor files a tax return. Actively earned income sources from part-time jobs, including work in the family firm, qualify for the building of RRSP room, which can be of assistance in reducing tax or maximizing tuition/education credits later.
- Gifts may be made to a minor child; however, resulting earnings in the form of dividends or interest are taxed back to the adult, until the child turns 18. The only exception to this rule is the earning of capital gains, which can accumulate in the hands of the child.
- Contribute to an RESP for your minor children, in order to take advantage of the Canada Education Saving Grant and tax-deferred accumulations of earnings.

Tax Planning Strategies for Net Incomes under $118,000

- These income ranges are in the "Clawback Zones": where marginal tax rates can increase dramatically as social benefits are clawed back through the tax system. This includes the value of The Age Amount, Canada Child Tax Benefits (CCTB), GST Credits, OAS receipts, EI Benefits.
- Maximize RRSP contributions, and any other tax deductions.
- Income diversification and income-splitting opportunities are vital in this income range. Find ways to legitimately transfer income to lower earners in the family.
- Utilize all tax deductions to reduce net income, including full RRSP room, to avoid clawbacks of refundable tax credits.
- Separated couples may wish to revisit old taxable support payment agreements in light of generous new federal/provincial Child Tax Benefits (CTB), particularly if recipient and payer are both in the lowest tax brackets. Enhanced Child Tax Benefits could bring more tax relief than the support payments deduction.
- Consider earning more taxable dividends or capital gains in your investment portfolio.
- Maximize non-refundable tax credits like medical expenses and charitable donations.
- Maximize Child Care Expense claims (up to $7,000 for children under the age of 7, $4,000 for those age 7 to 16 or over age 16 and mentally or physically infirm, and $10,000 for any child for whom a disability amount is claimable. Special provisions are available for students).

Tax Planning Strategies for Net Income over $118,000

- Always make your maximum RRSP contribution
- Plan to average realized taxable income in business and investment portfolios and consider adding Labour Sponsored Tax Credits to the mix

- Implement plans to give to charity, political parties, to maximize tax savings opportunties over a period of years
- Transfer medical expense credits to lower earners in the family
- Make sure any transferable credits (Age Amount, Pension Income Amount, Tuition & Education Credits and Disability Credits) are properly claimed and that lower earner's income levels are properly computed to maximize these claims.

Shelter Private Pension Income　Once you are ready to take a taxable pension by converting RRSP accumulations to a RRIF (Registered Retirement Income Fund) or annuity, you should decide what income level you will want to create with your withdrawals, being mindful of Tax-Free Zones for the lower-earning spouse, and tax bracket levels for the higher earner. It is generally best to withdraw the money from a sheltered plan in the hands of the lower earner first, to bring income up to either the Tax-Free Zone, if the person has no other income, or at least to within the upper limit of the first tax bracket. Remember, a tax free rollover of unused RRSP accumulations to a surviving spouse is possible upon the death of the first spouse. However, remaining amounts are taxable when the second spouse dies. Therefore, it is often more tax effective to realize RRSP income during your lifetime, as tax brackets and rates can skyrocket when large RRSP accumulations are added to the final return on death.

Tax Planning for Taxpayer's Death

- As a regular part of their tax and financial planning activities, individuals should prepare a tax projection every year to anticipate tax liabilities, should unexpected death occur, particularly if there are valuation changes in the non-registered investment portfolio.
- Life insurance policy requirements should be closely reviewed, to cover potential tax liabilities and for the purposes of leaving a tax-free estate to the family.
- RRSP/RRIF beneficiary elections should be made and wills updated to ensure hassle-free rollover of assets to the proper beneficiaries.
- Remember, RRSP/RRIF accumulations of the second surviving spouse may be subject to tax upon that person's demise. This generally means the estate will lose almost half of its accumulations to tax. Perhaps that survivor, who may be at a lower tax bracket in life, should consider generating the tax on the registered funds by withdrawing and reinvesting funds in a non-registered account, or possibly a universal life insurance policy.

- Bring forward unused capital/non-capital loss balances for use on the final return.
- Discuss planned giving for those whose estates are adequate and already cover family concerns. Remember, new capital gains tax exemptions available for donated shares from public companies on or after May 2, 2006.

No Such Thing as a "Stupid Tax Question"

Tax rules are always changing; so are personal lifecycles. Be prepared to ask your tax advisor lots of questions about the latest tax changes for your family members and discuss how they relate to lifecycle changes—births, deaths, marriages, divorces, new careers, new businesses, etc. Your goal is three-fold:

1. To reduce taxes in the current year
2. To recover overpaid taxes from prior years
3. To plan to save taxes in the future.

Also, make an attempt to understand current economic and political trends in order to recognize the impact of those trends on family tax filing profiles. Be sure to read federal and provincial budget summaries every year. You can do so at www.knowledgebureau.com

Recover, Correct and Amend

Finally, have you forgotten any of your available tax write-offs? Perhaps you have missed filing a tax return completely. Or maybe you have a guilty conscience about the overstated deductions or under claimed income on your return. If so, tap into CRA's Fairness Provisions. That is, you can apply to recover missed tax deductions and credits, file missed returns or amend returns for most provisions over a period of 10 calendar years, provided you forward an adjustment request (use from TI-AD) outlining the error or omission and attaching supporting documentation.

Consult the checklist of Tax Savers for Tax Adjustments on Prior Filed Returns on Fig 9.3.

ACTION PLAN: Summary of Often-Missed and Little Known Family Tax Deductions and Credits

Take a moment now to work through our family tax write-off checklist in Figures 9.3, 9.4 and 9.5.

For specific tax deductions allowed to investors and seniors, use the checklist in Figure 9.4 to double check grandpa and grandma's prior-filed returns.

Figure 9.3	Check List of Tax Savers* for Tax Adjustments on Prior Filed Returns

Tax Deductions

- ❏ RPP Contribution
- ❏ RRSP Contributions for each family member
- ❏ Union or professional dues paid
- ❏ Child Care Expenses paid
- ❏ Disability Supports Deduction
- ❏ Business Investment Losses
- ❏ Moving Expenses
- ❏ Spousal Support
- ❏ Child Support (agreements before May 1, 1997, or certain specific purpose or third party payments)
- ❏ Carrying Charges and Interest Expenses
- ❏ Exploration and Development Expenses
- ❏ Employment Expenses
- ❏ Clerics Residence Deduction
- ❏ Repayments of Employment Insurance
- ❏ Repayments of Old Age Security
- ❏ Repayments of Worker's Compensation
- ❏ Payments of Legal Fees for objecting to an assessment or appeal under the Income Tax, EI, CPP or QPP legislation, collection of late child support payments, collection or establishment of a right to retiring allowances or pension benefits
- ❏ Repayments of taxable scholarships, fellowships, bursaries, research grants, retiring allowances or Canada Pension Plan benefits
- ❏ Repayments of refund interest paid by CRA
- ❏ Refunds of undeducted RRSP contributions made after 1990 and received in the tax year.

Tax Credits

Non-Refundable Federal Credits

- ❏ Claim for Basic Personal Amount
- ❏ Claim for the Age Amount (65 & older)
- ❏ Claim for Spousal Amount
- ❏ Claim for Eligible Dependant Amount
- ❏ Claim for Infirm Dependant over 18
- ❏ Claim for the Pension Income Amount
- ❏ Adoption Expenses
- ❏ Claim for the Caregiver Amount
- ❏ Claim for the Disability Amount (be sure to obtain a Form T2201 signed by the attending medical practitioner)
- ❏ Claim for Tuition/Education and Textbook Amount
- ❏ Claim for Student Loan Interest Amount
- ❏ Claim for the new Canada Employment Amount, Amount for Public Transit Passes, The Fitness Amount
- ❏ Claim for Transfers from Spouse, including the Age, Disability, Pension Income and Tuition/Education and Textbook Amounts, depending on the spouse's net income
- ❏ Claim for Medical Expenses, the excess of total expenses for the best 12-month period ending in the tax year, over 3% of net income, to a maximum limitation
- ❏ Claim for Donations and Gifts, usually based on a limit of 75% of net income; this two-tiered credit can be calculated with unclaimed donations of the prior five years. Group family claims together to exceed $200 a year to maximize tax savings.

Refundable Tax Credits

- ❏ The Child Tax Benefit
- ❏ The Goods and Services Tax Credit
- ❏ Provincial Child Tax Benefits
- ❏ Overpayments of CPP Premiums
- ❏ Overpayments of EI Premiums
- ❏ The Refundable Medical Expense Supplement
- ❏ Refunds of investment tax credits
- ❏ Employee and partner GST/HST rebates
- ❏ Overpaid tax instalments
- ❏ Provincial/Territorial tax credits

* Attach supporting documentation
**Subject to indexing

Figure 9.4   Tax Write-Offs of Investors and Seniors

Tax Deductions from Income Lines

❑ Capital gains income is reduced by outlays and expenses like:
- brokerage fees or legal fees
- appraisal fees or surveyors fees
- finders fees or commissions
- advertising costs
- transfer taxes

❑ Revenue Property Owners may write off operating expenses like:
- mortgage interest, insurance, property tax
- maintenance and repairs
- accounting fees, advertising, office stationery costs, travelling expenses in certain cases, utility costs, condo fees
- management fees, landscaping fees.
- When claiming Capital Cost Allowances on assets, you may not create or increase a loss with this deduction

Deductions from Total Income

❑ Carrying Charges. Interest and dividend income can be offset by claiming interest expenses, safety deposit box fees, accounting fees, investment counsel and management fees for assets held outside an RRSP/RRIF/RESP.

Tax Credits (Non-Refundable)

❑ The Age Amount is claimable by those who attain age 65 during the year, but reduced at certain net income levels.

❑ The Pension Income Amount is claimable by those who received a periodic pension from superannuation, or those aged 65 or older who receive private periodic pension income sources. Those who receive these amounts as a result of the spouse's death will also qualify.

❑ The Caregiver Amount is claimable by those who provide in-home care to parents/grandparents over the age of 65 or other relatives over the age of 18. There is an upper net income ceiling level.

❑ The Disability Amount is claimable by those who have a disability that is severe and prolonged for a continuous period of at least 12 months.

❑ The Amount for Public Transit Passes will apply to the cost of transit starting in July 2006.

❑ Amounts Transferred from Spouse allows the higher income spouse to transfer unused credits for the Age Amount, Pension Income Amount, Disability Amount, and Tuition/Education and Textbook Amounts.

❑ Medical Amount is claimable for unreimbursed medical expenses of the family in the best 12-month period ending in the tax year.

❑ Charitable Donations provides a lower tax credit on the first $200 and 29% on the balance. Donations of shares from public companies can be made on a tax exempt basis.

Figure 9.5	Tax Deductions of the Self-employed

Tax Deductions

- ❑ Accounting Fees, Legal Fees
- ❑ Advertising, Marketing and Promotion
- ❑ Asset Repairs and Maintenance
- ❑ Assistant's or Other Employee's Salaries
- ❑ Auto Expenses
- ❑ Bad Debts
- ❑ Board and Lodging while on the road
- ❑ Bonding and Licensing
- ❑ Business Meals and Entertainment (50%)
- ❑ Canada Pension Plan contribution payable on self-employment income (one-half)
- ❑ Capital Cost Allowances on Assets are subject to time limitations for adjustments. Be sure to correct errors or omissions within 90 days of receipt of a Notice of Assessment/ Reassessment.
- ❑ Commissions paid to Sub-contractors
- ❑ Convention Expenses (2 per year)
- ❑ Disability-Related Expenses
- ❑ Insurance and Interest costs
- ❑ Leasing costs for building or equipment
- ❑ Office-in-the-Home expenses
- ❑ Telephone and other Communications Costs
- ❑ Other operating expenses

Tax Credits

- ❑ Canada Pension Plan contributions payable on Self-Employment income (one-half)
- ❑ Investment Tax Credits on specified asset purchases
- ❑ Taxes paid during the Year by Instalments.

For specific tax deductions for those reporting income from self-employment, use the checklist in Figure 9.5. Review business statements and the tax return itself to ensure the points in the checklist have been claimed in the past and are supported by receipts.

RECAP. YOU NEED TO KNOW:

- How to maximize each family member's tax free zone
- How to diversify income sources, and accumulate capital
- How to maximize new tax credits
- How to split income with family members, staying onside with the Attribution Rules
- How assets are taxed at death, and transferred to family members
- How to make decisions that help you maximize new taxation rules for dividends and capital gains
- How to maximize tax deductions, refundable and non-refundable tax credits

- How to avoid the clawback zones
- How to pay off non-deductible debt and make debt deductible
- How to use tax planning strategies all year long to reduce income taxes for each individual and the family unit as a whole

YOU NEED TO ASK: Your tax advisor about simple ways to make sure it's deductible for each family member by:

- Finding ways to maximize Tax-Free Zones using Personal Amounts
- Diversifying income sources
- Transferring income, deductions and credits from one family member to the other
- Minimizing realized income in the year
- Deferring income to the future
- Maximizing deferred investment vehicles and
- Maximizing the tax deductions and tax credits available to you.

CHAPTER 10

How to Create Serious Wealth

"Only you can hold yourself back, only you can stand in your own way. . .Only you can help yourself."
MIKHAIL STRABO

KEY CONCEPTS

- Recent tax changes provide excellent tax saving and deferral opportunities
- Every business owner should discuss the organization structure of the business with professional advisors
- Incorporation can offer more absolute tax savings, income diversification and tax deferral options
- Family ownership of the corporation can result in large tax free gains on sale of qualifying shares
- Retirement savings and significant family wealth creation can result

REAL LIFE: When Thomas started his electronic marketing company out of his basement office a couple of years ago, he would have never guessed what paths his business venture would take him on.

Those first years were so lean. Thomas barely scratched together enough money to lease his computer. But he had an idea, and a dream. This, together with his determination to create, led to the building of a base of institutional buyers of his custom-designed intellectual property. His income rose steadily. From a loss of $10,000 in the first year, to a profit of $60,000 in Year 2, $120,000 in Year 3 and before looking into Year 4, Thomas realized he was paying altogether too much tax.

Thankfully, it was at this point that he made some strategic tax-planning moves that really paid off. You see, quite out of nowhere, Thomas would be approached to sell his business.

THE PROBLEM

How can there possibly be a problem? Not only did you survive the start-up years, but you are bringing home more money than you ever did working for someone else. It gets even better: next year you'll bring home more, and as time goes on, you can see the ongoing expansion in your revenue and profits.

The problem is that many start-up entrepreneurs fail to anticipate just how quickly their business can take off. This is particularly true of those who start their enterprise due to negative circumstances — the loss of a job for example.

What's important is to understand that besides generating profits, every business owner has the potential to build equity. The technology, product, distribution method or client base contains value that some other firm may wish to acquire some day. This is an opportunity that has significant tax advantages, and if set up properly, the structure of the venture can greatly enhance your family's after-tax coffers.

THE SOLUTION

Every business owner should be discussing the best structure for the organization with his or her tax advisor every year. Should the business be incorporated or should you keep your proprietorship?

The answer is often one of timing. For example, you may wish to earn start-up losses in a proprietorship, in order to offset other income of the year — perhaps from a severance package. Or, if there are excess losses, you may wish to carry them back and offset employment income earned in the best of the last three tax years, to recover prior taxes paid.

You will also want to maximize your retirement savings opportunities, first through your RRSP contribution room, which as you have learned is generated from actively earned sources like employment income and self-employment income from a proprietorship.

As an unincorporated business grows, and start-up losses are absorbed, personal tax rates can become expensive. That's where a corporate entity can provide absolute tax relief, allowing the business owner to fund expenditures with larger after-tax dollars, diversify remuneration to earn employment income, tax free and taxable perks, dividends and capital gains, while taking advantage of some excellent tax deferral and income splitting opportunities.

Proprietors should therefore discuss the following opportunities with their tax advisors in considering incorporation and its timing:

❏ Who will own the shares?
❏ How can we think ahead to family income splitting opportunities?
❏ When should family trusts be used to hold shares for the benefit of adult children?
❏ What structures can be put into place to protect the family business in case of marriage breakdown or children's bankruptcy?
❏ What are the costs of incorporation and ongoing audit work?
❏ How are different income sources taxed and when, and what decisions can be made to maximize timing opportunities?
❏ What happens on sale of the company and/or shareholder's death?
❏ Under what circumstances can each member of the family tap into the $500,000 capital gains deduction?

In Thomas's case, the opportunity to sell his business came in Year 3. He was offered $2 million for his little software company. Due to his effective tax planning, Thomas's family kept much of that money for themselves.

THE PARAMETERS

Small business owners should become familiar with some of the key advantages for incorporating their small businesses. Consider the following as starting points in your exploration for the right opportunities to leverage your productivity and your investment in your business:

a) **Check Variations in Provincial and Rules for Personal Liability:** Corporations are set up under provincial laws, which vary from one province to another; this is true of their tax rates as well. Also, while one of the advantages of incorporation includes a limitation of personal liability, be aware that practicing members and shareholders of professional corporations are **not** so protected. Larger professional practices are more commonly organized as limited liability partnerships (LLPs), which protect individual partners by not holding them personally liable for the professional negligence of other partners. Check these variations with your lawyer and accountant.

b) **Lower Tax Rates:** Effective January 1, 2007 the first $400,000 of active business income earned within a Canadian-Controlled

Private Corporation that qualifies for the Small Business Deduction is subject to a lower corporate tax rate. The result is that business income is taxed more advantageously than if it was earned by the individual directly. In addition, recent tax changes will result in the reduction of the tax rate applicable to this active business income, the elimination of the large Corporations Tax and the elimination of the surtax:

Corporate Taxes: Summary of Federal Tax Rates

	2005	2006	2007	2008	2009	2010
On the first $400,000* of CCPC's active business income (Plus surtax)	12	12	12	11.5	11	11
Surtax rate	1.12%	1.12%	1.12%	0	0	0
Capital tax rate	0.175%	0	0	0	0	0
General income tax rate (before surtax)	21%	21%	21%	20.5%	20.0%	19.0%

c) **Increased Purchasing Power:** The rate applied to CCPC income earning the small business deduction is about 20%, versus a top marginal rate for a proprietor of about 45% (exact amounts depend on your province of residence). That provides you with a 25% tax deferral on every dollar reinvested in your business. Your larger after-tax dollars can therefore lower the costs of funding your operations, as well as expenditures that are otherwise non-deductible by you personally. This includes life insurance, 50% of meals and entertainment costs, employee loans, asset acquisitions, education and training, up to two conferences per year, and also group health or pension costs.

d) **Flexibility on Choosing Fiscal Year End:** Note that a corporation can choose any taxation year it wishes, as long as the first taxation year does not exceed 53 weeks after the corporation commenced. This means that you can choose July 1 to June 30, thereby deferring taxation of personal bonuses and dividends. However, a professional corporation which is a member of a partnership must end its taxation year at the end of each calendar year.

e) **Tax Deferral:** Your tax-efficient after-tax profits earned within the CCPC can be paid out as dividends to the individual. Timing plays an important role here. For example, if the corporation generates a profit at the end of its fiscal year (December 31) of

$50,000, the dividends could be declared and paid in January. This has the effect of deferring the payment of personal tax to April 30 of the next tax year. The money can be invested to earn income at lower tax rates within the corporation, employ additional resources, or reduce borrowing costs.

f) **Optimum Salary/Dividend Mix:** Dividends attract lower marginal tax rates than ordinary income from employment and other sources as a result of the gross-up and dividend tax credit. Where the dividend is not eligible (that is, is paid from income which attracted the small business deduction, or generated refundable tax) the gross-up and dividend tax credit reflect a combined federal-provincial rate of 20%, and an assumption that the individual's provincial tax is 50% of the federal tax paid. Where the dividend is eligible, the assumption is that the combined corporate tax rate is 32% and that the provincial dividend tax credit will be 63% of the federal dividend tax credit. Where these values are present, there is "perfect integration" between the corporate and personal tax systems. The theory is that an individual taxpayer will be indifferent as to whether s/he earns an amount of income personally or whether the income should be earned by a corporation, which then pays a dividend to the individual. In a perfect integration situation, the amount of total taxes paid by the individual and corporation will be identical to the total taxes paid by the individual alone, regardless of the individual's marginal tax rate. Taxpayers and their advisors have to carefully review the salary/dividend mix which generates taxable income each year and be aware of new rules, described below.

g) **Good News on Dividend Taxation:** Actual dividends paid out of income subjected to the Small Business Deduction are "grossed up" by 25% and those grossed up amounts qualify for an offsetting dividend tax credit of 13.33%. Under these rules, taxpayers can earn up to approximately $30,000 of dividend income tax free, when no other income sources are present. (Dividends paid to minors, however, attract "tax on split income", described in more detail under corporate attribution rules below).

But starting in 2006, shareholders will qualify for a new dividend gross up of 45%, offset by an 18.9655% dividend tax credit, on dividends distributed by public corporations and CCPCs in cases where income (other than investment income) is subject to tax at the general corporate rate. This provides even greater tax efficiencies to the shareholder, particularly in conjunction with reducing general corporate tax rates, which are to be phased in through to 2010.

The approximate effect of these rules on personal marginal tax rates (top tax bracket) appear below:

	Federal MTR	Approximate Federal and Provincial MTR*
Ordinary Income	29%	46.4%
CCPC Dividends	19.58%	31.34%
Public Dividends	14.49%	28.13%
Capital Gains	14.5%	23.2%

*Actual MTR depends on your province of residence, and the tax rates in effect each year.

h) **Bonus Planning:** Any income that exceeds the Small Business Deduction is subject to the general income tax rate as explained above. For more profitable corporations, then, it can make sense to "bonus down" to the small business limit ($400,000 in 2007; $300,000 for 2006) to reduce the corporation's tax burden. However, while deductible to the corporation, the bonus will be taxed personally. Bonuses must be paid within 180 days of the corporation's fiscal year end. The corporation gets the deduction now; shareholder reports the bonus later, and that's a great way to leverage your resources. In making this decision, ask your tax accountant to crunch some numbers to take into account the new dividend taxation rules which apply where taxable income exceeds the small business limit. This is discussed above. Will your net position—in the corporation and personally—be better if you take the bonus, the dividends or a combination of both?

I) **Bonus on non-active business income:** The reasonableness of a bonus could be challenged by CRA where it is used to reduce otherwise non-active income of a business, in cases where the owner manager does not have control over the income earned. Non-active business income is income that would be taxed in the corporation as investment income. These amounts include dividends, capital gains from the sale of assets and interest income to name a few.

j) **RRSP Planning:** You will want to earn salary of $105,556 in 2006 to maximize your 2007 RRSP contribution room of $19,000. To reduce the amount of tax that is required to be withheld from a bonus, consider paying a portion of the bonus contributed directly into an RRSP. The amount contributed to an RRSP will be deducted from the total bonus when determining the amount of tax to withhold. This is an excellent way to start earning tax-deferred retirement income immediately.

k) **Income Splitting:** Reasonable salaries paid to family members will reduce the corporation's taxable income, while splitting income subject to personal taxation and maximizing opportunities to save for retirement on a tax deferred basis with RRSP contribution room. Dividends, which do not qualify as earned income for RRSP purposes, can also be paid to adult shareholders, depending on your share structure, thereby diversifying income sources earned by each family member and averaging the overall tax burden downward (in most provinces).

l) **Corporate Attribution Rules:** There are a number of ways to split family income through a corporation, but there are some obstacles to clear. These are commonly referred to as corporate attribution rules. For example, if you make a low-interest or interest-free loan to a family corporation with the main purpose of reducing your income and benefiting your spouse or minor children, you will be deemed to receive interest on the loan at CRA's prescribed interest rates, reduced by any interest you actually receive on the loan. This must be reported on your tax return.

   The second obstacle is the "kiddie tax" introduced in the 1999 federal budget to prevent the transfer of income from high-income individuals to their children under the age of 18. Those rules provide that, rather than redirect the income to the parents' hands, the minors pay tax on the income at the highest marginal rate.

m) **Insurance Planning for Exit Strategies/Death of Shareholder.** The use of a buy-sell agreement should be an important part of any shareholder's agreement. This agreement can cover everything from death of a shareholder to exit strategies for the living. Insurance planning can play an important role when considering a buy-sell agreement especially when a shareholder dies, as the proceeds received from the insurance policy can be used to purchase the shares from the deceased shareholders' estate. Further, in the event of a living shareholder exiting the corporation, it is possible to insure someone else, usually older, and on their death, use the proceeds to purchase the shares.

n) **Use of Individual Pension Plans.** Discuss this option with your tax advisors as a way to contribute higher tax-deferred amounts towards your pension income planning than would normally be allowed under the RRSP rules. This is a good way to shore up your retirement, especially if investment returns in the RRSP have been poor. It is also possible to make past service contributions, which could be to your advantage once the corporation is profitable; however, a pension adjustment will result, which will in return reduce your RRSP contribution room for those years. Also, amongst the disadvantages, spousal contributions are not allowed, funds are usually locked in and administration costs, though tax deductible, can be higher.

o) **The $500,00 Capital Gains Deduction.** The $500,000 Capital Gains Exemption is available to taxpayers who own shares in a qualifying small business corporation, a qualified farm property or effective for dispositions after May 2, 2006, a qualified fishing property. Specific rules of eligibility must be met, however, before the claim for the deduction can be made.

Qualified Farm Property

For those taxpayers who disposed of qualified farm property during the year, the available Capital Gains Deduction (CGD) must be reduced by any Capital Gains Deduction previously claimed. If you are unsure of this information, contact CRA for a record of previously used amounts. Then the least of the following will determine the deductible amounts:

- annual gains limit from dispositions of qualified farm property during the current year
- the available CGD, and
- the cumulative gains limit.

The definition of "qualified farm property" that was acquired after June 17, 1987, includes real property owned by the taxpayer, spouse or child for at least 24 months immediately before sale.

Also, a gross revenue test must be met; that is, in at least two years prior to disposition, gross income earned by the individual by active farming operations must exceed net income from all other sources.

Third, all or substantially all of the fair value of the farm assets must be used in active business operations for at least 24 months prior to disposition.

Different rules exist for farms acquired before June 17, 1987. The $500,000 Capital Gains Exemptions will be allowed, but only if the farmland and buildings were used in an active farming business in Canada in the year of sale, and in at least five years prior to the disposition.

For 1988 and subsequent tax years, eligible capital property (for example, farm quotas) will constitute qualified farm property eligible for the deduction if used in the course of carrying on the business of farming in Canada.

Qualified Fishing Property

The May 2, 2006 federal budget extended to fishers each of the following benefits previously afforded farmers:

- $500,000 lifetime capital gains exemption on the disposition of Qualified Fishing Property, which includes real property, fishing vessels, interests in a fishing license and eligible capital property used principally in a fishing business carried on in Canada, if the individual or his/her family members were actively engaged on a regular and continuous basis in the enterprise. In addition, shares in family fishing corporations and interests in family fishing partnerships will qualify.
- Tax deferral of capital gains and recapture when Qualified Fishing Property is transferred to the fisher's spouse or common-law partner, child or grandchild, or nephews, nieces and in-laws who may have been under the taxpayer's custody and control while under 19, in cases where there is an active involvement on a regular and continuous basis. In these cases, it is possible to assign the value at the cost amount of the property; in the case of depreciable property, recapture can be deferred.
- Extension of the time for claiming reserves on the disposition of fishing property from five years to ten years.

The new term "Qualified Fishing Property" and the rollover and reserving rules will be defined to parallel similar definitions and rules as those for Qualified Farm Property.

Shares of Small Business Corporations

The $500,000 Capital Gains Exemption for individuals has been available on the disposition of qualified small business corporation shares after June 17, 1987. The allowable deduction is calculated as the least of the following four amounts:

- For 1988 and 1989, and between February 27 and October 17, 2000, $333,333 (66 2/3% x $500,000) less any amount claimed as a capital gains deduction in prior years (adjusted for increased inclusion rates). After 1989, and before February 28, 2000, the available deduction will be $375,000 (75% of $500,000) less any amount claimed as a capital gains deduction in prior years (adjusted for increased inclusion rates). After October 17, 2000, $250,000 (50% x $500,000) less any amount claimed as a capital gains deduction in prior years (adjusted for inclusion rate changes)
- The individual's cumulative gains limit less any amount deducted as a capital gains deduction in respect of qualified farm property for the year

- The individual's annual gains limit less any amount deducted as a capital gains deduction in respect of qualified farm property for the year
- Net taxable capital gains for the year from dispositions of qualified small business corporation shares after June 17, 1987.

What is a qualified small business corporation share? The share must be a share of the capital stock of a small business corporation owned by the individual, his/her spouse, or a partnership of which s/he was a member.

A small business corporation is defined to be a Canadian-controlled private corporation in which all or substantially all of the assets (90% or more) are used in an active business or carried on primarily in Canada by the corporation.

The share must not have been owned by any person or partnership other than the individual or a person or partnership related to him/her throughout the 24 months immediately preceding the disposition. During the holding period, more than 50% of the fair market value of the corporation's assets must have been used in an active business.

Finally, if the taxpayer disposes of shares of a small business corporation, some of which do not meet the holding requirement, the shares are deemed to be disposed of in the order in which they were acquired.

TAX ADVISOR

When setting up a qualifying small business corporation, it is important to give thought to the ownership of the shares, asset transfer provisions and compensation packages. The initiative is complicated and requires significant planning. However, Figures 10.1 and 10.2 serve to

Figure 10.1   Sole Shareholder Uses CGD

Tax Provision	Calculation
Proceeds of Disposition	$2,000,000
Adjusted Cost Base	$ 1
Capital Gain	$1,999,999
Taxable Gain (1/2)	$ 999,999
Less Capital Gains Deduction (1/2 X $500,000)	$ 250,000
Net Taxable Gain	$ 749,999
Taxes Payable @ 46%*	$ 345,000

* Consult with advisors for accurate calculation for your province of residence.

Figure 10.2	Capital Gains Split With Two Shareholders	
Tax Provision	**Thomas**	**Pat**
Proceeds of Disposition	$1,000,000	$1,000,000
Adjusted Cost Base	$ 1	$ 1
Capital Gain	$ 999,999	$ 999,999
Taxable Gain (1/2)	$ 499,999	$ 499,999
Less Capital Gains Deduction (1/2 X $500,000)	$ 250,000	$ 250,000
Net Taxable Gain	$ 249,999	$ 249,999
Taxes Payable @ 46%*	$ 115,000	$ 115,000

* Consult with advisors for accurate calculation for your province of residence.

make an important point: the use of the $500,000 Capital Gains Exemption can help qualifying small business owners accumulate serious wealth.

In the case of Thomas's sale, had he been the sole shareholder of his corporation, his tax liability would have been calculated as follows, assuming no prior use of the CGD.

Now, let's assume that Thomas and his wife Pat each were shareholders of this small business corporation. Each could split the gain and use their Capital Gains Exemptions, if available.

The family pockets $115,000 more in tax savings. They would have kept more of the $2 million if each of their adult children had also owned shares in this SBC. Therefore, it pays to set up your business in anticipation of future windfalls. Ask your advisor about minimum tax and any net income tax implications.

The transfer of assets from a proprietorship to a corporation, the timing of such an event and the structure of the shareholders' agreements and compensation structures all need careful consideration. These matters should therefore be discussed with your tax advisor.

RECAP. YOU NEED TO KNOW:

- How to position your business structure to minimize tax on business income and maximize your tax position upon sale or transfer of the business
- How to handle start-up losses in the most tax-efficient way
- How to time the transfer of the business from a proprietorship to a corporation
- The difference in tax rates applied to corporations and personal income

- How the choice of corporate fiscal year ends can facilitate tax reductions and deferral
- How to diversify income sources earned from the corporation
- How to determine the optimum salary, dividend, bonus mix
- What the new rules for dividend taxation are and how they affect taxpayers
- How astute RRSP planning can help you
- How to ensure your small business qualifies for the capital gains exemption

YOU NEED TO ASK: Your tax advisor about the best way to minimize tax using a small business corporation by:

1. Maximizing tax advantages the proprietorship may have (i.e., excess loss carry-overs), before incorporation.
2. **Structuring your salary** within a Small Business Corporation at least to maximize annual RRSP contribution room.
3. **Consider distributing shares** of the company to your spouse and adult family members in order to multiply the claims for the $500,000 Capital Gains Exemption.
4. **Knowing the value of your business enterprise** after Year 1, Year 3 and Year 5 and determining valuation methods and reporting requirements with your advisors. Be ready when a potential buyer appears on the scene.
5. **Anticipating the changes that rapid growth** will mean to the management of the company. Also consider what structural changes the growth of your business will require in the short term, including financing for expansion.
6. **Creation of a Family Trust and estate plan**

Remember, Think Big. . .it takes as much effort as thinking small, and it's much more fun!

CHAPTER 11

How to Turn a Tax Audit into a Profitable Experience

"To know is to control."
SCOTT REED

KEY CONCEPTS

- CRA may question whether an outlay was made to incur income from a business or property, and whether the expenses were really personal or living expenses of the taxpayer
- CRA has the power not to accept your tax return as filed and may make its own assessment of the amount of tax it believes you should pay
- Section 152(8) of the Income Tax Act makes the assumption that CRA is correct in its assessments, unless those assessments are challenged by the taxpayer
- Therefore, while the Burden of Proof is on you to disprove CRA's assessment, it is also your duty to defend your right to pay only the correct amount of tax.
- The taxpayer and his/her advisor must keep up with tax law and its changes over a period of years in order to determine the best final outcome for an audit, which can span many years, and ensure tax cost averaging is applied to the family's best benefit.

REAL LIFE: Rubin was staring down his tax auditor's nose. "I have every receipt for every number I claimed on my tax return, every deposit of income. There should be absolutely no problem with any of the numbers on the tax returns you are checking so thoroughly." It was hard to hide the disdain from his voice. Three years earlier, Rubin had been through a similar tax audit, just as he was turning the corner on the popular acceptance of his passionate compositions.

After years of working at the Symphony as an employed classical guitarist, and writing music in between performances, Rubin got his first major break. A popular singer from Vancouver heard his piece, *Majestic Moonlight*. Despite incurring nothing but losses for his efforts over the previous three-year audit period, that chance meeting opened doors to a recording contract. The royalties from Rubin's first CD were just starting to flow when CRA reassessed Rubin's previously filed tax returns, and disallowed his business losses. Citing no reasonable expectation of profit from what they considered to be his "hobby" of songwriting, Rubin faced a tax bill of $18,000, due to the disallowed business losses that he had used to reduce his other income.

At the time, Rubin fought a hard battle with CRA. Together with his tax advisor, he successfully proved there was a reasonable expectation of profit, forfeiting only his auto expense claim, because he had failed to keep an auto log. Not long after this, Rubin got his first royalty cheque: $55,000—more than what he earned at his day job in a year! Then the new opportunities started to roll: an offer to become Composer in Residence for the Toronto Symphony Orchestra, concert dates, radio interviews. . .Rubin had survived his first tax audit and was on his way to international fame and fortune!

Which brought him back to the present. Three months ago, he was visited again by CRA. In the excitement of the developments in his career, he had failed to file tax returns over the past several years. When he did comply, after several reminders, CRA decided to scrutinize his figures closely. Rubin had been concerned about the visits from the auditor, who observed his recording studio, located in his newly renovated home. Three weeks before Christmas, Rubin learned that he had become the subject of a *net worth assessment,* when a reassessment proposal indicated he faced another potentially devastating, retroactive tax bill.

THE PROBLEM

Sometimes a taxpayer can get the feeling s/he's between a rock and a hard place. While struggling to make a business run in the early years, one of the biggest threats s/he faces in a CRA tax audit, assuming documentation requirements are met, is the possibility that an auditor will disallow legitimate business losses by using the "no reasonable expectation of profit" argument. The onus of proof, however, is on the taxpayer to show there was a reasonable expectation of profit from commercial rather than personal activities, at the time the expenditures, and the effort, occurred.

Then, wouldn't you know it, a few years later, having made a success of the struggle to succeed, the taxpayer faces a completely different problem, but similar subjectivity: the danger of being accused of under-reporting income, due to a subjective assessment of living standards, under the Net Worth Assessment process. The onus of proof that income was not under-reported? Again, it's on the taxpayer.

As a result, many taxpayers shiver with dread when they anticipate the receipt of a tax audit notice. The potential for a subjective dismissal of their documented claims is often enough reason to underclaim expenses. For this reason, many taxpayers give up their rights under the law and deliberately overpay their taxes. . .year in and year out.

While the law grants the privilege of self-assessment on the self-employed, "grey areas" in the law can create uncertainty and unfairness. The taxpayer should be able to have the peace of mind and the confidence that comes with knowing the tax return was filed to his or her best benefit under the framework of the law, and is audit-proof.

THE SOLUTION

In complying with tax law, the self-employed person automatically accepts the Burden of Proof that income reported is correct and that deductions were allowable, reasonable, incurred to earn income from a commercial venture with a reasonable expectation of profit, and backed up with documentation.

That Burden of Proof is actually your best weapon against a subjective judgement from CRA. It presents an opportunity for you to explain your business motives, and therefore to exercise your full legal rights under the Income Tax Act. Because nobody knows your business and its potential to earn profits in the future as well as you do, you have a distinct advantage going into a tax audit. You have the opportunity to control the outcome.

When you combine the expert knowledge you have of your business vision for today and tomorrow, with meticulous bookkeeping and the excellent tax expertise of your financial advisors, the result should be audit-proof tax returns that reduce your overall tax costs (and the time you spend complying with the law) over the period of years in which you run your business. That allows you to focus on what you do best: build your business. It is critical, though, that the audit strategy both you and your advisors will employ is decided upon *at the time your tax returns are being filed*. This is the key to winning a tax audit.

THE PARAMETERS

In assessing your tax-filing game plan throughout the year and during tax-filing season, there are three things to analyze and discuss with your tax advisors:

Your Audit Risks

Anticipate these facts: a civil servant, your tax auditor, is mandated to determine whether your business is viable or whether you are operating on a "hobby" basis for the purposes of determining loss deductibility, without understanding the risks and challenges you may be facing in the marketplace today. While he or she will have historical and industry statistics at their disposal to assist in assessing whether your business is viable or not, or to test whether you are indeed reporting all of your income or overstating your deductions; in fact, you and your advisor must help the auditor understand your unique circumstances. Your auditor's interpretation of your business activities can initiate a long and costly dispute that could be left to the courts to decide who is right. You can avoid this by providing formal budgeting and business planning documentation.

Your Audit Tests

When your taxes are in dispute there are five tests you must pass:

1. that the activities of the business will result in a source of income
2. that there is a reasonable expectation of profit over time
3. that deductions claimed are reasonable under the circumstances, and supported by receipts
4. that all income from the venture is being reported
5. that all personal use components of any expenditures are removed.

We have discussed most of these concepts in previous chapters.

Your Tax Audit Strategy

To go into an audit battle with a winning strategy, arm your defense team with a number of deft weapons:

- the story of the evolution of your business: yesterday, today and tomorrow
- full use of your appeal rights
- research of precedents set in similar cases by the courts
- a summary of the tax law of the day, current tax law and future tax proposals
- an Action Plan that includes your Tax Audit Strategy.

The Evolution of Your Business   We have suggested earlier that your Daily Business Journal will go a long way in helping to inform your tax auditor about the motive and intent you have in operating your business. So will the log of networking activities, business plans, budgets, cash flow projections, marketing plans and human resource plans you pull together with your bookkeeper, as previously discussed. Don't wait for a tax audit to put these documents in place. File them with your tax return each and every year, *in anticipation of an audit*. Be prepared.

These documents will also help you make better business decisions, underscoring your commercial viability.

Rights to Appeal   There are a number of important rights you should be aware of and discuss with your tax advisor. Here are just a few of them:

Right to Voluntary Compliance   If you have indeed overstated your business deductions or under-reported your income, you need not fear any penalties for gross negligence or tax evasion, if you contact CRA first and ask that your tax return be corrected. There may be some interest charges, and CRA will expect you to either pay any resulting bill or make satisfactory arrangements to pay it over time. There may also be a late-filing penalty if you failed to file on time. However, the best policy is to correct and amend those tax returns to comply with the law, as soon as possible, even if you have to do this in retrospect. However, be sure to speak to your tax advisor about these matters before contacting CRA.

Right to a Fairness Committee Review   If you have suffered an unusual hardship beyond your control—illness, natural disasters, death of a family member and so on—and as a result of this were unable to file a tax return, interest and penalty costs can be waived through a decision of CRA's Fairness Committee.

Right to Object to the Assessment or Reassessment   Discuss with your advisors the appeal routes available to you should you run into a dispute with CRA. See Figure 11.1 for a summary.

Consequences of Non-Compliance   Throughout this book we have assumed the reader is a law-abiding citizen who endeavours to file a correct tax return to his family's best tax advantage, as allowed under the law. The consequences of failure to comply with tax law are outlined in Figure 11.2, for those who want to know the parameters:

Figure 11.1	Summary of a Taxpayer's Appeal Rights

Method of Appeal	Basic Parameters
1. Informal Objection	When you perceive a mistake has been made in the initial assessment of your return, have your tax advisor write to CRA to request an adjustment. If CRA refuses to make the adjustment, and you still believe they are incorrect, contact your tax professional again to discuss further options. Do this immediately.
2. Notice of Objection	This is a formal objection to the Chief of Appeals at the local Tax Services Office. It must be filed within one year after the taxpayer's filing due date or 90 days after the day of the mailing of the Notice of Assessment or Reassessment, whichever is later. You may indicate in this Notice that you wish to appeal directly to the Tax Court of Canada.
3. Appeals to the Tax Court of Canada	An appeal may be made after the Minister has confirmed the assessment or reassessment, or within 90 days after the service of a Notice of Objection to which no reply has been received. This court has an informal procedure, for federal taxes in dispute of $12,000 or less, and a general procedure for amounts over this, which requires the services of a lawyer. This court may dispose of the appeal by either dismissing it or allowing it in whole or part.
4. Appeals to Federal Court of Appeal	If you have lost an appeal at the Tax Court level, informal procedures, you have 30 days from the date the decision was mailed to you or your representative to appeal to the Federal Court. A lost case under the general procedure may be appealed to the Federal Court within 30 days from the date on which the judge signs the decision. The months of July and August are omitted; so if the decision date was June 30, the taxpayer would have until September 30 to file the appeal.
5. Appeals to the Supreme Court of Canada	Appeals to the Supreme Court require the granting of permission to hear the appeal by the Supreme Court itself. The taxpayer has 60 days from the date of the judgement at the Federal Court of Appeal to file an application. The month of August is left out.

Penalties for Misrepresentation by a Third Party

Persons (including partnerships) who, after June 29, 2000, participate in planning and/or valuation activities that lead to the reduction, avoidance, or deferral of taxes are subject to civil penalties under the Income Tax Act, which defines "culpable conduct," subject to penalties, as activities:

- tantamount to intentional conduct
- show an indifference as to whether the Income Tax Act is complied with, or
- show a wilful, reckless or wanton disregard of the law.

The penalties levied under this section are as shown in Figure 11.3.

Figure 11.2 Consequences of Non-Compliance

Circumstance	Penalty
Failure to file a return on time	5% of unpaid taxes plus 1% per month up to a maximum of 12 months from filing due date, which is June 15 for unincorporated small businesses
Subsequent failure to file on time within a 3-year period	10% of unpaid taxes plus 2% per month to a maximum of 20 months from filing due date
Failure to provide information on a required form	$100 for each failure
Failure to provide Social Insurance Number	$100 for each failure unless the card is applied for within 15 days of the request
Failure to provide information with regard to foreign-held property	$500 per month for a maximum of 24 months; $1,000 a month for a maximum of 24 months if there is a failure to respond to a demand to file plus an additional penalty of 5% of the value of the property transferred or loan to a foreign trust or the cost of the foreign property where failure to file exceeds 24 months
False statements or omissions with regard to foreign properties	5% of the value of the property, minimum of $24,000
Gross negligence: false statement or omission of information in the return	50% of tax on understated income with a minimum $100 penalty
Late or insufficient instalments	50% of interest payable exceeding $1,000 or 25% of interest payable if no instalments were made, whichever is greater.
Tax Evasion	50% to 200% of tax sought to be evaded and imprisonment for up to 5 years
Failure to deduct or remit source deductions	10% of amount not withheld, or remitted
Second such failure in same year	20% of amount not withheld or remitted if this was done knowingly or through gross negligence.

Figure 11.3 Third Party Penalties

Circumstance	Penalty
Misrepresentation in tax planning arrangements if made at the time of the planning or valuation activity	$1,000 or the total that the person is entitled to receive from the planning or valuation activity, whichever is more
Misrepresentation in tax planning arrangements if not made at the time of the planning activity	$1,000

Figure 11.3	Third Party Penalties (Cont'd)
Participating in misrepresentation	Greater of $1,000 and lesser of • the penalty the taxpayer would be liable for if that person made the statement and knew it to be false or • the total of $100,000 and the amount that the person is entitled to receive from the planning or valuation activity

Research Precedents on Tax Law

It can really pay to ask your tax advisors how taxpayers in similar businesses to yours have argued their cases in the courts. Probably one of the most contested concepts in Canadian income tax law is CRA's enthusiasm for charging "no reasonable expectation of profit" as the condition for disallowing the losses of small business owners. It is useful to see what conclusions the judges of the Canadian court system have come up with over the years.

Contemporary Jurisprudence.   Since 1978, the tax department has used the "Reasonable Expectation of Profit" test to determine whether the interest expenses incurred for an investment were deductible. In a pair of landmark decisions on May 23, 2002 (Stewart v Canada and Walls v Canada), the Supreme Court changed the rules of the game. The court said that the REOP test "should not be used to second-guess the business judgment of the taxpayer. It is the commercial nature of the taxpayer's activity which must be evaluated, not his or her business acumen." The court went on to say: "Where the nature of an activity is clearly commercial, there is no need to analyze the taxpayer's business decisions. Such endeavours necessarily involve the pursuit of profit."

The Department of Finance did not agree and attempted to change the law to require a subjective test: Reasonable Expectation of Cumulative Profit (REOCP), which would require an assessment of profitability both annually and over the ownership period of the asset. However, this drew heavy criticism in a consultative exercise and has not yet, at the time of writing, been implemented.

Based on these circumstances, a new test has been adopted to determine if a person's activities are related to a source of income in order to determine whether or not the activity is a commercial activity or a personal activity. Where it clearly is a commercial activity, a non-capital loss should be allowed, without the second-guessing of business decisions in hindsight. Where there is "mixed activity", the taxpayer must be prepared to show a reasonable expectation of profit.

You might glean the following guidance from these outcomes:

- Your motive and conduct will influence reasonable expectation of profit
- Profits and losses, as well as your qualifications to run the business and your investment in income-producing assets will help to establish the probability of future taxable income sources, and its commercial viability
- Do not mix personal and business affairs. Remove personal costs from expenses you are deducting.
- Strive to properly present your economic situation in real terms, but as it relates to the evolution of your business over a period of years. Tax cost averaging is important. Take full advantage of carryover provisions, and tax deferral opportunities.

Know the Tax Law of Yesterday, Today and Tomorrow

One of the interesting aspects about going through a tax audit is the fact that the auditor is usually focused only on assessing the tax years in question. This is generally the current year and/or two years back. He or she is not necessarily concerned with the concept of "tax cost averaging." This is where you and your advisor come in. Make sure the auditor prepares your reassessed return with the most advantageous tax provisions allowed by the law of the day and subsequent tax law.

It is also important to note that, while adjustments to current year CCA claims must generally be made within 90 days after receipt of Notice of Re/Assessment, a tax auditor will generally allow adjustments to the CCA statements during a tax audit. If a tax bill results, for example, you may wish to pull out all the stops and claim full CCA for the year. You'll also want to claim as many carry-over provisions as possible and review claims with family members, especially if there are transferable provisions available.

You and your tax advisor must see to it that the end result of a tax audit reflects all multi-year tax-planning provisions that are available to you. See Chapter 12 for summaries of significant provisions.

Also remember that while the Burden of Proof is on the taxpayer to disprove CRA's reassessment of taxes, it is CRA that must prove any additional facts that are raised during the audit, or in tax evasion cases, that there was wilful intent on the part of the taxpayer to defraud the government. The taxpayer may also challenge the appropriateness of CRA's penalties under the circumstances and to request that these be removed if they are excessive or incorrect.

Be Proactive

Remember, *the Income Tax Act makes the assumption that CRA is correct in its assessments, unless those assessments are challenged by the taxpayer.* Therefore it is most important that the taxpayer make a pro-active effort to prove the tax return was correct as filed.

TAX ADVISOR

The taxpayer and his/her advisors should follow certain steps proactively in ensuring the taxpayer's rights under the law are upheld during a tax audit. Initiate your Tax Audit Strategy in two parts:

I. Initial Audit Assessment Steps

1. **Act immediately.** Go to see your tax advisor with all the records you can find for the tax years being audited.
2. **Determine key dates to be met:** the deadline for filing a Notice of Objection, for example, is the first milestone. Determine whether this document should be filed, and when.
3. **Have your advisor request an extension** from CRA, in order to pull together the documents required. This will take some of the pressure off, and allow you to continue with your normal income-producing activities while you put together the tax audit case. But from here on in, do not miss any agreed upon dates or tasks in your dealings with CRA.
4. **Identify the problem areas in your position**, like missing receipts or logbooks, as well as the subjective issues: no reasonable expectation of profit or the accuracy of the auditor's net worth assessment.
5. **Identify the problem areas in CRA's position**, including misinterpretation of the actual facts, errors in assumptions made, omissions of facts in making the assumptions, and so on.
6. **Anticipate your outcomes:** Quantify your upside and your downside. Your upside would be one of two things:
   * No changes are made to the return
   * You uncover a tax-filing method, provision, or new receipts that have been previously missed, and use these to actually have your taxes decreased for the year.

   Your downside could be one of three things:
   * Taxes are increased because source documents are missing
   * Taxes are increased because tax losses are disallowed
   * Taxes are increased because income reported is adjusted upward, or tax deduction or credits are disallowed.

Put numbers to these circumstances to analyze your tax risk.

7. **Identify the tax provisions that were new for the tax year in question,** to ensure you took advantage of them all, and understand their carry-over potential. Keep a list of these in your tax files. The Top 10 Questions you should ask your tax advisor follow later in this Chapter.

8. **Set aside the time to work with your tax advisor** in putting together the appeal.

9. **Be prepared to go back and look through old files,** recover duplicate receipts, create auto logs from the information in your Daily Business Journal, etc. A tax audit will require your personal resources of time and money.

10. *Determine and agree upon your Tax Audit Action Plan.*

II. Tax Audit Action Plan

1. *File the Notice of Objection* once all the documentation has been gathered.

2. *Organize your evidence*: the documents that support your tax return as filed, any other additional documents, a listing of all relevant facts in your case to support your filing position, and a listing of facts that will reply to CRA's assumptions. It would be a good idea for all of these facts and replies to be organized in such a manner that they can be referred to quickly and often. A tabular numbering system, set out at the start of the process, generally saves everyone a lot of time.

3. *Ask CRA for information*: a taxpayer is within his/her rights to ask CRA to disclose the facts behind all of their findings, and the exact provision in the law that supports these facts.

4. *Stick to the facts at all times.* You and your tax advisor must separate emotion from fact to win the case. Remember, you have more facts than CRA does and you know the truth: what actions were taken in the past and why, and what potential there is for the business for the future. Judges understand that you did not have the benefit of hindsight when you acted as you did.

5. *Do not express personal opinions on tax law within your written materials* or at the audit interview (see below). Word your positions to say "Our position is the following." This keeps your presentation at a high level of professionalism.

6. *Correspond with CRA in writing* throughout the audit. For example, ask CRA to put any requests for additional information in writing.

7. *Identify your weaknesses at the outset.* If you don't have an auto log, say so. Often, the auditor will allow the taxpayer to go back and look through any documentation that will show a business driving pattern, and submit a summary of this. Another strategy that

sometimes will work is to start keeping an auto log immediately, even if this is throughout the audit period. A long shot, it will at least give the auditor a trend to look at.

8. *Identify any tax provisions you may have missed* in that tax year, or prior years. This is a good idea at any time, as you always want to be in a position to recover missed provisions. In fact, it may pay to find a reason to do this to assist in your audit position. For example, if you missed claiming your safety deposit box fees, prepare an adjustment to your prior-filed returns to claim these. Now you have 90 days from the date on the Notice of Reassessment to open up claims for Capital Cost Allowances elsewhere on the return. This could reduce your net income, CPP liability, tax liability, perhaps even create or increase your spouse's claims for the Spousal Amount, and so on.

During the Audit Interview

Generally, once all the information is gathered, the taxpayer's advisor will meet with the auditor to impart the information and have a discussion about the file. It is usually not a good idea for the taxpayer to participate in this process: let your hired advisor do the communicating at this point. Consider the following as constructive ways to help your advisor represent you successfully:

1. *Meet with your advisor before the interview* with the auditor and overview the materials and the strategy once more. This is a good rehearsal for your advisor, who may have some last-minute questions. What you are hoping for at this point is that you have communicated the story of your business, your intent for its future, and why the tax return should be accepted as originally filed. Because you will have all of these facts in writing, you should have peace of mind and confidence in your advisor to represent you with all the details you feel are important to express to the auditor.

2. *Overview first*. The advisor should begin the presentation of the materials with a solid overview of the essence of the taxpayer's position, and what information is enclosed to support this position. It is important that this information is assembled so that the auditor can review it easily, as mentioned earlier.

3. *Relate to the File*. Once the facts of the position and the supporting documents are identified, the advisor should proceed to explain how these items relate to the way the tax return was actually filed. It is at this time that new provisions to be included should be identified, or prior errors on returns should be corrected.

4. *Bring more information.* The advisor has the opportunity to gather additional information needed by the auditor to come to his/her conclusions about the file. Therefore, if the advisor doesn't know the answer to the question, or the auditor needs additional information, this is confirmed with the auditor — in writing — and the pieces of information required to satisfy the request gathered within a new timeline. Make it easy to your advisor to comply.

5. *Clearly articulate the conclusion* the taxpayer wishes to see, including the details of specific provisions (additions or deletions) and how they should be filed. With regard to subjective conclusions, the advisor should be prepared to stand firm on the reasons why the return was filed the way it was, and in the case of tax losses why the taxpayer is within his right to believe his assumption of reasonable expectation of profit from the venture. The advisor may cite previous cases that address the theory of the law, present information about changes in the tax law that apply to the taxpayer, as well as the documents that support the future growth of the business.

6. The case of *Johns-Manville Canada Inc.* established that where there is reasonable doubt, the case should be resolved in favour of the taxpayer. This is especially true if the law is ambiguous or uncertain. In the end, the judge of a dispute must look to the Income Tax Act for guidance in coming to a decision. If it can be shown that the taxpayer attempted to comply with the intent of law as it stands (without the benefit of hindsight at the time his/her actions were taken) and that the law does support the taxpayer's position, CRA's subjective interpretation of the Act is the weaker position.

Examples of Cases in Which Taxpayers Profited From the Audit Experience

While the following are based on true stories, all characters and circumstances have been changed for anonymity, and any similarities to actual circumstances are purely coincidental.

REAL LIFE: Taxpayer A had succeeded in receiving a patent for an invention

After attempting on numerous occasions to manufacture the invention through a third party — only to find one manufacturer was about to go bankrupt, another failed to perform after numerous delays in the schedule — the taxpayer proceeded to manufacture the invention on his own. He invested the money required to redraw plans, bought the required materials and set out to build the prototype, and in the process claimed all the expenses on his tax return. This created an operating loss which offset the income from the inventor's day job — working as a letter carrier. CRA disallowed those losses citing no reasonable expectation of profit.

In contesting this reassessment, the taxpayer was able to show, despite sketchy records, the motives and intent in attempting to find a manufacturer for the invention, and that the invention would already have been in the marketplace had it not been for the aborted manufacturing attempts with the first two companies. In fact, the taxpayer had detailed cash flows and projections to show how close he was to bringing the invention to market. He was about to close a contract to sell 50 of his inventions to a national distributor on a consignment basis. In fact, in the time since he filed the tax returns in question, a number of steps had been taken to enhance the expectation of profit. All of these events since the taxes were filed formed part of his audit strategy.

At the end of the process, the auditor agreed that there was indeed a reasonable expectation of profit from the business, and the taxpayer's returns were reassessed, only this time more advantageously than when he first filed. That's because his sharp tax advisor had caught a little-known provision about writing off the costs of a patent. Rather than using a straight-line method over the life of the patent, which is the usual course of actions, a fast write-off allowed the taxpayer to claim the costs over a shorter period. After this adjustment was made, CRA actually owed the taxpayer money!

REAL LIFE: Taxpayer B had a farming enterprise

The farmer claimed losses for years, as he faced one calamity after another. From bad weather to insects to bottomed-out world market pricing, this taxpayer fought to stay afloat. In fact, he came close to losing his asset on several occasions. While he was under this economic siege, he failed to file tax returns. A badly disorganized bookkeeper, Taxpayer B simply ignored CRA's requests to file a return until one day he was faced with a Net Worth Assessment.

This is a little-known audit tool CRA employs from time-to-time under the powers given to it under the Act. This process begins like any other tax audit: income verification as well as receipts are requested. Then, the tax auditor sits back and takes a close look at the taxpayer's perceived surroundings and lifestyle. What they saw in Taxpayer B's circumstances was vast landholdings, Christmas vacations financed by his wife's earnings as a government worker, and a paid off-mortgage. . .which, in truth, was the result of a family inheritance.

Taxpayer B was a classic case for a net worth assessment. He owned tax-paid holdings, but had little evidence of income to justify the apparent wealth. Further, he failed to give an explanation when questioned about it. The auditor took a stab at assessing the value of his lifestyle, guessing at what he thought income might have been in the audit period, to pay for it all. Given the powers in the Act, the auditor computed income, deductions and credits accordingly, and sent out a bill for tens of thousands of dollars. Taxpayer B fought back tears in his advisor's office.

The good news is that at the end of a very lengthy challenge to disprove the net worth assessment, which included combing through crates of disorganized receipts, bank records, contracts and asset transactions, CRA owed Taxpayer B over $15,000. To his great relief, even after paying his tax deductible accounting fees, Taxpayer B's net worth actually took a jump when the audit process was finished.

Has he been a regular tax filer since? You guessed it. . .no! Some people are just their own worst enemies!

RECAP. YOU NEED TO KNOW:

- How to meet the Burden of Proof in a tax audit
- How to develop an Audit Strategy with your tax advisor
- How to link your business activities to revenue and profitability
- How to appeal an assessment or reassessment you think is unfair or incorrect
- What the consequences of non-compliance are
- How to hold your tax advisor accountable for misrepresentation
- How contemporary jurisprudence has ruled in grey areas
- How to profit from a tax audit with tax cost averaging

WHAT YOU NEED TO ASK:

Like it or not, the fact that you are in business for yourself increases your chance of a tax audit. One way to deal with this fact is to continually prepare yourself for a potential audit, together with your tax advisor, as you file your income tax returns annually. Remember these rules as you coach your advisor:

1. **Know your rights under the law.** The four basic provisions in the Income Tax Act which give the self-employed taxpayer guidance in self-assessment of their tax burden are the following:

   - A taxpayer's income for a taxation year from a business or property is the taxpayer's *profit* from that business or property
   - No deduction for an outlay or expense will be allowed unless it was made for the purpose of gaining or producing income from a business or property that has *a reasonable expectation of profit*. These deductions must not include personal living expenses

- No deduction for an outlay or expenses will be allowed except to the extent that it was *reasonable* under the circumstances
- Whether you filed a return or not, CRA may reassess the taxes payable arbitrarily because they are *not bound to accept a return* as filed by the taxpayer.

2. **Never cave.** It is critical to be proactive when you're audited. Know that under Section 152(8), CRA's assessment of your taxes will be accepted as fact, unless you exercise your burden of proof and challenge CRA's assumptions.

3. **Make it a point to be a model tax-filing citizen.** File a tax return source and sales tax remittance every year, on time, to minimize penalties and build up points for when you really need them. . .at tax audit time. Disorganization is absolutely no excuse. Be sure to hire help if you can't — or don't want to — keep your own records in order. Besides, for small business owners it's deductible!

4. **Make sure it's all deductible**. . .defend your right to claim losses in the current year and the carry-over years by emphasizing the source of income created by your activities and that by its very presence you meet the "reasonable expectation of profit test."

5. **Gain confidence from the facts.** A judge must give the taxpayer the benefits of reasonableness, if you are making an effort to comply with the Income Tax Act. Your Burden of Proof puts you in a position of power to win a tax audit. . .provided that you stick to the facts, and remain highly professional in your approach. In many cases, CRA owes money to the tax filer at the end of the audit session.

6. **Never give CRA a reason to question your integrity.** The Income Tax Act allows you tremendous leeway to reduce gross income with legitimate tax deductions and credits that will average out your tax burden over time. Tax fraud is just not worth it. Make sure you support all income sources—cash, cheque, credit card, barter—with paper documentation and deposit to separate bank accounts (that is, never co-mingle business and personal funds). Keep receipts for all personal non-taxable sources, like inheritances, so that you can prove that what you have is fully tax paid or tax exempt. When it comes to your tax compliance burden, honesty is the best—and cheapest—policy over the long term.

7. **Know why they audit taxpayers.** The answer is quite simple: to promote a level playing field for all business owners in Canada. To illustrate, we'll leave you with this story:

Karl is in the construction business. He bases his quotes and his profit margins on the fact that he'll be paying GST and income taxes every year. His competitor, Shady Sal, on the other hand, quotes "under the table." That is, he'll cut the price in half to get the job, and he figures he can do this because he's paying no GST and no income taxes. Can Karl compete? The answer is apparent.

The integrity of the tax system depends on the CRA's ability to crack down on characters like Shady Sal, and to protect honest taxpayers like Karl. Auditing tax returns of the self-employed is a part of this process.

CHAPTER 12

Taxpayers and Their Advisors: The Top Check Lists

"Don't forget until too late that the business of life is not business, but living."
B.C. FORBES

KEY CONCEPTS

- Given that tax will be your largest lifetime expense your relationship with your professional tax advisor can be the most profitable one you have
- Choose that person carefully and begin with a review of prior filed returns to recover overpaid taxes on errors or omissions from the past decade
- Communicate your business and financial goals for the short and long term
- Stay current on tax changes for the future and stay in tune with tax cost averaging options
- Make financial decisions in tandem with your tax savings opportunities
- Build on your productivity and that of your business with smart tax planning

REAL LIFE: Marshall, a self-employed plumber, was getting married. . .and he had a deep, dark secret that he didn't want his bride to know about. In fact he was so worried about this, he found himself waking up frequently in the middle of the night, in a complete sweat. Now, his wedding date was fast approaching, and he had to confess to somebody. . .Marshall hadn't filed a tax return. . .ever.

You cannot imagine the relief on poor Marshall's face after he found out that the statute of limitations required that he only file for the current year and two years back. He had done the right thing the last time he woke up in a sweat: he called a local tax accountant with a very good reputation and an understanding demeanour. He explained that he just didn't want to go into his new marriage with this terrible burden hanging over him.

A week later, when his returns were filed, he just couldn't believe that CRA actually owed him money! In fact, due to the application of tax credits both federally and provincially, Marshall was going to receive enough to finance a short honeymoon.

Now that he understood how the tax system could work in his favour, Marshall wanted to know more about what he had missed. Perhaps he could have claimed more, if he had known more about the rules. Had he only turned his tax files over to an advisor sooner!

THE PROBLEM

Tax is just one of those things. . .everyone has to deal with it; most people have difficulty doing so enthusiastically. While many pay an advisor to help them. . .they often pay their fees grudgingly. They perceive the entire experience like a double negative. . .the only thing worse than paying taxes is paying someone to figure out how much you have to pay!

How do you choose a tax advisor, someone with whom you'll have a long-term relationship in the quest to pay only the correct amount of tax over time. . .and not one cent more? How do you communicate with your tax advisor so that you can learn the rules to help you make tax-wise decisions all year long? How can you best leverage the professional fees you are paying to achieve peace of mind that your tax affairs are in order and that the tax system is working for you, not against you?

How do you turn the double negative around to work proactively with your tax advisor in building tax-efficient profits and equity in your business?

THE SOLUTION

You may be surprised at the solution to this dilemma. To find the right tax advisor you have to decide what it is that you want from the service you seek. In short, it's your money and it is within your control to get the most out of your professional relationships. However, like most other relationships, this may take a bit of research at the start. There are numerous levels of tax-preparation, tax-accounting and tax-planning services to choose from in the marketplace. Which of these will best suit your needs today and into the future?

It goes without saying that every taxpayer who pays for a professional service expects a tax return that is 100% correct. However, there can be a big difference between a return that is just mathematically correct, and one done to your family's best advantage over the long term.

Find an advisor who will be as precious to your financial health as your doctor is to your physical health. Your tax advisor should be someone who knows you and your goals for your family and your business very well. S/he should be someone who has earned your trust and respect by keeping up with the latest in tax law, and CRA's interpretation of the law, its policies and procedures as well as your own personal, business and financial evolution. This person will also play an integral role with your other professional team members—your financial planner and lawyer for example.

In short, your professional tax advisor can be one of the most important people in your lifetime. For this reason, you should take some time to define this relationship carefully.

THE PARAMETERS

To find such a trusted advisor, consider this action plan:

- **Seek Referrals.** Ask your friends and business associates for referrals; check out the yellow pages and Chamber of Commerce or Board of Trade in your area for the names of well-respected tax advisors.
- **Expertise and Services Needed.** Find out what level of expertise you need: bookkeeping and payroll services, commercial tax preparation, accounting and auditing, corporate as well as personal returns, trust returns and estate planning.
- **Reputation and Experience.** Interview at least three professionals in your area. This can include independents, partners in a partnership, financial institutions, and so on. It's best to include one from every group to get the best overview of potential service, quality and price. You will receive a broad sampling of services and fees and, most important, an opportunity to judge the effectiveness of communications with you.
- **Ask Questions.** Come to the interview prepared to ask your top taxation concerns.
- **Listen Well.** When you ask your questions, take note of the way the answers are communicated to you. Can you learn from this person? Is the person willing to help you learn? Is the person interested in you and your business? Does s/he make suggestions to you? Does s/he have a strong background in taxation? The last thing you need is to feel intimidated or unclear about the way your concerns were addressed. You are looking for peace of mind and a professional partner for the future of your business and personal affairs.

- **Find Out About Service.** Ask about fees, guarantee of service, billing practices, errors or omissions insurance, size of organizations, additional services provided. What happens when errors occur?
- **Integrated Services.** Ask about the professional's ability to interact with others: lawyers, financial planners, insurance advisors and so on, should you need these services.
- **Make the Decision.** Choose the advisor you are most comfortable with.
- **Give a Trial.** Ask the advisor to complete a small job, to see if there is integrity behind the quality of the work, the ability to meet deadlines and to work with you on follow-up procedures.
- **Review the Accuracy of the Work.** Listen and learn as the advisor explains the results of the work to you.

TAX ADVISOR

Compile a "Top 10" list of questions to ask your potential advisor, such as:

1. What are the latest tax changes that will apply to my business operations this year?
2. What is the tax rate I will pay on each source of income I earn in the coming year?
3. What tax provisions should I be carrying forward from previous filing years?
4. What are the latest tax changes for our family unit to take advantage of?
5. How can our family members split income and transfer deductions and credits this year?
6. What are the retirement savings strategies we should be working towards?
7. How can we plan new investments in registered and non-registered accounts to increase tax-deferred income sources?
8. How can we reduce tax withholding/tax instalment payments this year?
9. How should asset acquisitions and dispositions be timed to make the most tax sense?
10. What audit-proofing procedures should we be putting in place this year?

RECAP. Ten Skill Testing Questions to Discuss with Your Advisors

True False?

1. ❑ ❑ A small business owner can diversify income sources, defer the reporting of taxable income, and split income with family members more easily than an employee.

True. Any investment advisor will tell you that the way to spread risk and accumulate wealth is to pay close attention to your asset mix. You want to earn income from a variety of sources: employment or self-employment, pensions, dividends, capital gains, interest and so on. When you start a small business, you'll be creating two types of income: on-going profits from the operations of the venture; and the potential for capital gains on the future sale of your business. This is a great way to diversify your taxable income sources, defer taxation of accrued wealth into the future and reduce your overall tax burden through income-splitting with family members.

True False?

2. ❑ ❑ A myriad of tax deductions that fall under general and unspecific statutory guidelines are available to the self-employed.

True. Business owners are only taxed on net profits, which are added to taxable income annually, and taxed at the appropriate marginal tax rate. The rules governing tax deductibility of expenditures are very general, and found in about a half a dozen sections of the Income Tax Act. They centre around two basic concepts: your ability to explain to a tax auditor why the expense you wish to deduct was reasonable under the circumstances, and how it was used to create income for your business, which has a reasonable expectation of profit, now or in the future. You must also show the auditor that any personal use component of the expenditure has been removed.

True False?

3. ❑ ❑ The self-employed can't write off the value of their own labour.

That's true of unincorporated small businesses. The proprietor gets to keep the net profits (after taxes are paid) and can make draws from this throughout the year. As the business grows, the proprietor may wish to incorporate, in which case s/he can become an employee of the corporation, which is a separate legal entity, and also pay him or herself dividends, which are after tax distributions of a corporation's profits.

Under both forms of business organization, equity in the value of the business grows on a tax-deferred basis. However, when a qualifying small business corporation is sold, a $500,000 capital gains exemption is available. This is not available to the proprietor. Speak to your tax advisor about all of your options for today and the future.

True   False?

4. ❑   ❑   The self-employed must finance all the risk of building their business, without tax relief.

Not so. Here's why. What is your most precious commodity? Is it your time? Your money? Your health? Likely it's all of those things. The key to preserving your resources is to use them wisely; to multiply them if possible, and to have them work for you. A small business provides you with the vehicle to leverage time, money and human resources needed to build appreciating equity over time. And best of all, the costs of leveraging — hiring staff, paying interest on an operating loan, leasing computers, marketing your services — are tax deductible if you earn income from your venture, which has a reasonable expectation of profit, and keep proper records.

True   False?

5. ❑   ❑   It's much better to arrange for one person in the family to earn $50,000 than for two people to earn $25,000.

False. If you understand a little about our progressive tax system, you'll know it's best to minimize realized income in the hands of one taxpayer and to "spread the wealth" into the hands of many. The taxpayer who earns $50,000 pays tax at a higher marginal rate. The potential return on the process of income splitting is pretty good *and* it's legal. You'll want to strive to split income with your family members. In fact, by starting a home-based business, you have the potential to reap double-digit returns in tax savings, simply by giving family members an opportunity to work for you.

True   False?

6. ❏   ❏   Keeping up with tax law and its continuous change is a pointless effort.

False. Most Canadians have the educational qualifications to understand their own tax system. Motivation to understand it and use it to their advantage is often a bigger problem, which is puzzling. True, it is not possible for every taxpayer to be a tax expert. That's not your goal, nor was it the goal of this book to make you one. (I'm sure you're relieved.)

However, the essence of opportunity lies within the structure of our tax system: it is based on voluntary compliance and self-assessment. It is your legal right and duty to arrange your affairs within the framework of the law to report the least amount of tax possible. By learning more about the existing provisions within our Income Tax Act, you'll be empowered to make tax-wise decisions throughout the year. Your motivation to do so? Simple. . .it's money; *your money.*

True   False?

7. ❏   ❏   Small business owners can reap tax savings of 22% to over 45% on each and every dollar they spend in their small business ventures, depending on their province of residence and income levels.

Yes. Because each qualifying business expenditure reduces business income dollar for dollar, you'll reap double-digit returns for each receipt you keep. It's important to know the income parameters you need to reach to maximize the return on your expenditures, and how each different income source you earn will be taxed in the future.

True   False?

8. ❏   ❏   The cost of your computer purchase can be written off in full against business revenues.

False. Many business owners fail to classify their expenditures into two main categories: operating expenses and capital expenditures. This error can be expensive in a tax audit. The former are 100% deductible against revenues of the business, and can even be used to create a loss. Capital cost allowances, the partial deduction allowed for the wear and tear on depreciable assets, also can increase an operating loss, but are taken at your option.

This allows you to defer the use of the deduction to a more advantageous year. So, a percentage of the computer's costs can be written off to a prescribed maximum; or if you choose, no deduction can be taken.

True   False?

9. ❑   ❑   It's difficult to justify claims for car and in-home business workspaces.

No, it's really quite easy to comply. All you have to do is separate your personal use of the assets from your business use. In the case of the auto, this is done by keeping a distance log which reports all your driving for both business and personal purposes. At the end of the tax year all expenses relating to the vehicle are totalled, and prorated according to the business kilometres driven divided by the total kilometres driven in the year. A similar process, based on square footage of the workspace in the home over the total living area, will help you claim the properly deductible portions of home expenses. The recordkeeping process can be easily recorded in your Daily Business Journal.

True   False?

10. ❑   ❑   Most taxpayers lose their tax audit appeals when they go to court.

Unfortunately this is true. CRA wins appeals at the Tax Court level about 70% of the time.* However, the odds for winning are much better locally. Appealing under a Notice of Objection to the Chief of Appeals in your area reaps a successful conclusion result the majority of the time. This negotiated approach to solving taxes in dispute can pay off for both parties, particularly when it comes to the grey areas of the law. For that reason, taxpayers should never back away from filing a Notice of Objection to a reassessment of their taxes, if they believe their tax return was correct as filed.

Tax Fact Sheets

Automobile Operating Cost Benefits

Period	Regular Employee	Automobile Salesperson
2006	22¢	19¢
2005	20¢	17¢

* As at time of writing.

2003–2004	17¢	14¢
2001–2002	16¢	13¢
2000	15¢	12¢
1997–1999	14¢	11¢
1996	13¢	10¢

Limit on Automobile Allowances. A per-kilometre automobile allowance which is not taxable to an employee is not deductible if it exceeds the following amounts. Note that where the automobile is driven in the Northwest Territories, the Yokon Territory or Nunavut, each amount shown is increased by 4¢.

Period	First 5,000 km	Excess
2006	50¢	44¢
2005	45¢	39¢
2003–2004	42¢	36¢
2001–2002	41¢	35¢
2000	37¢	31¢
1997–1999	35¢	29¢
1996	33¢	27¢

Automobile Capital Cost Allowance Limit. In each case, the dollar amount is increased by the amount of GST or HST, plus the amount of provincial retail sales tax, that is payable on the limit shown.

Period	Dollar Limit (add GST/HST/PST)
2001–2006	$30,000
2000	$27,000
1998–1999	$26,000
1997	$25,000
1995–1996	$24,000

Automobile Interest Expense Limit. The maximum monthly interest that can be deducted on a loan taken out to purchase an automobile.

Period	Dollar Limit
2001–2006	$300
1997–2000	$250
1995–1996	$300

Automobile Leasing Limit. The maximum monthly lease payment that can be deducted with respect to an automobile.

Period	Dollar Limit (add GST/HST/PST)
2001–2006	$800
2000	$700

1998–1999	$650
1997	$550
1995–1996	$650

Employment Insurance Premiums. Employed individuals and their employers contribute to the Employment Insurance fund. The employer's contribution is calculated by applying the Employer's Rate Factor to the employee's contribution.

Year	Maximum Insurable Earnings	Minimum Insurable Earnings	Premium Rate	Maximum Premium	Employer's Rate Factor
2006*	$39,000	$2,000	1.87%	$729.30	1.4
2005	$39,000	$2,000	1.95%	$760.50	1.4
2004	$39,000	$2,000	1.98%	$772.20	1.4
2003	$39,000	$2,000	2.10%	$819.00	1.4
2002	$39,000	$2,000	2.20%	$858.00	1.4
2001	$39,000	$2,000	2.25%	$877.50	1.4
2000	$39,000	$2,000	2.40%	$936.00	1.4
1999	$39,000	$2,000	2.55%	$994.50	1.4
1998	$39,000	$2,000	2.70%	$1,053.00	1.4
1997	$39,000	$2,000	2.90%	$1,131.00	1.4
1996	$39,000	$2,000	2.95%	$1,150.50	1.4

*Starting in 2006, rates for Quebec employees will vary. The Quebec premium rate for 2006 is 1.53%.

Canada Pension Plan Contributions. Both employed and self-employed individuals contribute to the Canada Pension Plan. Where an individual is employed, the employer matches the employee's contribution. Where an individual is self-employed, the individual funds both parts of the contribution.

Year	Maximum Pensionable Earnings	Basic Exemption	Contribution Rate	Maximum Employee Contribution	Max Self Employed Contribution
2006	$42,100	$3,500	4.95%	$1,910.70	$3,821.40
2005	$41,100	$3,500	4.95%	$1,861.20	$3,722.40
2004	$40,500	$3,500	4.95%	$1,831.50	$3,663.00
2003	$39,900	$3,500	4.95%	$1,801.80	$3,603.60
2002	$39,100	$3,500	4.70%	$1,673.20	$3,346.40
2001	$38,300	$3,500	4.30%	$1,496.40	$2,992.80
2000	$37,600	$3,500	3.90%	$1,329.90	$2,659.80
1999	$37,400	$3,500	3.60%	$1,186.50	$2,373.00
1998	$36,900	$3,500	3.20%	$1,068.80	$2,137.60
1997	$35,800	$3,500	3.00%	$969.00	$1,938.00
1996	$35,400	$3,500	2.80%	$893.20	$1,786.40

Foreign Exchange Rates. *The Income Tax Act* does not prescribe a method for translating into Canadian dollars transactions that are denominated in foreign currencies. CRA accepts that a taxpayer may use the rate in effect at the date a transaction takes place, or an average rate for the period in which the transaction occurs. The following are average annual exchange rates for the U.S. dollars as computed by the Bank of Canada.

2005	1.2116
2004	1.3015
2003	1.4015
2002	1.5704
2001	1.5484
2000	1.4852
1999	1.4858
1998	1.4831
1997	1.3844
1996	1.3636

RRSP Contribution Limits.

The following table reflects the maximum RRSP contribution limits, assuming an individual is not covered by an RPP or DPSP.

2006	$18,000
2005	$16,500
2004	$15,500
1995–2003	$13,500

Federal Tax Brackets and Rates: Personal

Year	Bracket	Rate
2006	First $36,378	15.25%
	36,379–72,756	22%
	72,757–118,285	26%
	Excess	29%
2005	First $35,595	15%
	35,596–71,190	22%
	71,191–115,739	26%
	Excess	29%
2004	First $35,000	16%
	35,001–70,000	22%
	70,001–113,804	26%
	Excess	29%
2003	First $32,183	16%
	32,184–64,368	22%

Federal Tax Brackets and Rates: Personal (Cont'd)

Year	Bracket	Rate
	64,369–104,648	26%
	Excess	29%
2002	First $31,677	16%
	31,678–63,354	22%
	63,355–103,000	26%
	Excess	29%
2001	First $30,754	16%
	30,755–61,509	22%
	61,510–100,000	26%
	Excess	29%
2000	First $30,004	17%
	30,005–60,009	25%
	Excess	29%
1995–99	First $29,590	17%
	29,591–59,180	26%
	Excess	29%

Federal Corporate Tax Rates

	Years	Rate
General corporate rate	2006–1995	38%
General rate reduction	2010	9%
	2009	8%
	2008	7.5%
	2007	7%
Abatement for income earned in a province	2006–1995	10%
Surtax (Note 1)	2006–1995	4%
Manufacturing and processing credit	2006–1995	7%
Small business deduction (Note 2)	2006–1995	16%
Tax on small business income up to $33,000 (Note 3)		12%
Small business tax rate reduction	2009	1%
	2008	0.5%
Refundable surtax on investment income (Note 4)	2006–1996	6–2/3%

Notes

1. The current surtax rate of 1.12% for small and medium-sized corporations will be eliminated effective January 1, 2008.

2. The annual business limit for the small business deduction was $200,000 from 1995 through 2002, $225,000 for 2003, $250,000 for 2004 and $300, 000 for 2005 and 2006. Effective January 1, 2007 and subsequent years, this limit will increase to $400,000.

3. The tax rate applicable to the small business deduction will be reduced to 11.5% in 2008, and 11% in 2009.

4. The refundable surtax on the investment income of a Canadian controlled private corporation applies only from July 1, 1995.

Conclusion

Within the next 15 years, more than half of Canada's small business owners are expected to retire, with approximately $1.2 trillion in business assets expected to change hands.

In a 2005 report by CIBC World Markets only 2 in 5 small business owners have scouted out a clear succession plan for their businesses, with 60% of entrepreneurs aged 55 to 64 to yet have a discussion about their existing plans with their family members or business partners. Only 15% of those have definite plans to transfer or sell the business to a family member.

Canada, in fact, finds itself home of the highest percentage of baby boomers in its total population, with 9.8 million individuals. Although the United States, due to its sheer size, has the largest overall baby boom population, (the U.S. population aged 65 and over is projected to grow from 34.6 million in 1999 to 40.4 million in 2011, to 70.3 million in 2030, and to a staggering 82.0 million by 2050 (Wells, 2000).

Given that there are only 23 million tax filers in Canada, this disappearing demographic will soon lead to a disappearing tax base, a phenomenon which has been described as an "economic time bomb."

To keep up our current standards of living, recent federal budget documents have suggested a focus on increasing employment opportunities and productivity. Sustainability of employment in the near future, according to the learned people at the Department of Finance, will depend on

- boosting job opportunities for Aboriginal people
- integration of highly skilled immigrants into the workforce
- ensuring that older Canadians may continue to work

Increasing productivity, on the other hand depends on economic growth, and therefore a strong and healthy business community working in harmony with governments within a fair and efficient tax system. This is critical, given all of the other challenges business owners face.

According to Statistics Canada, of all firms that were created in Canada during the 1990s, roughly one-quarter ceased to operate within the first two years, just over one-third of these firms survived five years or more, and only one-fifth were still in operation after 10 years. Being in business is tough, staying in business even tougher.

We all have an interest in this, as healthy businesses proliferate the tax base. Clearly, our investment in time and money must be more productive to ensure existing standards of living well into the future. For this reason, take the time to *Make Sure It's Deductible*...paying only the correct amount of tax—not one cent more—within your small business and the family unit. By protecting your precious energy and the wealth you create from tax erosion, you will be in a position to secure not only your own future, but also that of your employees and suppliers.

I sincerely hope that this book has helped you to do that.

Evelyn Jacks

Index

About Evelyn Jacks

Throughout her varied career, Evelyn Jacks has established an international reputation as an award-winning entrepreneur, a consistently best-selling author, speaker, educator, and educational publisher in the tax preparation and financial services industries. She can be contacted at 1-866-953-4769 or by website: www.knowledgebureau.com.

Evelyn is the founder and president of The Knowledge Bureau, Canada's leading educator in the tax and financial services industry. The company is home of the Distinguished Financial Advisor Certificate CE and Designation Programs. Evelyn's companies have specialized in publishing continuing education for professional tax and financial advisors for over 25 years.

The Knowledge Bureau has recently partnered with the Schulich Executive Education Centre, rated #1 in the world in public programming, to offer a Masters Certificate in Tax or Investment Services. The Knowledge Bureau also hosts the Distinguished Advisor Conference, an annual international education conference for tax and financial advisors.

Evelyn Jacks is also one of Canada's most prolific national authors and publishers. She has written close to 40 books on the subject of personal taxation, as well as published over 100 certificate vocational courses on the subject of tax, tax accounting, tax planning, and business practices for tax accountants and financial planners. This year she has also coauthored an international title on team leadership and management: *Get Your People to Work Like They Mean It.*

Evelyn is an internationally recognized, award-winning entrepreneur, several times over, houring won many awards, including the prestigious Rotman School of Business National Canadian Entrepreneur of the Year Award in Toronto, and an International Business Leadership Award by the Canadian Embassy in Washington, DC.

In 1999, she was appointed a Commissioner for the Lower Tax Commission, by the Premier of the province of Manitoba.

In November 2005 she was chosen as The Winnipeg Free Press's Inspiring Woman.

Evelyn has maintained significant influence in the national media through her years as a highly respected featured commentator on tax policy in newspapers, on radio and television. She has written thousands of articles and analysis for newspapers, magazines and internet portals. She is well known to millions of Canadians from coast to coast as the leading resource on personal taxation.

Currently she is active in a number of volunteer leadership positions including Governor of the Manitoba Club. She is also a Cabinet Member of the United Way of Winnipeg.